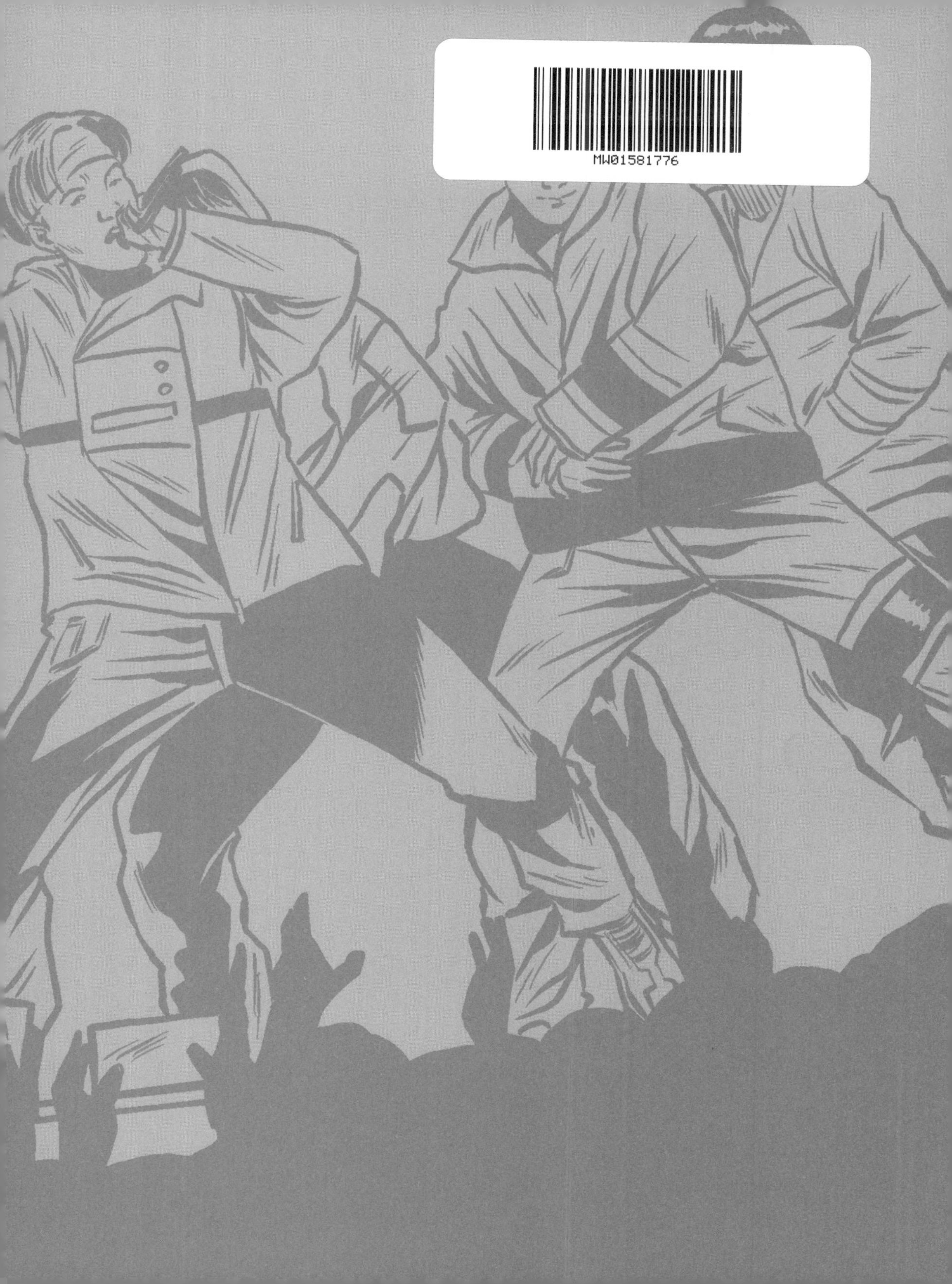

Quarto

First published in 2025 by White Lion Publishing,
an imprint of The Quarto Group.
One Triptych Place, London, SE1 9SH,
United Kingdom
T (0)20 7700 9000
www.Quarto.com

EEA Representation, WTS Tax d.o.o., Žanova ulica 3, 4000 Kranj,
Slovenia

Design copyright © 2025 Quarto Publishing Plc
Text and illustrations copyright © 2025 BesideBooks Srl, Milan – Italy
Edited by Balthazar Pagani
Text by Filippo Zambello. Translated from the Italian by Jamie Richards
Illustrations by Mattia Ferrari
Graphic Design by Bebung

BesideBooks Srl have asserted their moral right to be identified as the owner of rights on text & illustrations of this Work in accordance with the Copyright Designs and Patents Act 1988.

All rights reserved. No part of this book may be reproduced or utilised in any form or by any means, electronic or mechanical, including photocopying, recording or by any information storage and retrieval system, without permission in writing from White Lion Publishing.

Every effort has been made to trace the copyright holders of material quoted in this book. If application is made in writing to the publisher, any omissions will be included in future editions.

A catalogue record for this book is available from the British Library.

ISBN 978-1-83600-104-1
Ebook ISBN 978-1-83600-105-8

10 9 8 7 6 5 4 3 2 1

Publisher: Jessica Axe
Commissioning Editor: Andrew Roff
Senior Editor: Laura Bulbeck
Senior Designer: Renata Latipova
Senior Production Controller: Rohana Yusof

Printed in China

Disclaimer: This publication and its contents are not licensed, authorised or connected with BTS or their work. This publication includes elements of BTS' life, and that of others, which have been fictionalised.

BTS

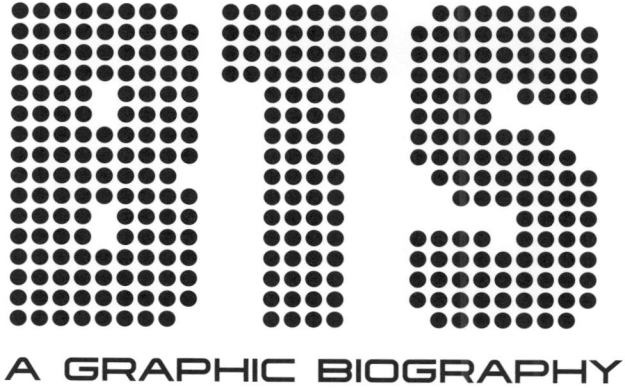

A GRAPHIC BIOGRAPHY

TEXT BY
FILIPPO ZAMBELLO

ILLUSTRATIONS BY
MATTIA FERRARI

EDITED BY
BALTHAZAR PAGANI

WHITE
LION
PUBLISHING

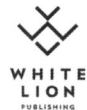

CONTENTS

P. 8
BTS

PROLOGUE – P. 14
THE RAP DEN

SIGNING WITH BIG HIT ENTERTAINMENT
AND LIFE IN THE DORMS.

CHAPTER 1 – P. 28
RM

FROM RUNCH RANDA TO RAP MONSTER TO RM.

CHAPTER 2 – P. 40
SUGA

FROM BASKETBALL TO MIDI TO BTS IDOL.

CHAPTER 3 – P. 52
J-HOPE

FROM TENNIS PLAYER TO STREET DANCER TO SINGER.

CHAPTER 4 – P. 64
JUNG KOOK

FROM TIRELESS ATHLETE
TO HEARTBREAKER TO HONEST WORKER.

CHAPTER 5 – P. 76
V

FROM THE SAXOPHONE TO SINGING TO BTS.

CHAPTER 6 - P. 88

JIN

FROM ASPIRING ACTOR TO CELEBRITY, CROSSING THE CATWALK.

CHAPTER 7 - P. 100

JIMIN

FROM ASPIRING DANCER AND PERFORMER TO IDOL,
VIA THE JUST DANCE ACADEMY
AND THE BUSAN HIGH SCHOOL OF ARTS.

EPILOGUE - P. 112

BEYOND THE SCENE

13 JUNE 2013: BTS MAKES THEIR OFFICIAL DEBUT
ON A MUSIC BROADCAST.

BTS

SEVEN REASONS WHY

Over the course of the 1990s, the international spread of dance music made massive changes to the South Korean pop scene. While the music in vogue until then was simply for listening, dance music complemented the aural with a visual component, quickly captivating audiences with irresistible rhythms and original choreographies.

By the decade's end, Korean entertainment companies had begun selecting and training dance music performers directly, with auditions and singing and dance courses taught by industry professionals. This created generations of artists or 'idols' trained for show business from adolescence and stealing the hearts of fans with their performances.

THE FIRST GENERATION OF IDOLS IN THE 1990S GENERATED INNOVATIVE AND TREND-SETTING MUSIC, YET THE SECOND, IN THE 2000S, MADE KOREAN POP A TRULY VIRAL PHENOMENON, LOVED BY YOUNG PEOPLE ALL OVER THE WORLD.

The rhythm and spontaneity of the lyrics, with their catchy, memorable choruses, captivated audiences as much as the simple yet fun-to-copy dance moves.

―――――

BUT THE GREATEST IMPACT ON AUDIENCES HAS COME WITH THE THIRD-GENERATION IDOLS, WHO ARE HIGHLY PRESENT ONLINE, RELEASING NEW SONGS ON MUSIC STREAMING SERVICES AND ACTIVELY ENGAGING WITH FANS ON SOCIAL NETWORKS. BY ENTERING PEOPLE'S LIVES AND HEARTS, THIS COHORT OF ARTISTS HAS, IN A RELATIVELY SHORT TIME, BUILT A LARGE AND LOYAL FANBASE.

―――――

Belonging to this third generation is BTS, one of the most popular idol groups in recent memory, a massive youth phenomenon and cornerstone of Korean pop culture. Since their debut as a boy band in June 2013 in South Korea, RM, Jin, SUGA, j-hope, Jimin, V and Jung Kook have been warmly and widely embraced, their dazzling performances and strong bond with fans enabling them to overcome language barriers and national borders.

THE 'BULLETPROOF BOYS' EXPLORE A VARIETY OF MUSICAL GENRES AND THEMES IN THEIR SONGS, LIKE TEEN ANGST AND SOCIAL STRUGGLES, MENTAL HEALTH AND FREEDOM OF EXPRESSION, SHOWING THEIR VULNERABILITY WITHOUT SHAME AND PROVIDING YOUNG PEOPLE WITH A USABLE TOOLKIT FOR THE CHALLENGES OF GROWING UP.

———

With their 2017 Top Social Artist win at the *Billboard* Music Awards — one of the most prestigious globally-recognised accolades in the industry — they threw open the doors for K-pop to enter the mainstream U.S. market. The incredible appeal of these seven young men, each with their own particular speciality and musical style, has been powered by drawing on their individual personalities, making them a touchstone and an inspiration for audiences all over the world.

ARE YOU READY TO BE INSPIRED BY THEIR STORY?

This graphic biography will take you on a journey through the most exciting moments of their lives as they soared to global stardom.

Filippo Zambello

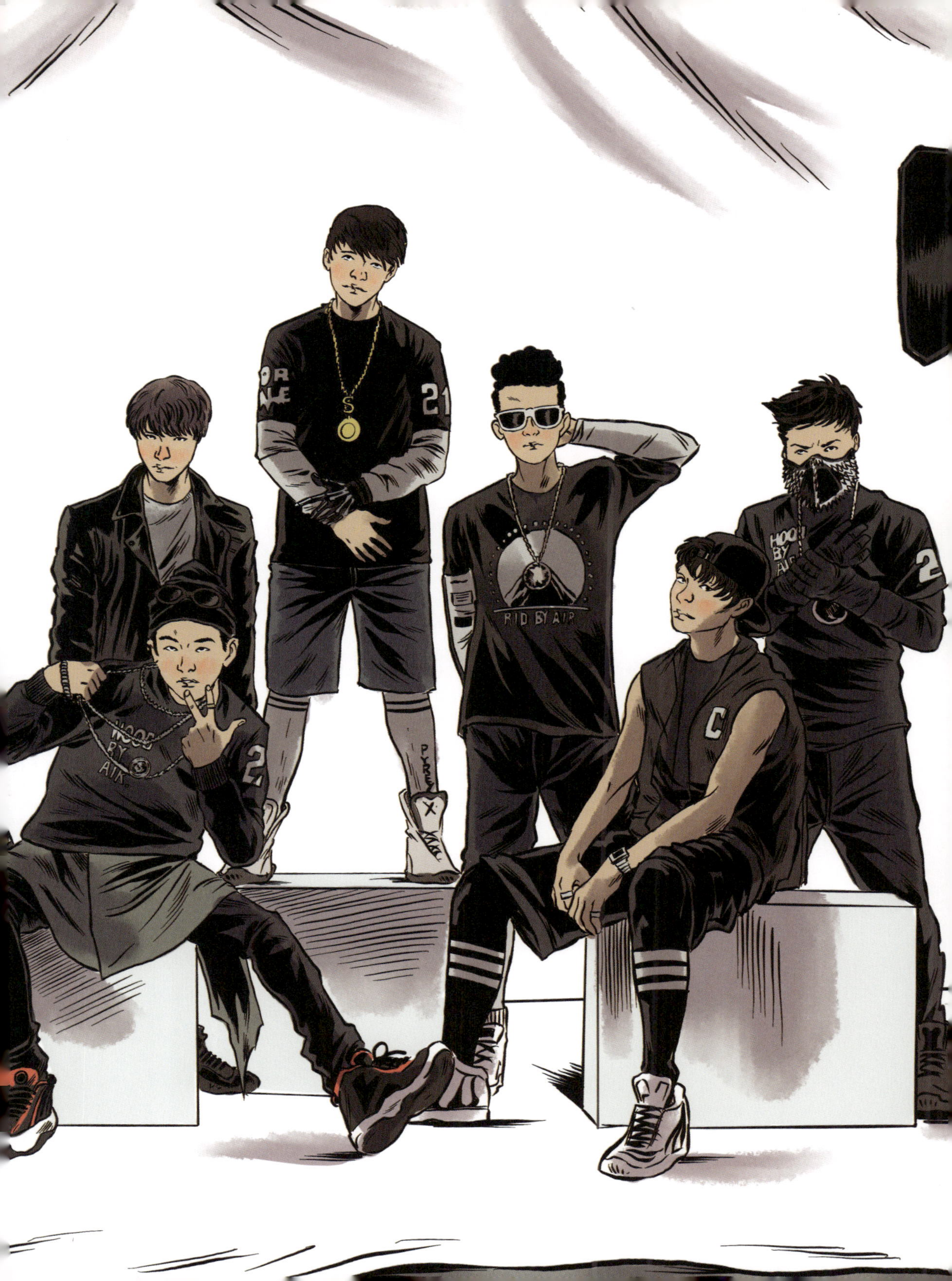
21
RID BY AIR
C

PROLOGUE

THE RAP DEN

SIGNING WITH BIG HIT ENTERTAINMENT
AND LIFE IN THE DORMS.

THE 'MAGNIFICENT SEVEN', FROM HOPEFULS TO IDOL
TRAINEES, FROM *BIG KIDZ* AND *YOUNG NATION* TO
OFFICIALLY BECOMING THE 'BULLETPROOF BOYS'
(BANGTAN SONYEONDAN).

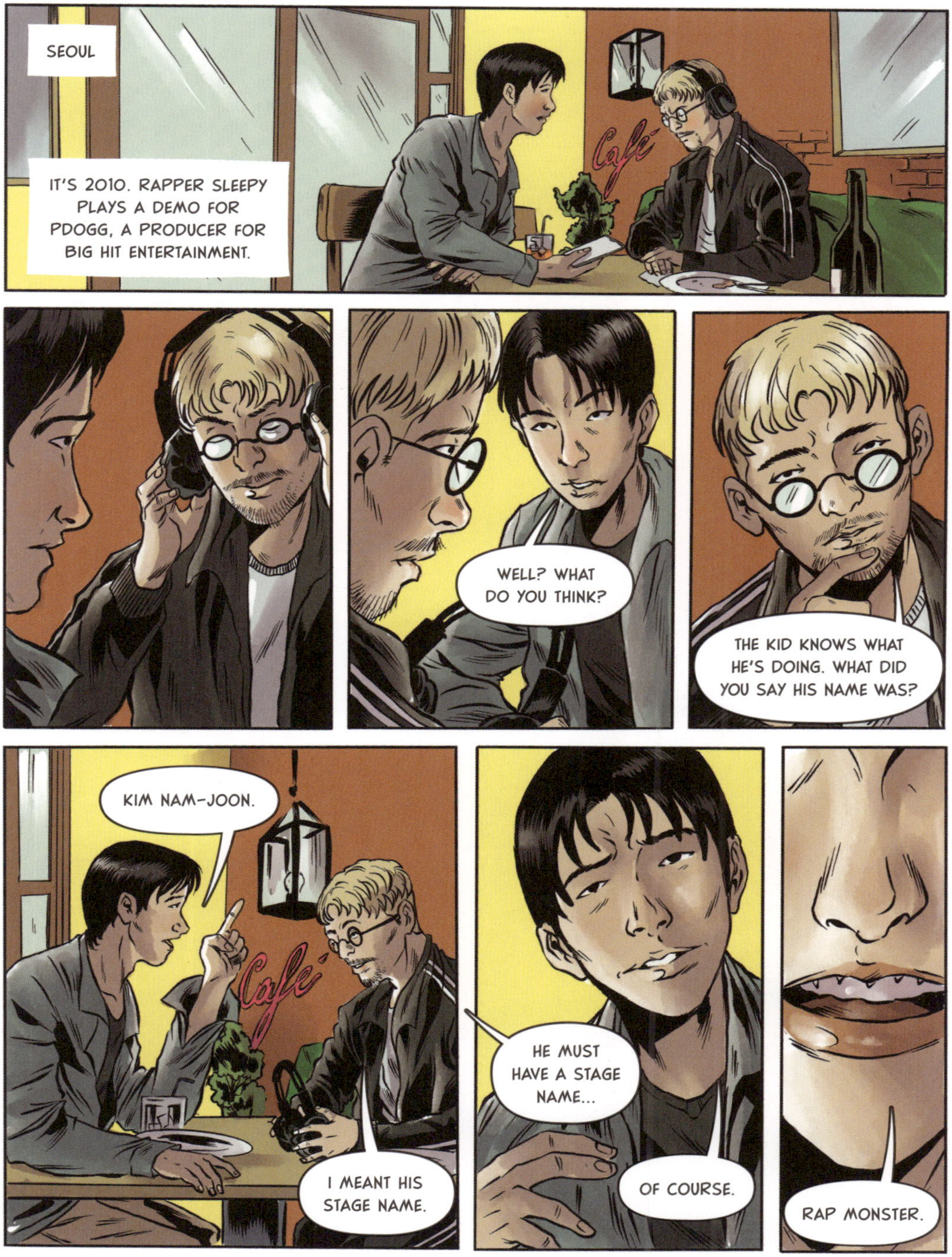
SEOUL
IT'S 2010. RAPPER SLEEPY PLAYS A DEMO FOR PDOGG, A PRODUCER FOR BIG HIT ENTERTAINMENT.
Café
WELL? WHAT DO YOU THINK?
THE KID KNOWS WHAT HE'S DOING. WHAT DID YOU SAY HIS NAME WAS?
KIM NAM-JOON.
Café
I MEANT HIS STAGE NAME.
HE MUST HAVE A STAGE NAME...
OF COURSE.
RAP MONSTER.

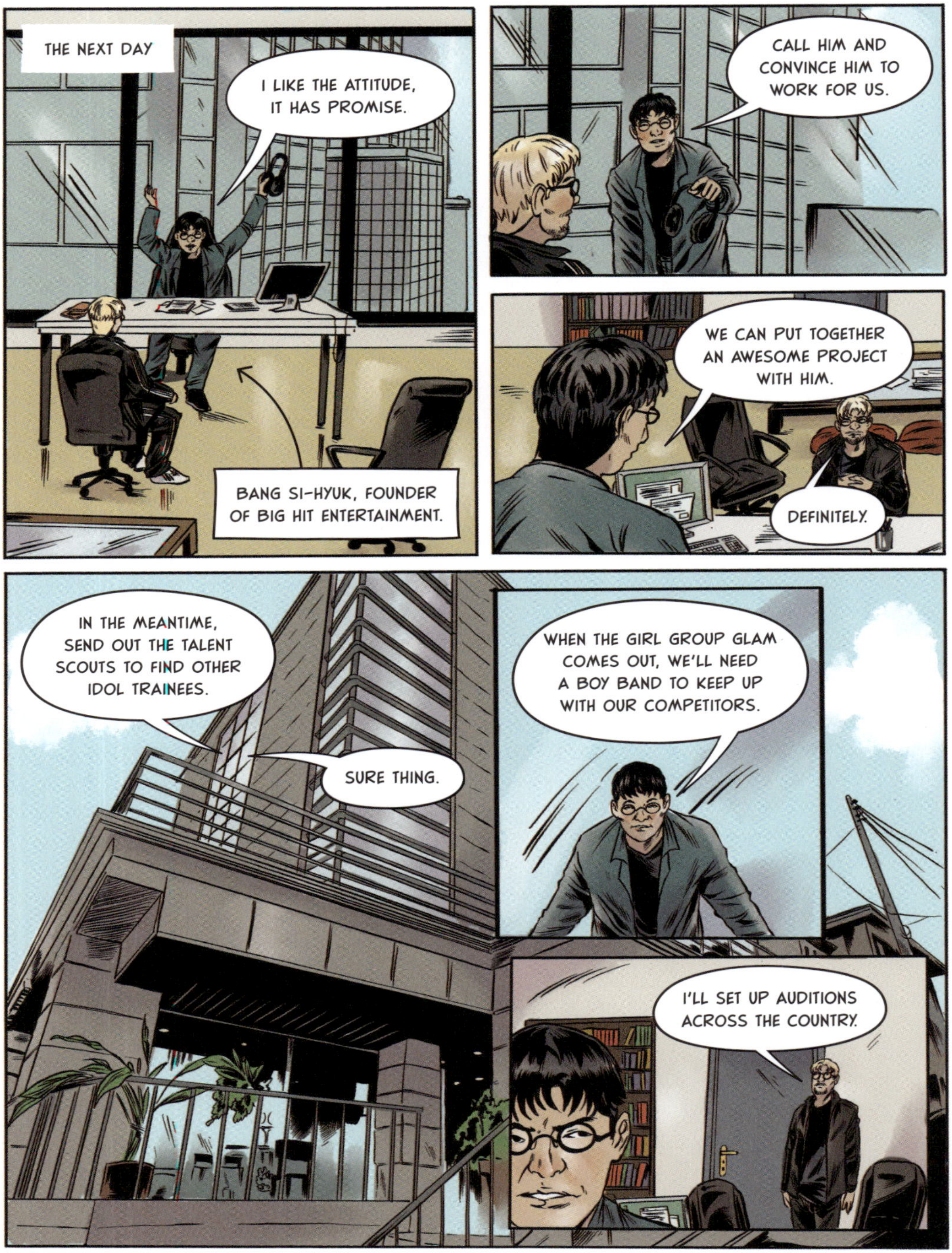

THE NEXT DAY
I LIKE THE ATTITUDE, IT HAS PROMISE.
BANG SI-HYUK, FOUNDER OF BIG HIT ENTERTAINMENT.
CALL HIM AND CONVINCE HIM TO WORK FOR US.
WE CAN PUT TOGETHER AN AWESOME PROJECT WITH HIM.
DEFINITELY.
IN THE MEANTIME, SEND OUT THE TALENT SCOUTS TO FIND OTHER IDOL TRAINEES.
SURE THING.
WHEN THE GIRL GROUP GLAM COMES OUT, WE'LL NEED A BOY BAND TO KEEP UP WITH OUR COMPETITORS.
I'LL SET UP AUDITIONS ACROSS THE COUNTRY.

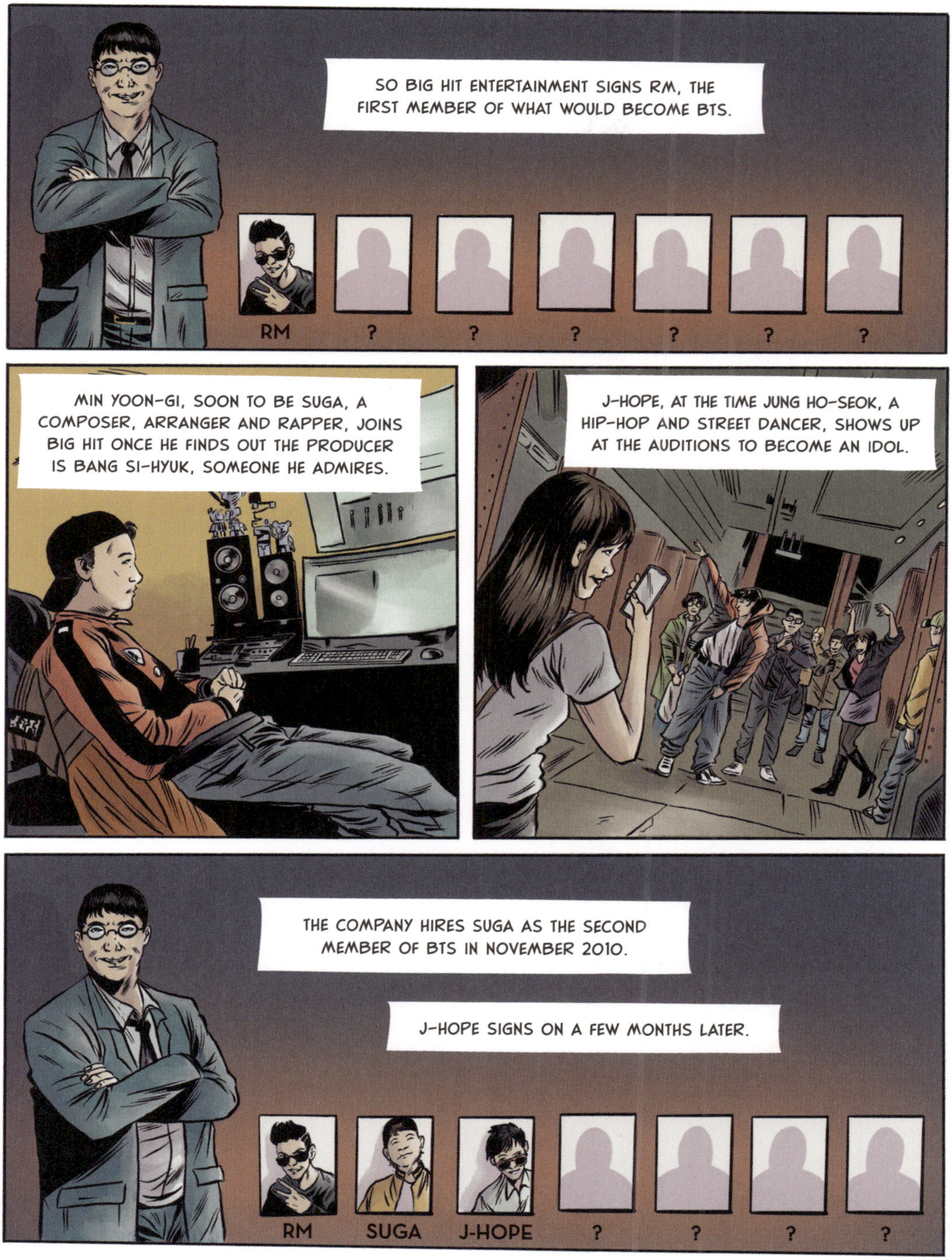
SO BIG HIT ENTERTAINMENT SIGNS RM, THE FIRST MEMBER OF WHAT WOULD BECOME BTS.
RM
?
?
?
?
?
?
MIN YOON-GI, SOON TO BE SUGA, A COMPOSER, ARRANGER AND RAPPER, JOINS BIG HIT ONCE HE FINDS OUT THE PRODUCER IS BANG SI-HYUK, SOMEONE HE ADMIRES.
J-HOPE, AT THE TIME JUNG HO-SEOK, A HIP-HOP AND STREET DANCER, SHOWS UP AT THE AUDITIONS TO BECOME AN IDOL.
THE COMPANY HIRES SUGA AS THE SECOND MEMBER OF BTS IN NOVEMBER 2010.
J-HOPE SIGNS ON A FEW MONTHS LATER.
RM
SUGA
J-HOPE
?
?
?
?

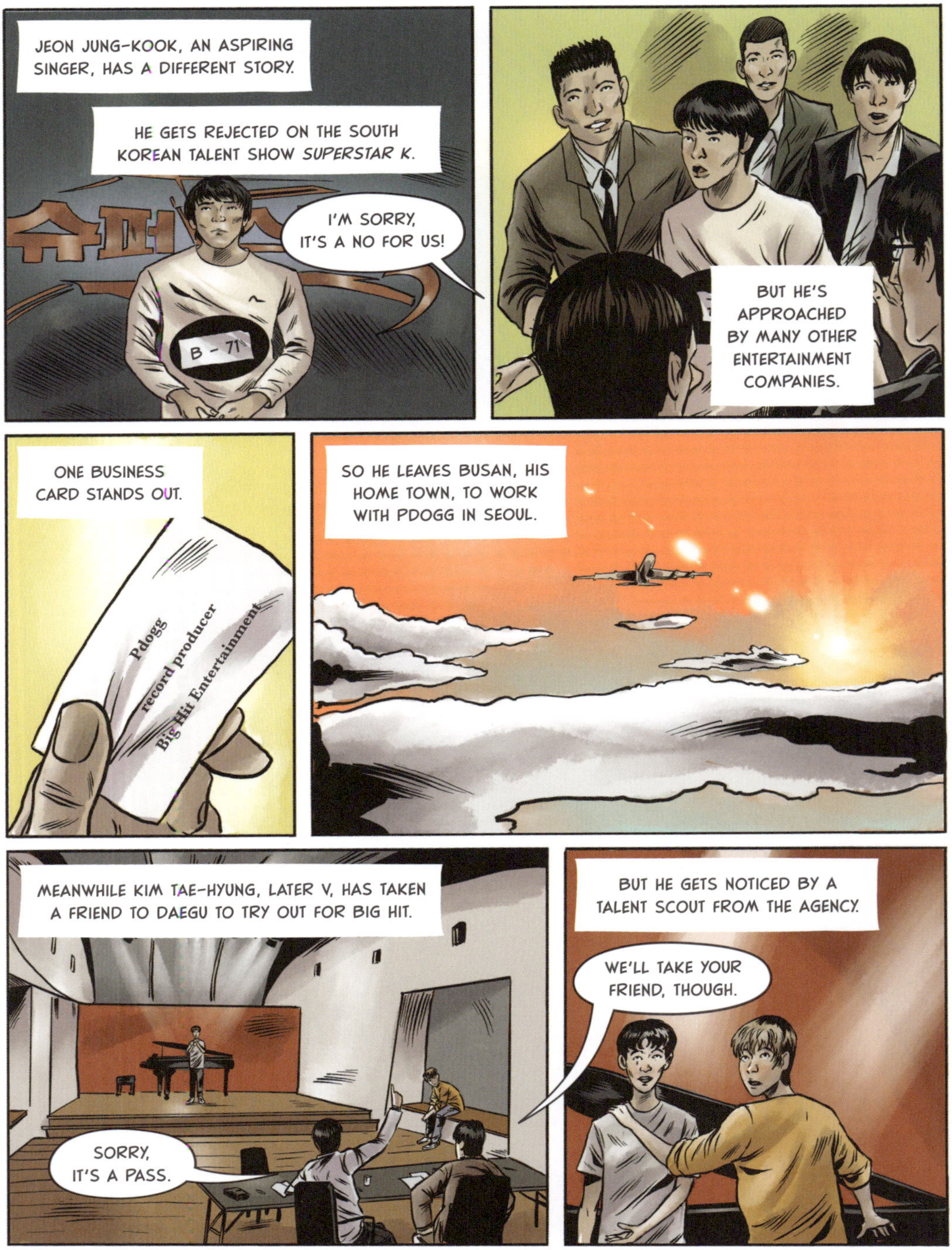

JEON JUNG-KOOK, AN ASPIRING SINGER, HAS A DIFFERENT STORY.
HE GETS REJECTED ON THE SOUTH KOREAN TALENT SHOW *SUPERSTAR K*.
B - 71
I'M SORRY, IT'S A NO FOR US!
BUT HE'S APPROACHED BY MANY OTHER ENTERTAINMENT COMPANIES.
ONE BUSINESS CARD STANDS OUT.
Pdogg
record producer
Big Hit Entertainment
SO HE LEAVES BUSAN, HIS HOME TOWN, TO WORK WITH PDOGG IN SEOUL.
MEANWHILE KIM TAE-HYUNG, LATER V, HAS TAKEN A FRIEND TO DAEGU TO TRY OUT FOR BIG HIT.
SORRY, IT'S A PASS.
BUT HE GETS NOTICED BY A TALENT SCOUT FROM THE AGENCY.
WE'LL TAKE YOUR FRIEND, THOUGH.

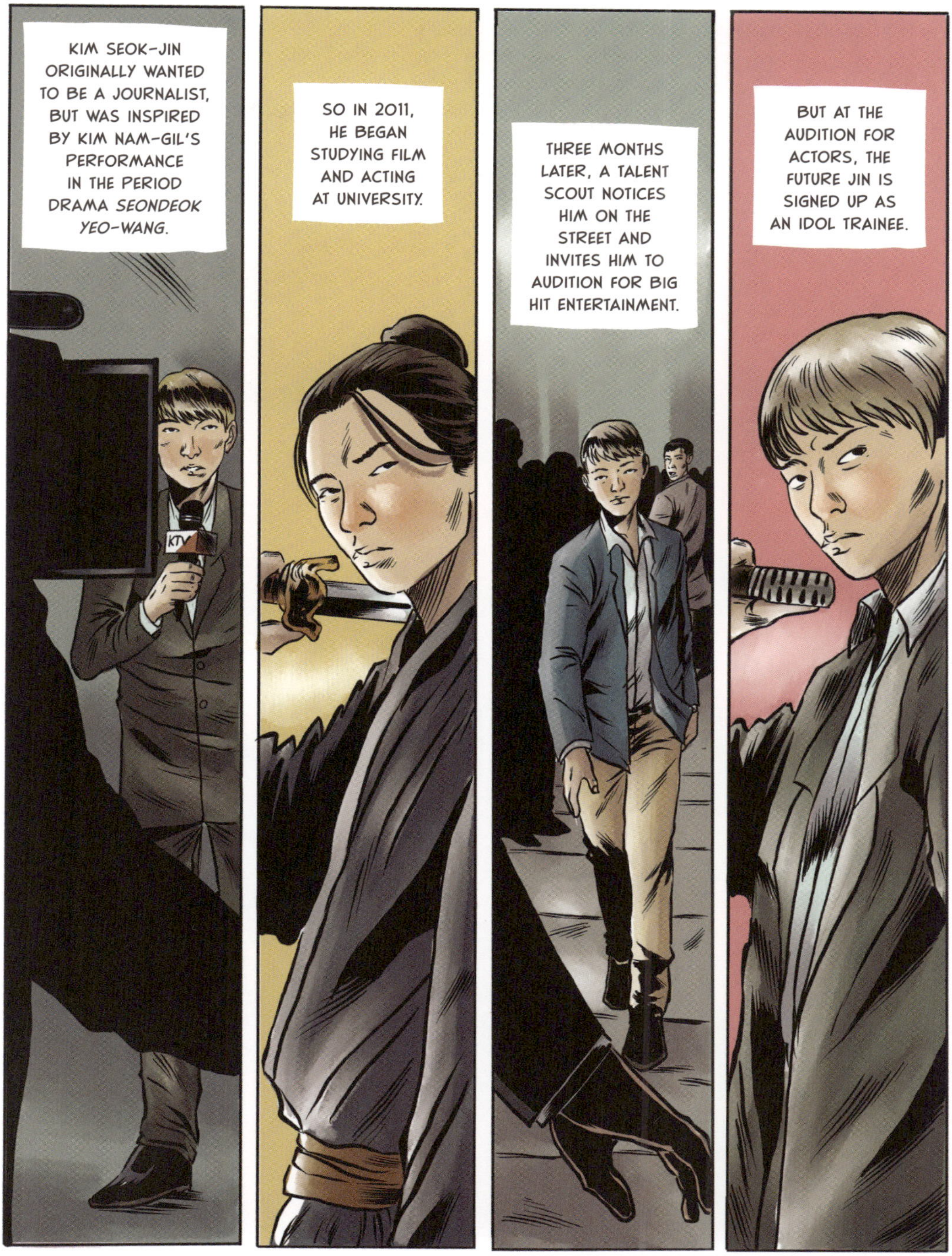
KIM SEOK-JIN ORIGINALLY WANTED TO BE A JOURNALIST, BUT WAS INSPIRED BY KIM NAM-GIL'S PERFORMANCE IN THE PERIOD DRAMA *SEONDEOK YEO-WANG*.
KTV
SO IN 2011, HE BEGAN STUDYING FILM AND ACTING AT UNIVERSITY.
THREE MONTHS LATER, A TALENT SCOUT NOTICES HIM ON THE STREET AND INVITES HIM TO AUDITION FOR BIG HIT ENTERTAINMENT.
BUT AT THE AUDITION FOR ACTORS, THE FUTURE JIN IS SIGNED UP AS AN IDOL TRAINEE.

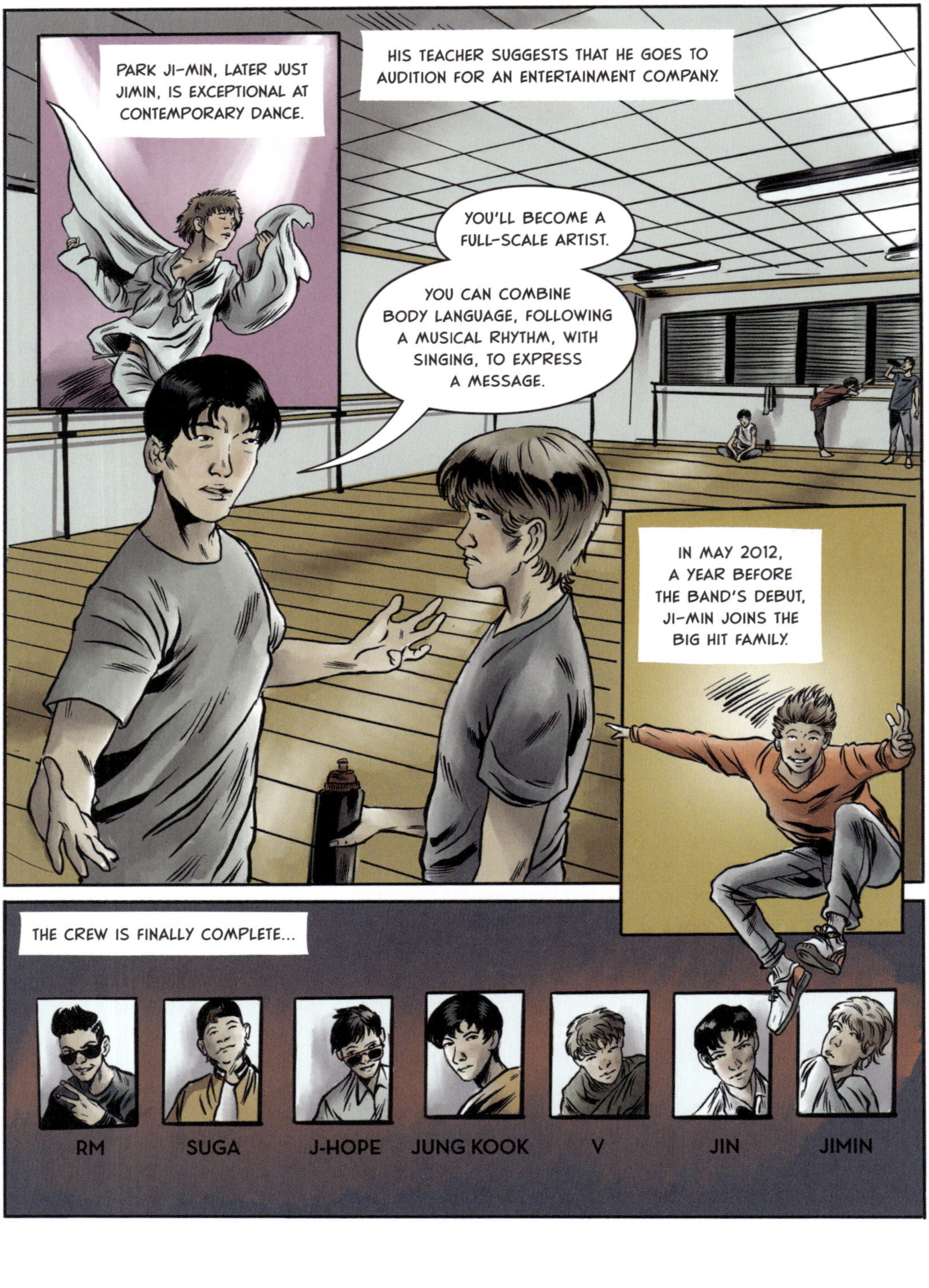
PARK JI-MIN, LATER JUST JIMIN, IS EXCEPTIONAL AT CONTEMPORARY DANCE.
HIS TEACHER SUGGESTS THAT HE GOES TO AUDITION FOR AN ENTERTAINMENT COMPANY.
YOU'LL BECOME A FULL-SCALE ARTIST.
YOU CAN COMBINE BODY LANGUAGE, FOLLOWING A MUSICAL RHYTHM, WITH SINGING, TO EXPRESS A MESSAGE.
IN MAY 2012, A YEAR BEFORE THE BAND'S DEBUT, JI-MIN JOINS THE BIG HIT FAMILY.
THE CREW IS FINALLY COMPLETE...
RM
SUGA
J-HOPE
JUNG KOOK
V
JIN
JIMIN

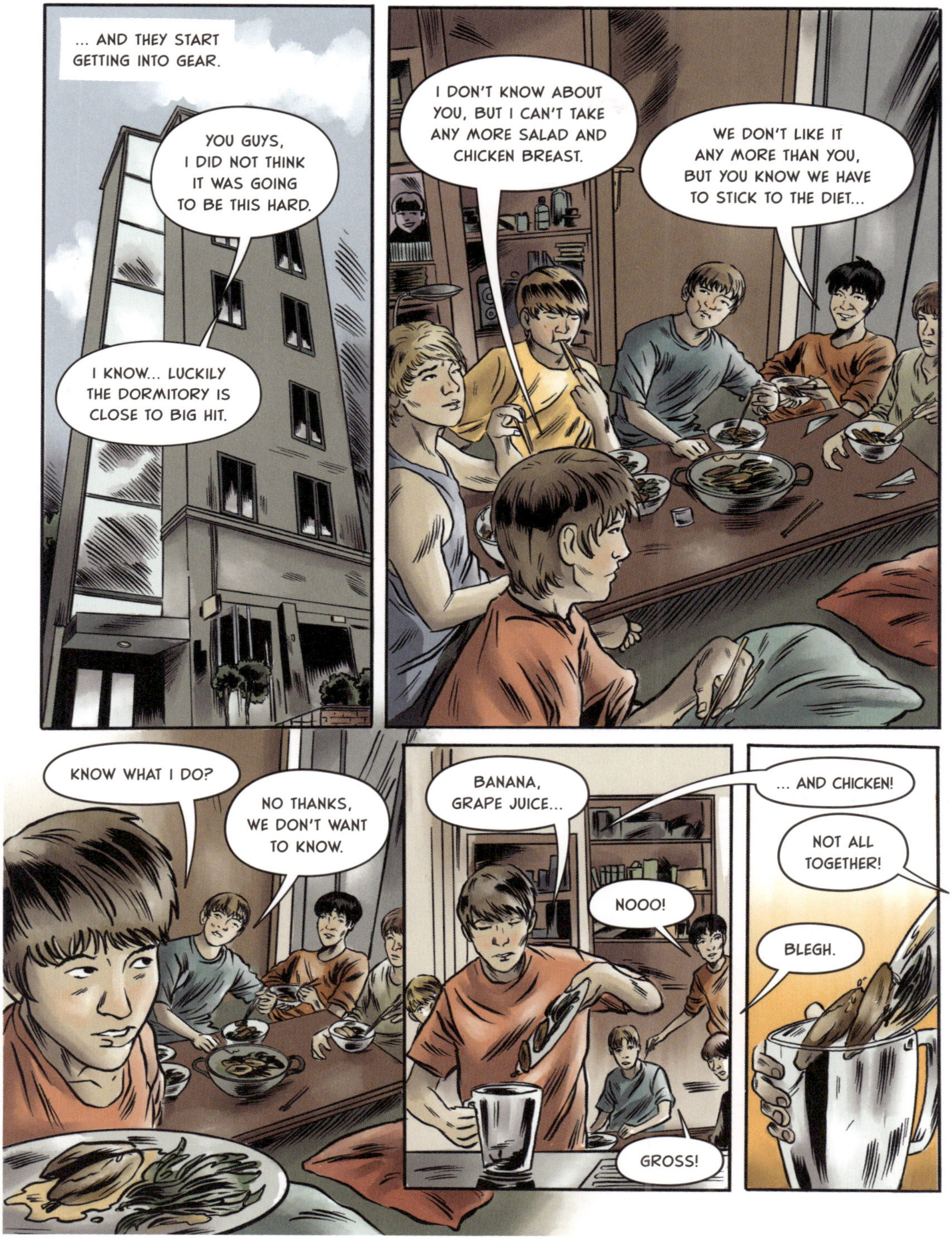
... AND THEY START GETTING INTO GEAR.
YOU GUYS, I DID NOT THINK IT WAS GOING TO BE THIS HARD.
I KNOW... LUCKILY THE DORMITORY IS CLOSE TO BIG HIT.
I DON'T KNOW ABOUT YOU, BUT I CAN'T TAKE ANY MORE SALAD AND CHICKEN BREAST.
WE DON'T LIKE IT ANY MORE THAN YOU, BUT YOU KNOW WE HAVE TO STICK TO THE DIET...
KNOW WHAT I DO?
NO THANKS, WE DON'T WANT TO KNOW.
BANANA, GRAPE JUICE...
... AND CHICKEN!
NOOO!
GROSS!
NOT ALL TOGETHER!
BLEGH.

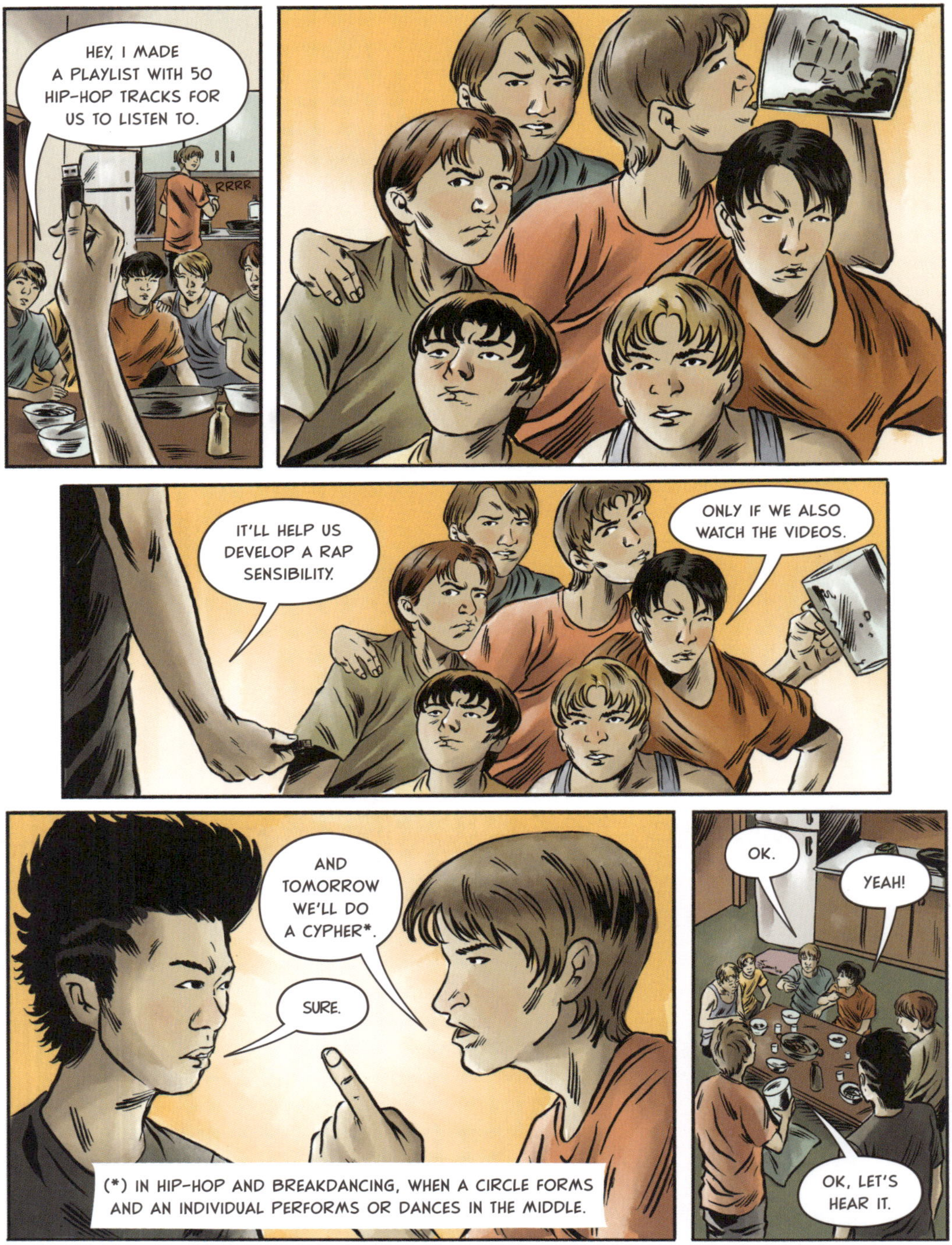
HEY, I MADE A PLAYLIST WITH 50 HIP-HOP TRACKS FOR US TO LISTEN TO.
RRRR
IT'LL HELP US DEVELOP A RAP SENSIBILITY.
ONLY IF WE ALSO WATCH THE VIDEOS.
AND TOMORROW WE'LL DO A CYPHER*.
SURE.
(*) IN HIP-HOP AND BREAKDANCING, WHEN A CIRCLE FORMS AND AN INDIVIDUAL PERFORMS OR DANCES IN THE MIDDLE.
OK.
YEAH!
OK, LET'S HEAR IT.

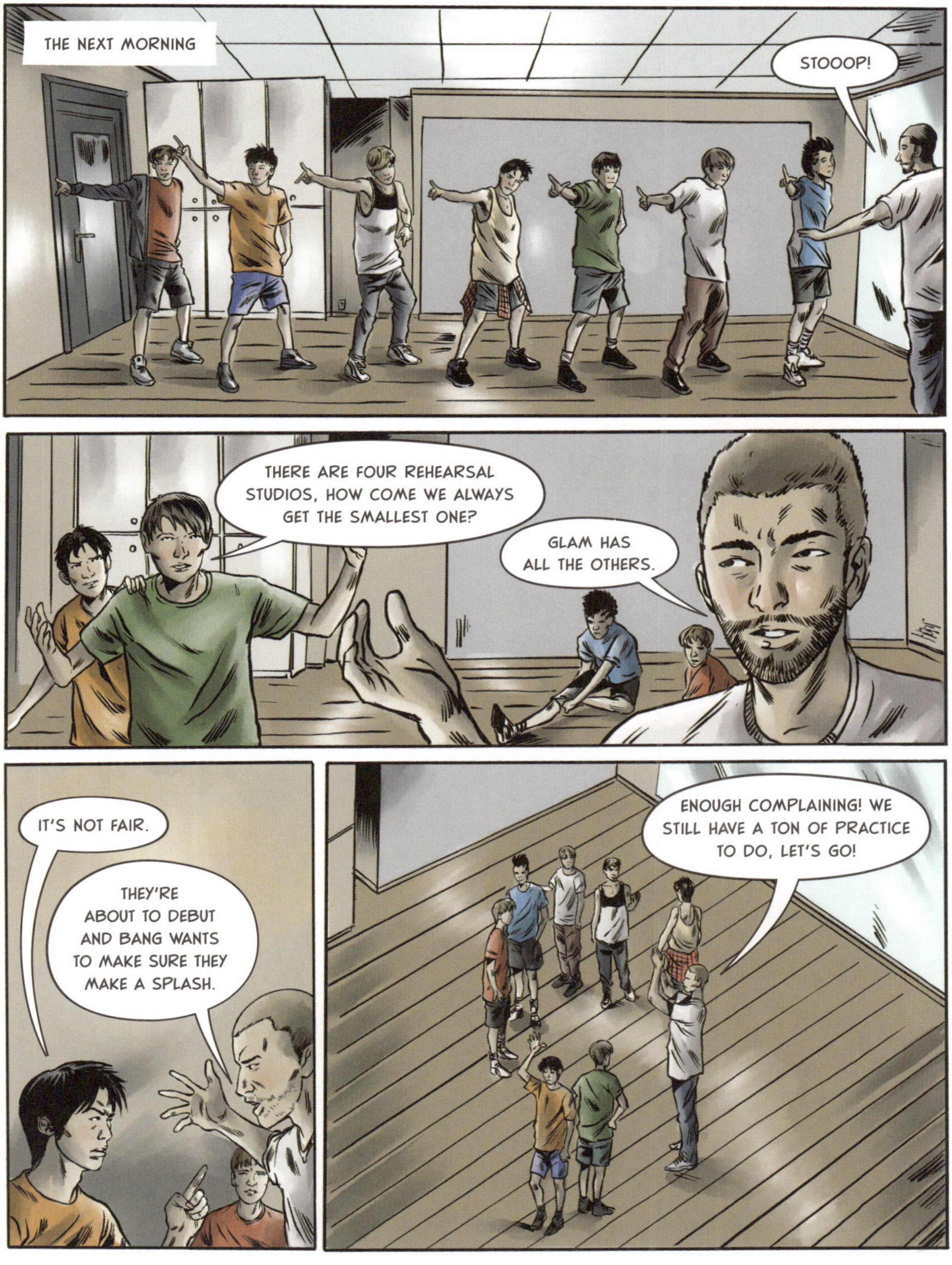
THE NEXT MORNING
STOOOP!
THERE ARE FOUR REHEARSAL STUDIOS, HOW COME WE ALWAYS GET THE SMALLEST ONE?
GLAM HAS ALL THE OTHERS.
IT'S NOT FAIR.
THEY'RE ABOUT TO DEBUT AND BANG WANTS TO MAKE SURE THEY MAKE A SPLASH.
ENOUGH COMPLAINING! WE STILL HAVE A TON OF PRACTICE TO DO, LET'S GO!

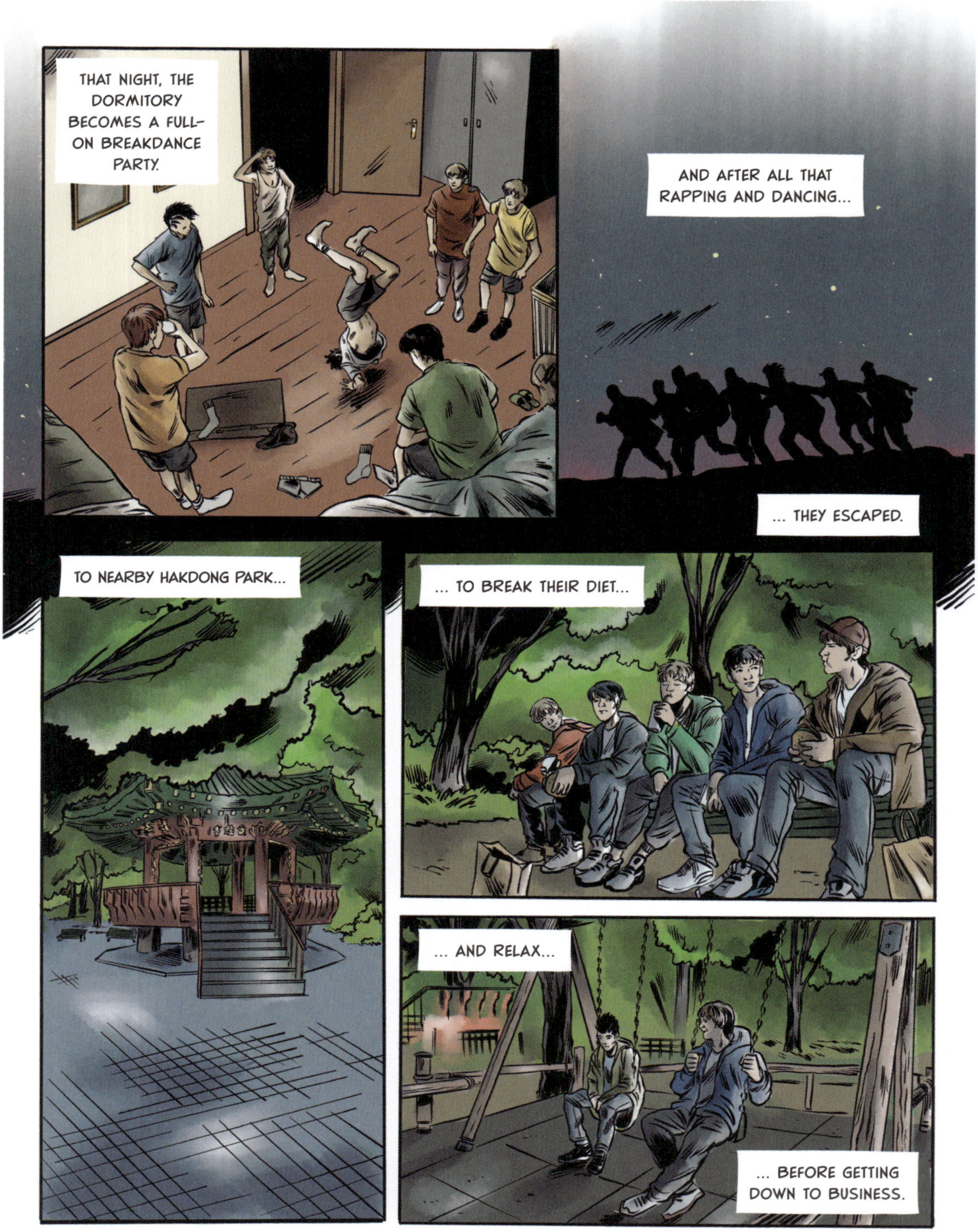
THAT NIGHT, THE DORMITORY BECOMES A FULL-ON BREAKDANCE PARTY.
AND AFTER ALL THAT RAPPING AND DANCING...
... THEY ESCAPED.
TO NEARBY HAKDONG PARK...
... TO BREAK THEIR DIET...
... AND RELAX...
... BEFORE GETTING DOWN TO BUSINESS.

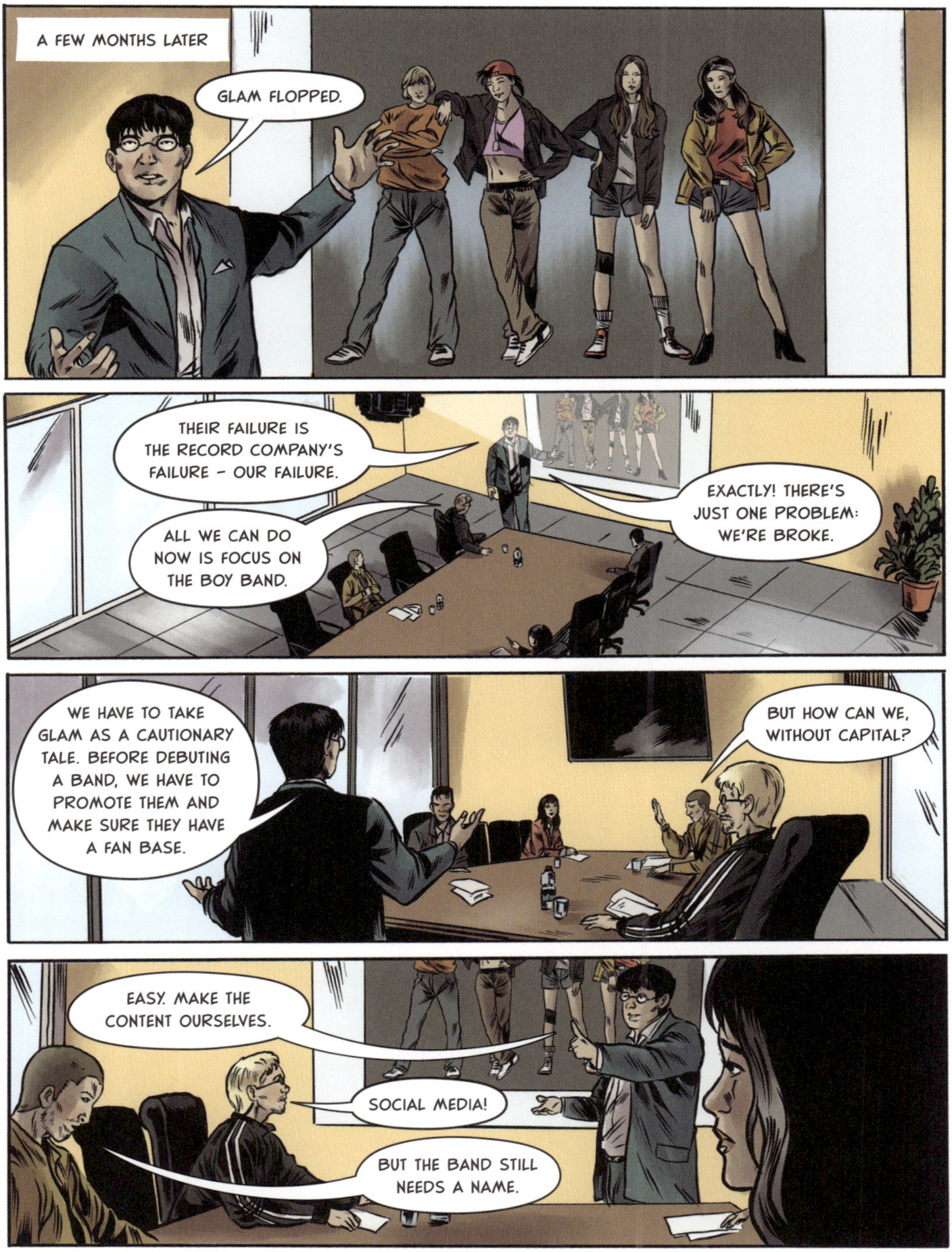
A FEW MONTHS LATER
GLAM FLOPPED.
THEIR FAILURE IS THE RECORD COMPANY'S FAILURE - OUR FAILURE.
ALL WE CAN DO NOW IS FOCUS ON THE BOY BAND.
EXACTLY! THERE'S JUST ONE PROBLEM: WE'RE BROKE.
WE HAVE TO TAKE GLAM AS A CAUTIONARY TALE. BEFORE DEBUTING A BAND, WE HAVE TO PROMOTE THEM AND MAKE SURE THEY HAVE A FAN BASE.
BUT HOW CAN WE, WITHOUT CAPITAL?
EASY. MAKE THE CONTENT OURSELVES.
SOCIAL MEDIA!
BUT THE BAND STILL NEEDS A NAME.

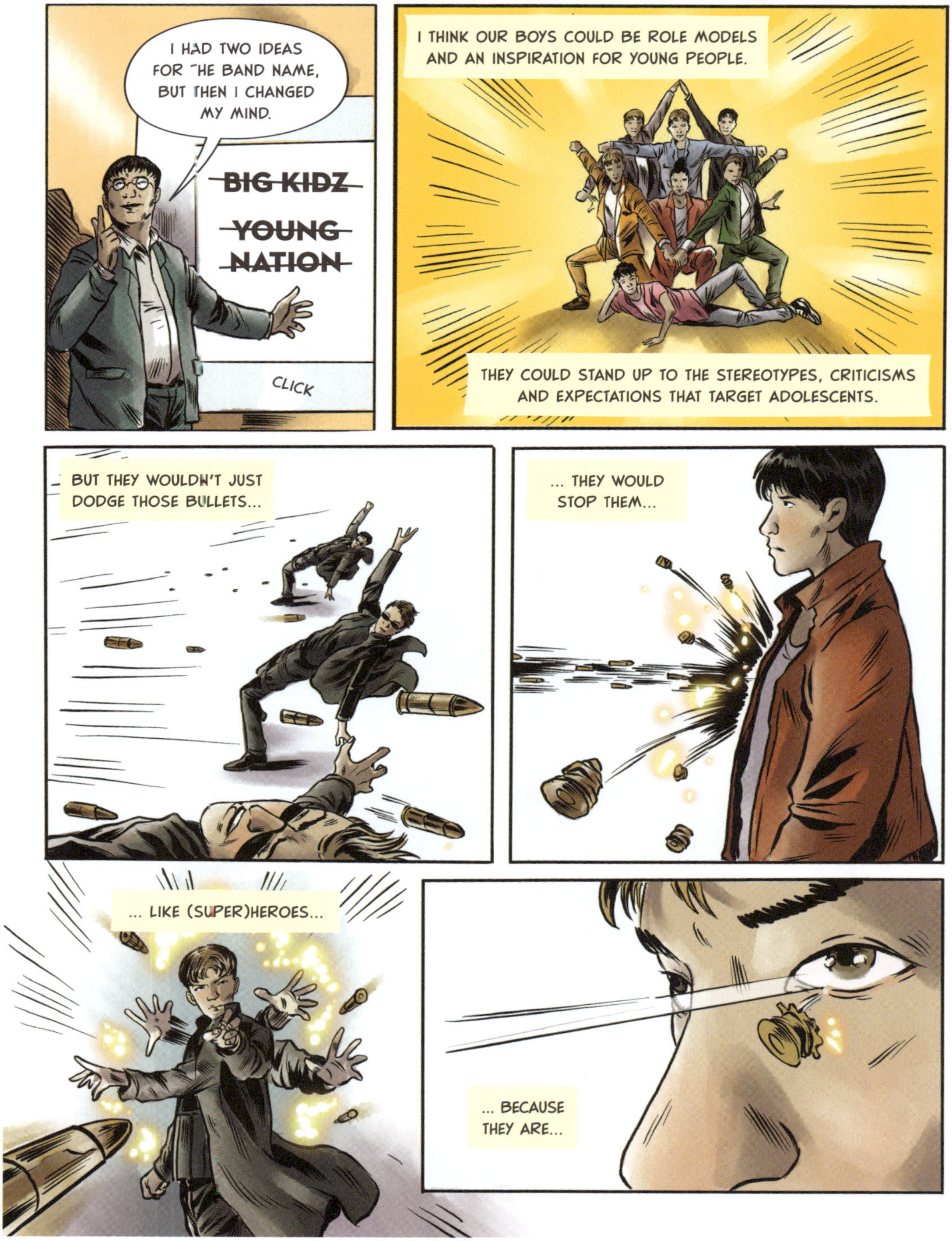
I HAD TWO IDEAS FOR THE BAND NAME, BUT THEN I CHANGED MY MIND.
BIG KIDZ
YOUNG NATION
CLICK
I THINK OUR BOYS COULD BE ROLE MODELS AND AN INSPIRATION FOR YOUNG PEOPLE.
THEY COULD STAND UP TO THE STEREOTYPES, CRITICISMS AND EXPECTATIONS THAT TARGET ADOLESCENTS.
BUT THEY WOULDN'T JUST DODGE THOSE BULLETS...
... THEY WOULD STOP THEM...
... LIKE (SUPER)HEROES...
... BECAUSE THEY ARE...

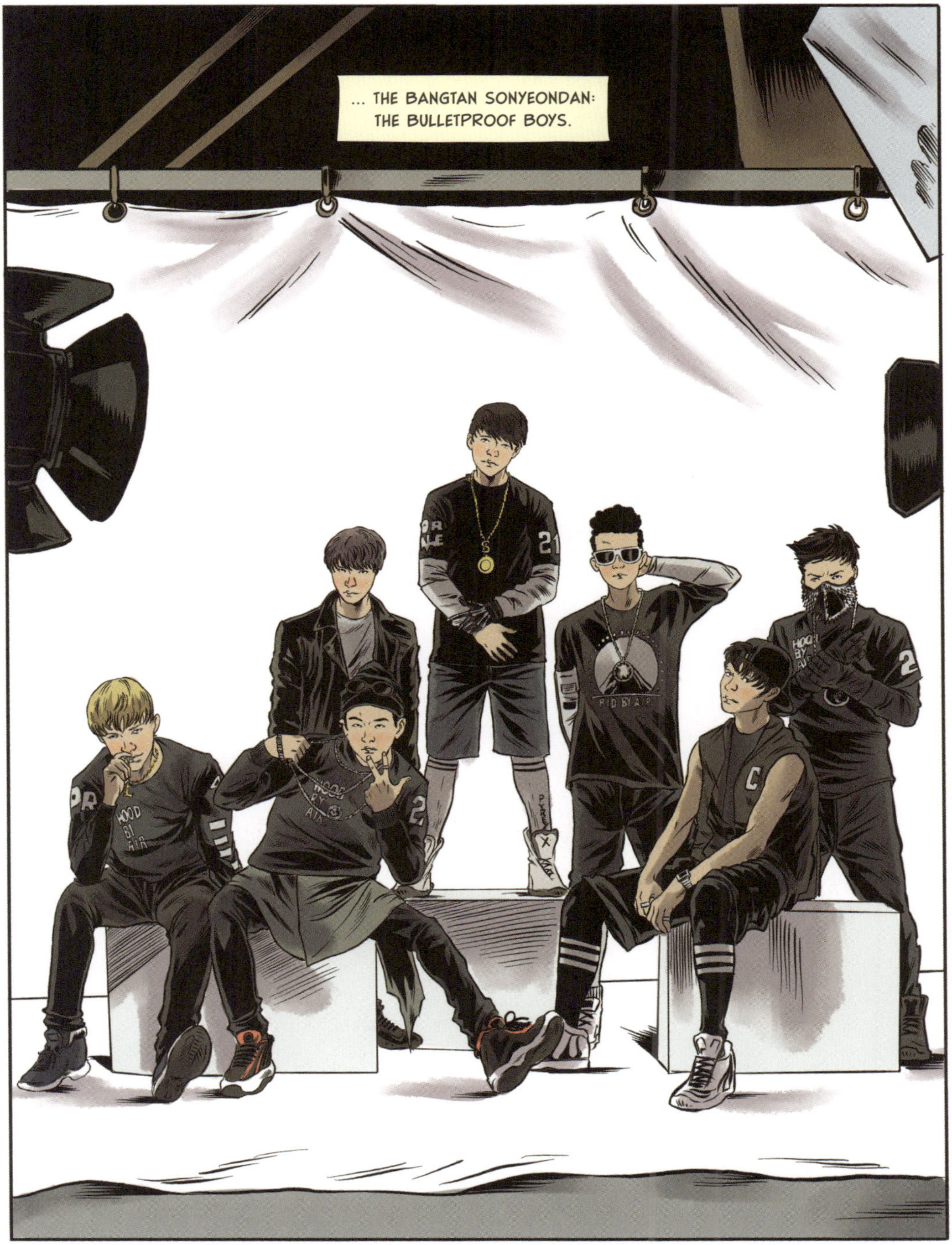
... THE BANGTAN SONYEONDAN: THE BULLETPROOF BOYS.

RM

KIM NAM-JOON

FROM RUNCH RANDA TO RAP MONSTER TO RM.

THIS IS NAM-JOON'S CULTURAL AND MUTUAL JOURNEY TO THE DISCOVERY OF HIS TRUE IDENTITY AS A TOTAL ARTIST.

HIS LOVE AND SUPPORT FOR CONTEMPORARY ART, HIS TRIPS TO MUSEUMS AND GALLERIES, HIS CHOICES OF READING AND HIS STUDIES (SHARED ON SOCIAL MEDIA), HAVE BOOSTED HIS FANS' INTEREST IN CONTEMPORARY ART, DRAWING HUNDREDS OF VISITORS TO THE EXHIBITIONS HE ATTENDS AND JUST AS MANY BUYERS OF THE BOOKS HE READS.

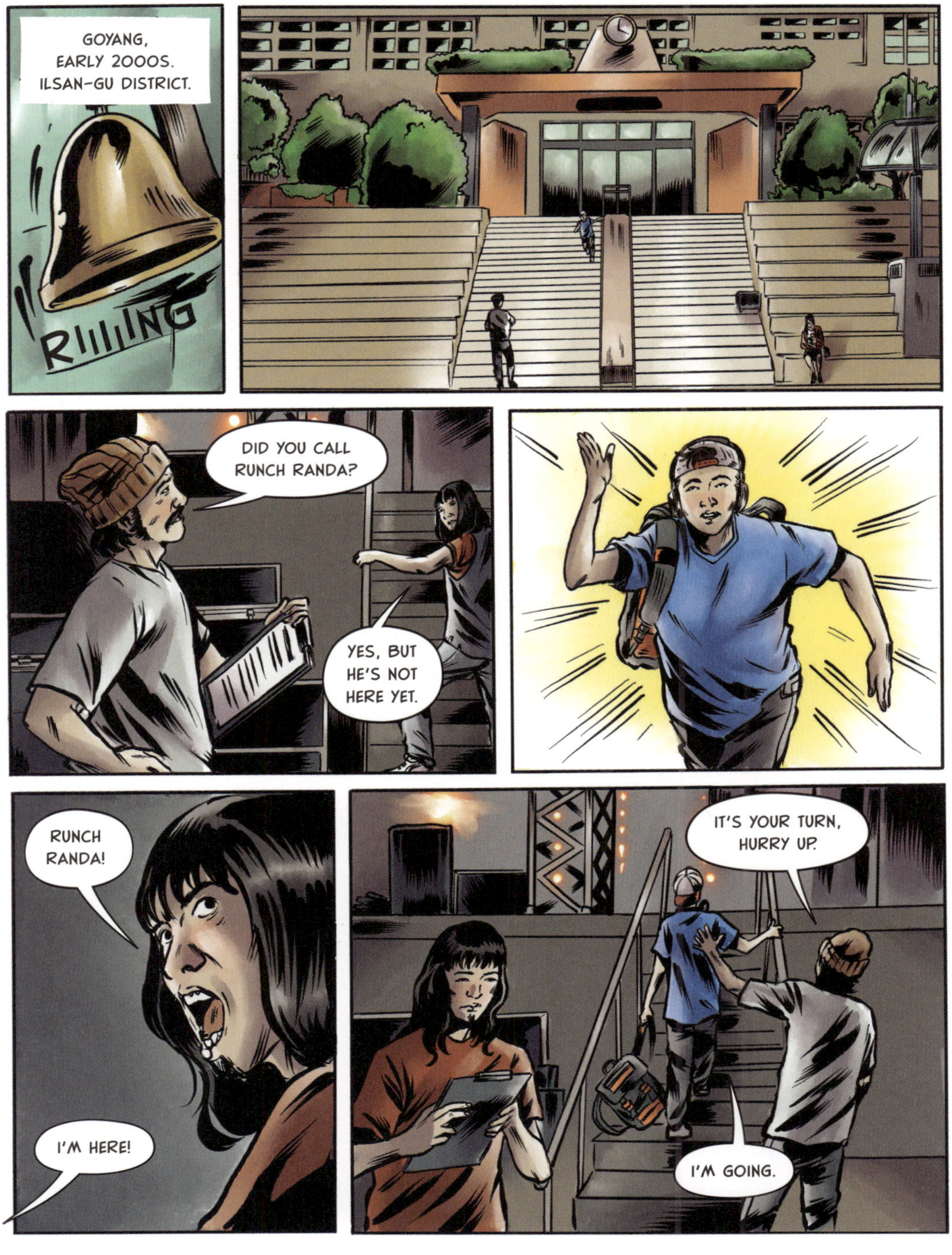
GOYANG, EARLY 2000S. ILSAN-GU DISTRICT.
RIIIING
DID YOU CALL RUNCH RANDA?
YES, BUT HE'S NOT HERE YET.
RUNCH RANDA!
I'M HERE!
IT'S YOUR TURN, HURRY UP.
I'M GOING.

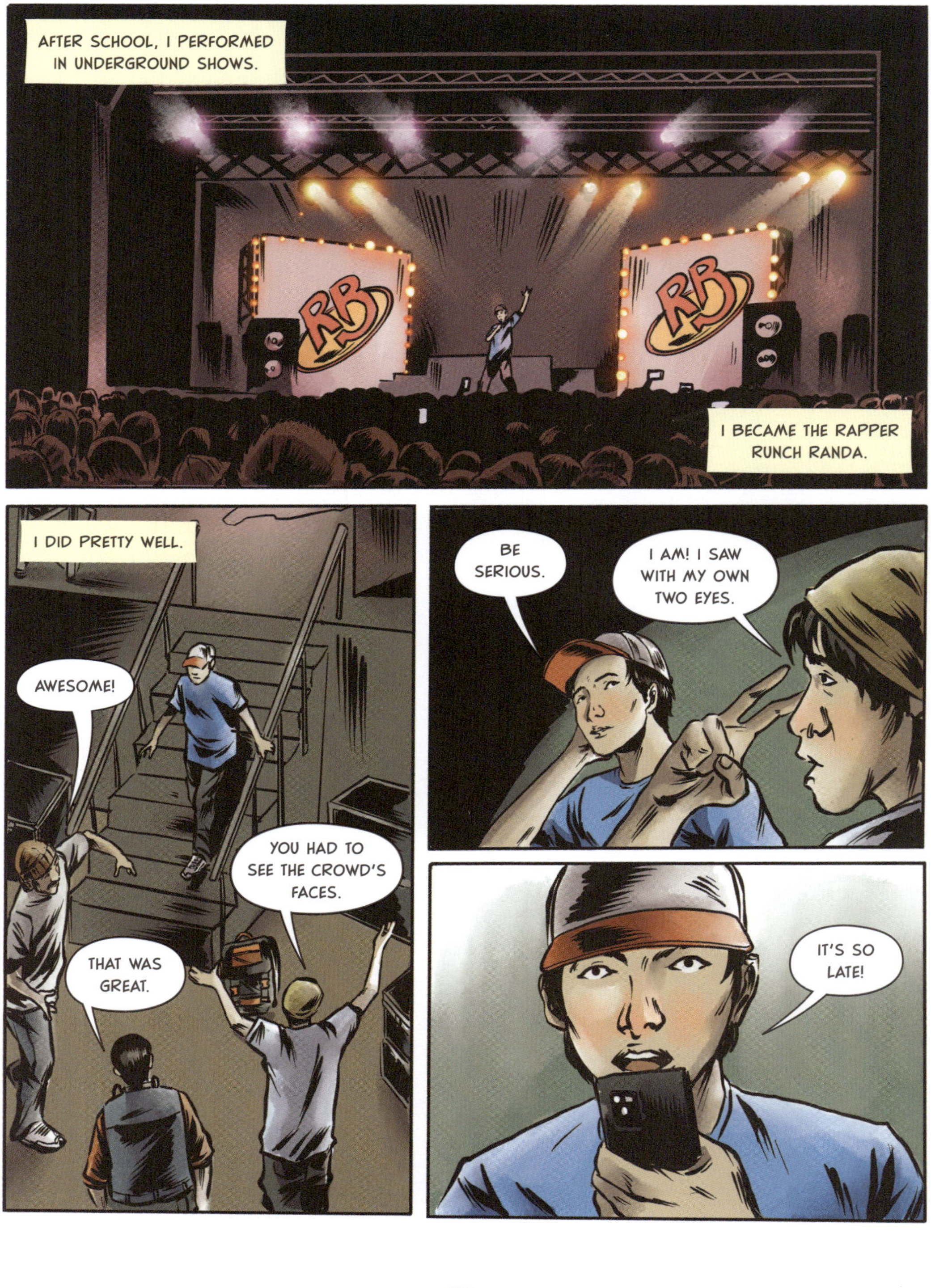
AFTER SCHOOL, I PERFORMED IN UNDERGROUND SHOWS.
RB
RB
I BECAME THE RAPPER RUNCH RANDA.
I DID PRETTY WELL.
AWESOME!
YOU HAD TO SEE THE CROWD'S FACES.
THAT WAS GREAT.
BE SERIOUS.
I AM! I SAW WITH MY OWN TWO EYES.
IT'S SO LATE!

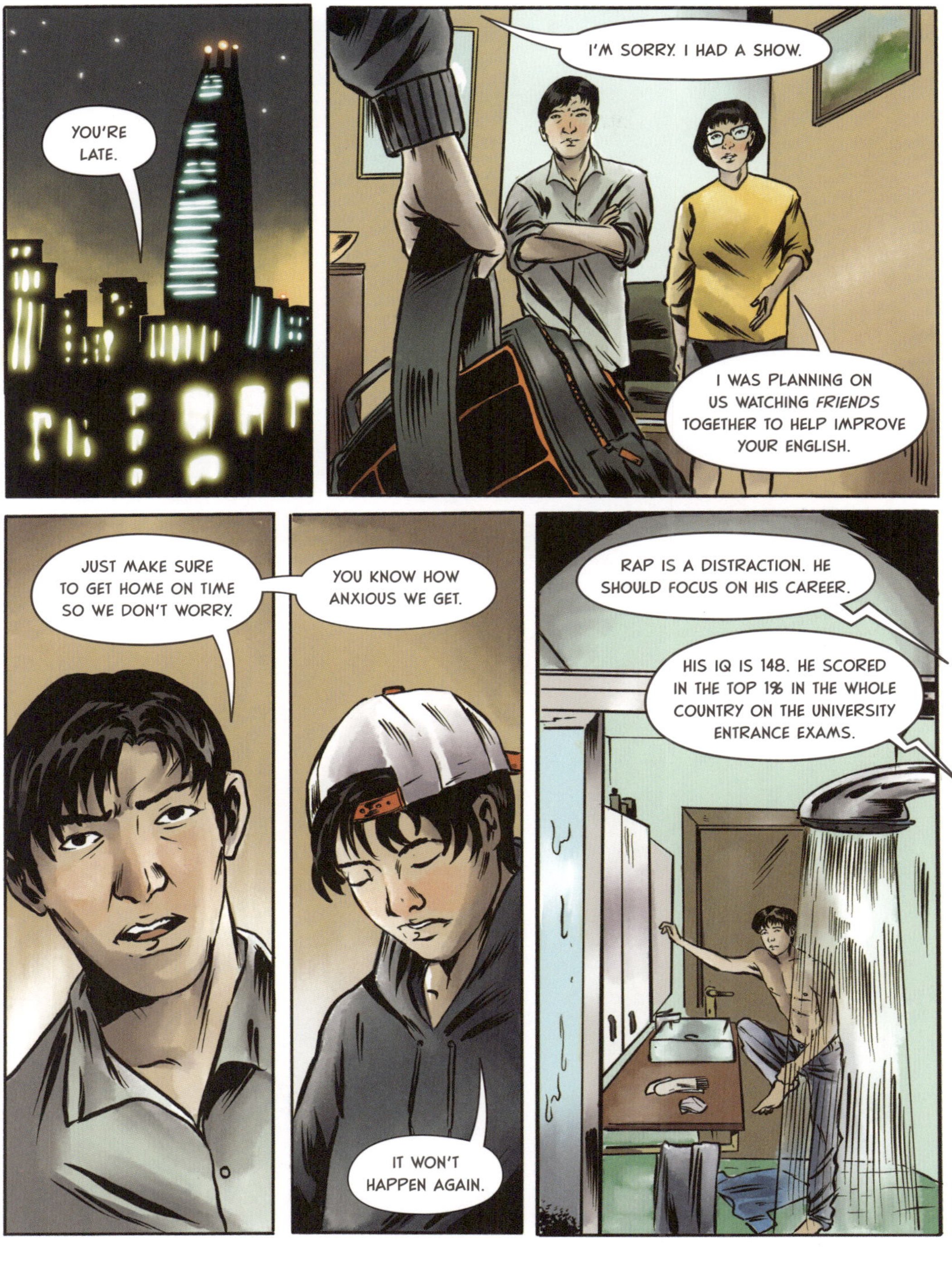
YOU'RE LATE.
I'M SORRY. I HAD A SHOW.
I WAS PLANNING ON US WATCHING *FRIENDS* TOGETHER TO HELP IMPROVE YOUR ENGLISH.
JUST MAKE SURE TO GET HOME ON TIME SO WE DON'T WORRY.
YOU KNOW HOW ANXIOUS WE GET.
IT WON'T HAPPEN AGAIN.
RAP IS A DISTRACTION. HE SHOULD FOCUS ON HIS CAREER.
HIS IQ IS 148. HE SCORED IN THE TOP 1% IN THE WHOLE COUNTRY ON THE UNIVERSITY ENTRANCE EXAMS.

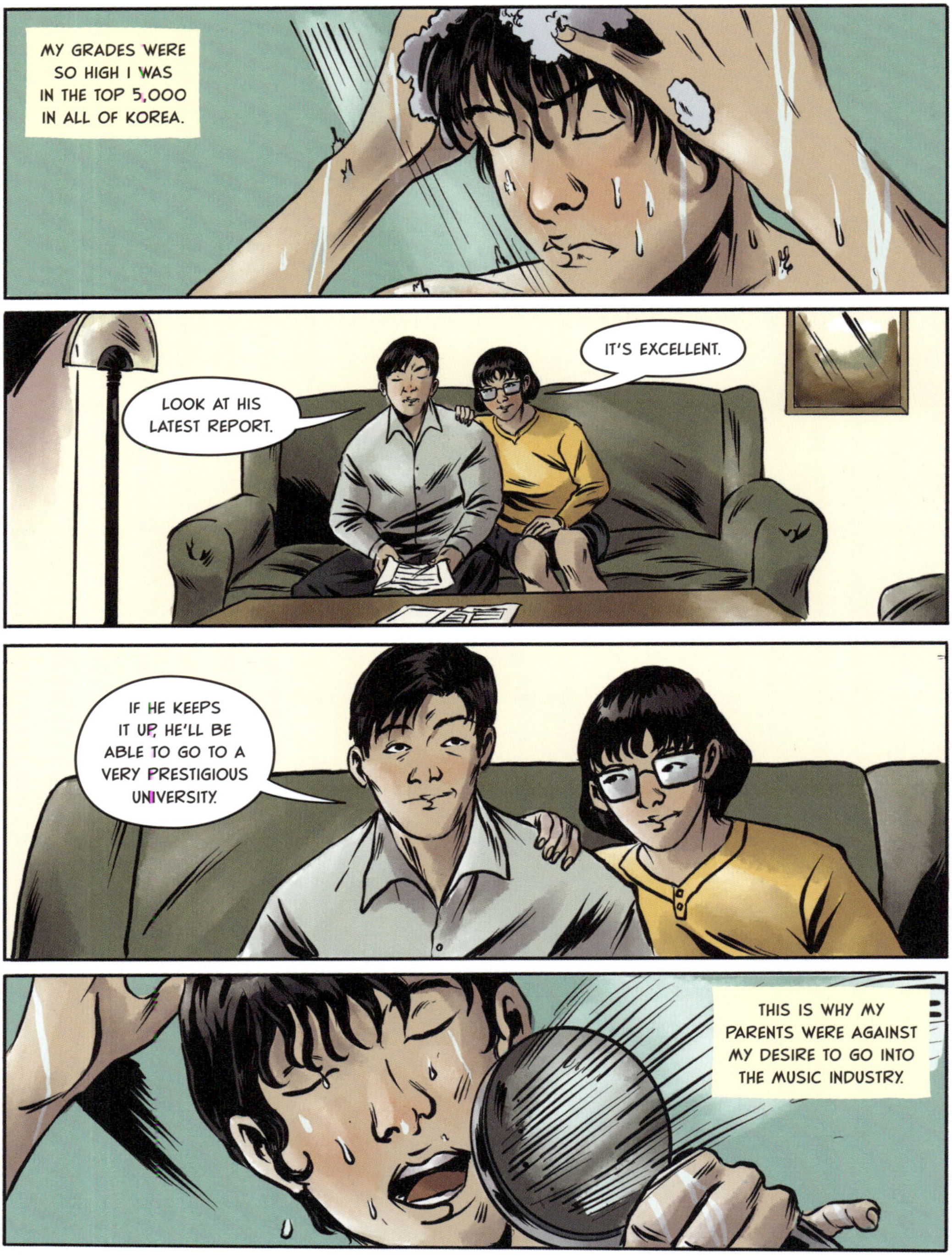
MY GRADES WERE SO HIGH I WAS IN THE TOP 5,000 IN ALL OF KOREA.
LOOK AT HIS LATEST REPORT.
IT'S EXCELLENT.
IF HE KEEPS IT UP, HE'LL BE ABLE TO GO TO A VERY PRESTIGIOUS UNIVERSITY.
THIS IS WHY MY PARENTS WERE AGAINST MY DESIRE TO GO INTO THE MUSIC INDUSTRY.

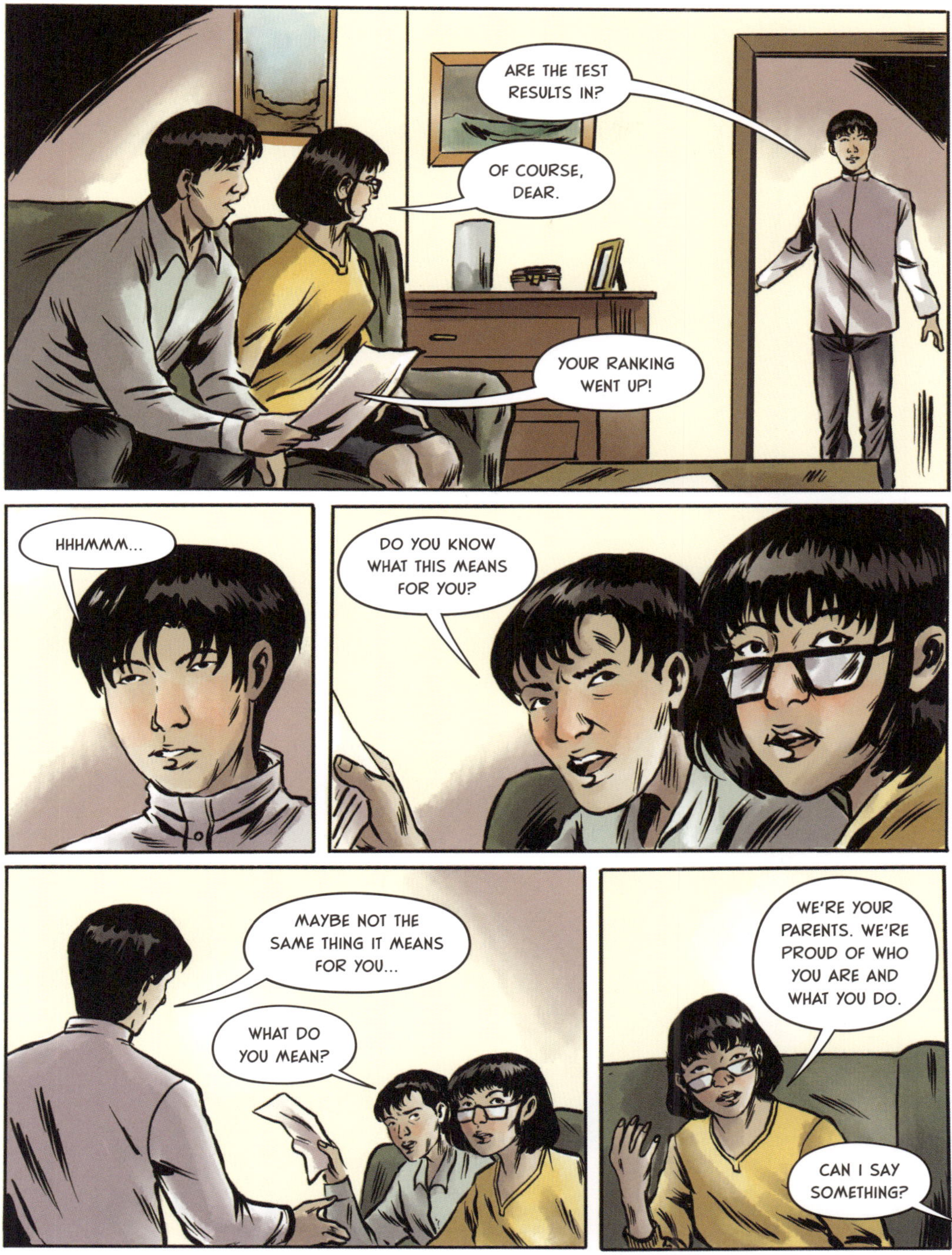
ARE THE TEST RESULTS IN?
OF COURSE, DEAR.
YOUR RANKING WENT UP!
HHHMMM...
DO YOU KNOW WHAT THIS MEANS FOR YOU?
MAYBE NOT THE SAME THING IT MEANS FOR YOU...
WHAT DO YOU MEAN?
WE'RE YOUR PARENTS. WE'RE PROUD OF WHO YOU ARE AND WHAT YOU DO.
CAN I SAY SOMETHING?

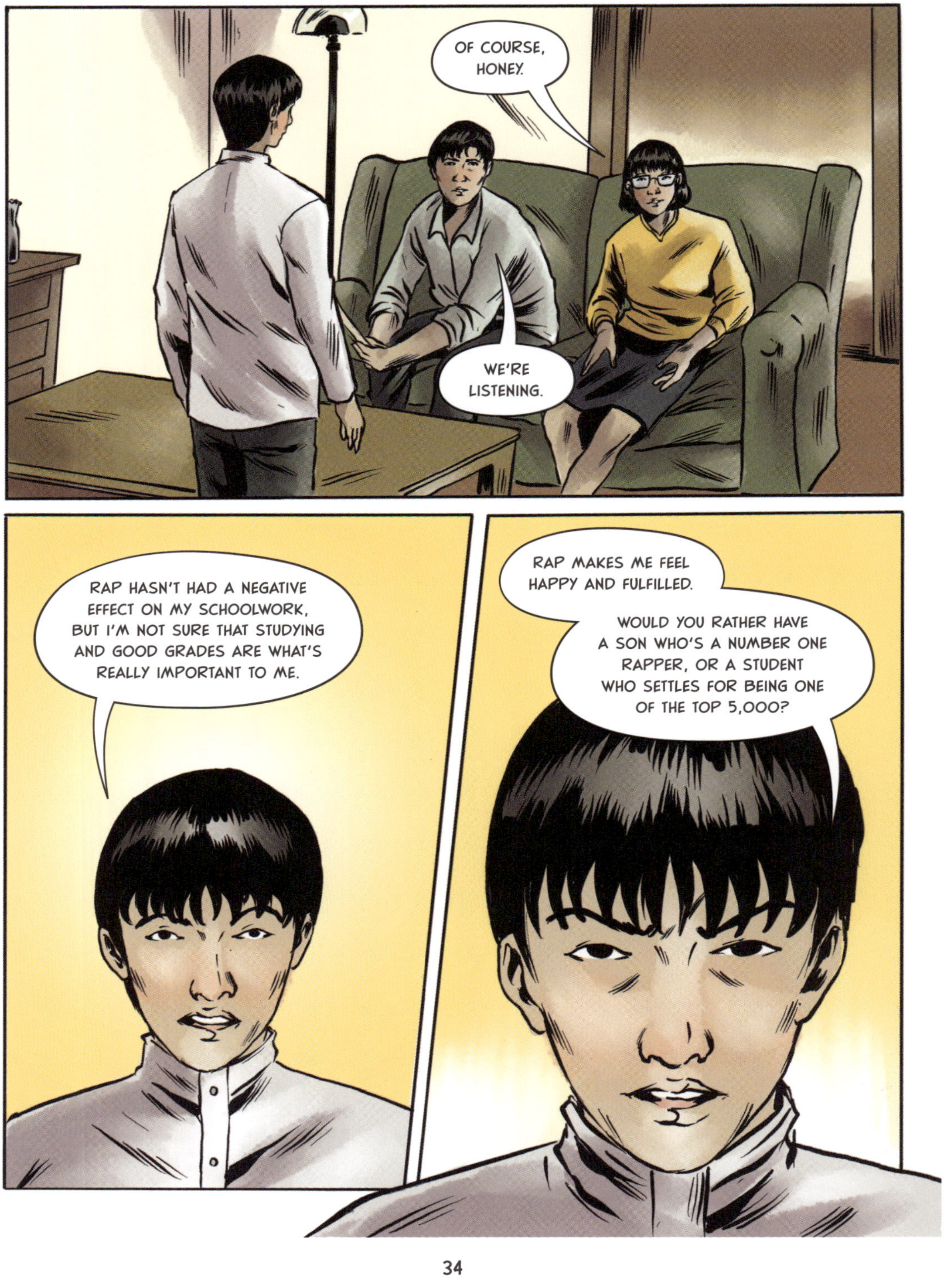
OF COURSE, HONEY.
WE'RE LISTENING.
RAP HASN'T HAD A NEGATIVE EFFECT ON MY SCHOOLWORK, BUT I'M NOT SURE THAT STUDYING AND GOOD GRADES ARE WHAT'S REALLY IMPORTANT TO ME.
RAP MAKES ME FEEL HAPPY AND FULFILLED.
WOULD YOU RATHER HAVE A SON WHO'S A NUMBER ONE RAPPER, OR A STUDENT WHO SETTLES FOR BEING ONE OF THE TOP 5,000?

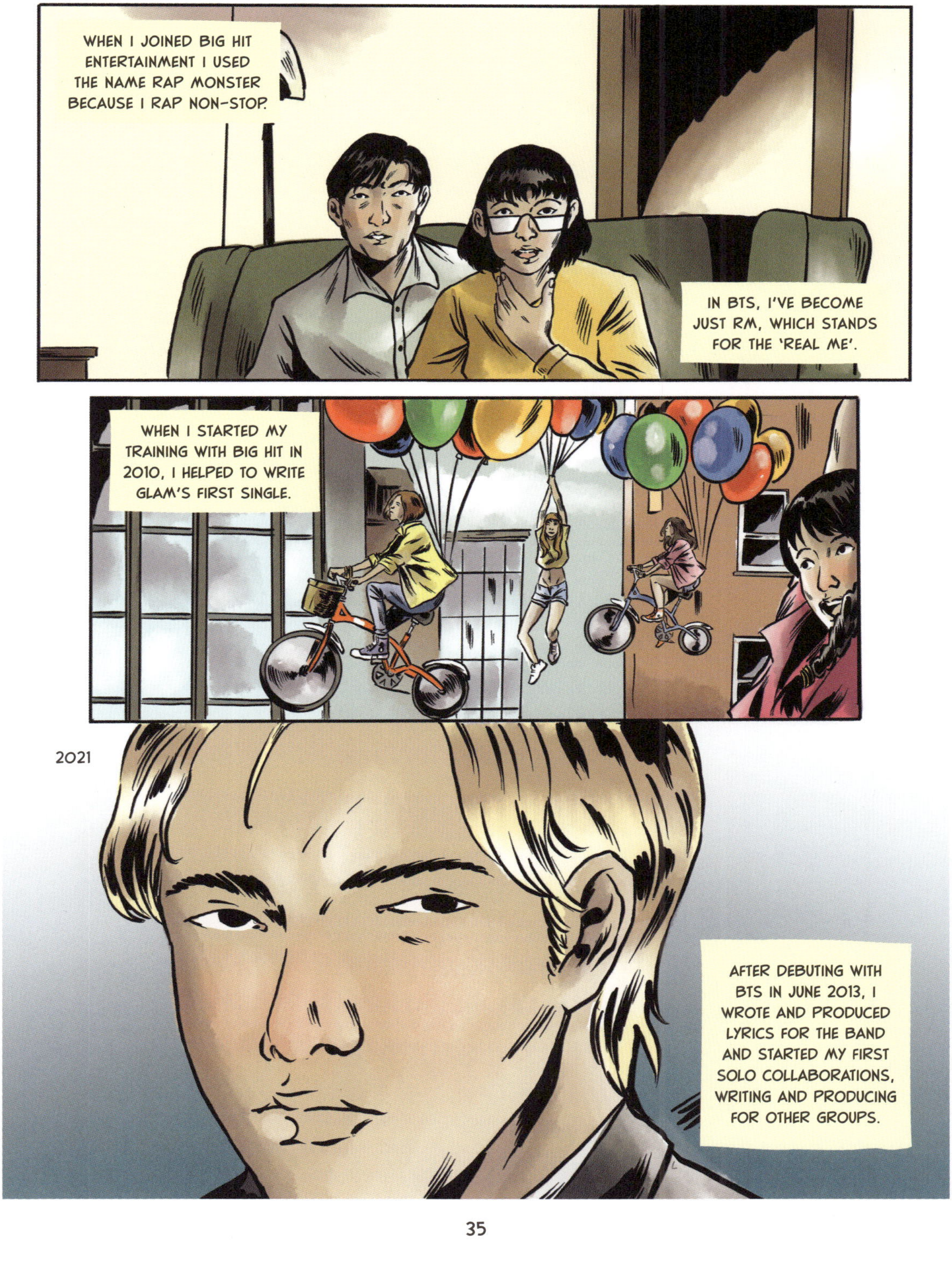
WHEN I JOINED BIG HIT ENTERTAINMENT I USED THE NAME RAP MONSTER BECAUSE I RAP NON-STOP.
IN BTS, I'VE BECOME JUST RM, WHICH STANDS FOR THE 'REAL ME'.
WHEN I STARTED MY TRAINING WITH BIG HIT IN 2010, I HELPED TO WRITE GLAM'S FIRST SINGLE.
2021
AFTER DEBUTING WITH BTS IN JUNE 2013, I WROTE AND PRODUCED LYRICS FOR THE BAND AND STARTED MY FIRST SOLO COLLABORATIONS, WRITING AND PRODUCING FOR OTHER GROUPS.

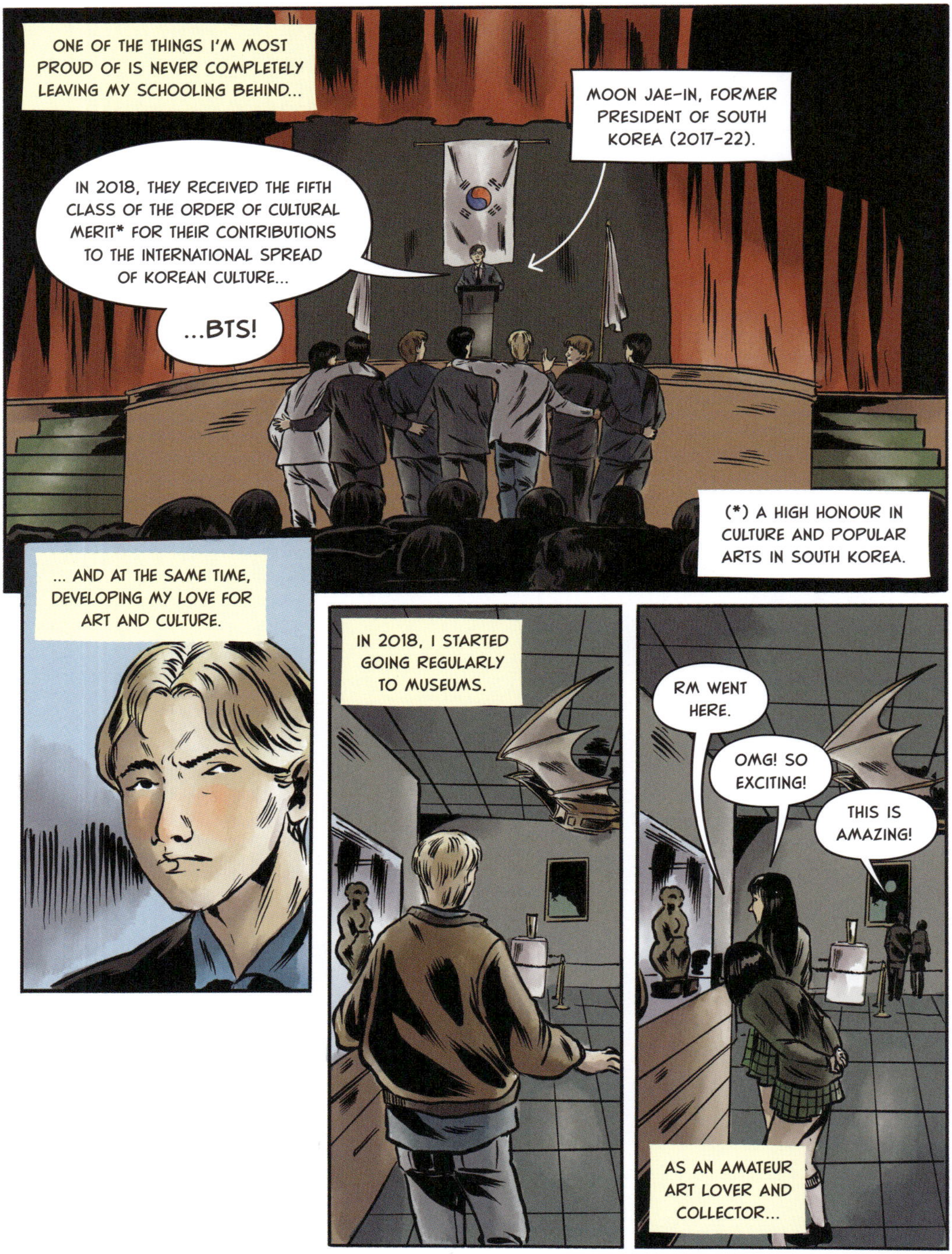
ONE OF THE THINGS I'M MOST PROUD OF IS NEVER COMPLETELY LEAVING MY SCHOOLING BEHIND...
MOON JAE-IN, FORMER PRESIDENT OF SOUTH KOREA (2017–22).
IN 2018, THEY RECEIVED THE FIFTH CLASS OF THE ORDER OF CULTURAL MERIT* FOR THEIR CONTRIBUTIONS TO THE INTERNATIONAL SPREAD OF KOREAN CULTURE...
...BTS!
(*) A HIGH HONOUR IN CULTURE AND POPULAR ARTS IN SOUTH KOREA.
... AND AT THE SAME TIME, DEVELOPING MY LOVE FOR ART AND CULTURE.
IN 2018, I STARTED GOING REGULARLY TO MUSEUMS.
RM WENT HERE.
OMG! SO EXCITING!
THIS IS AMAZING!
AS AN AMATEUR ART LOVER AND COLLECTOR...

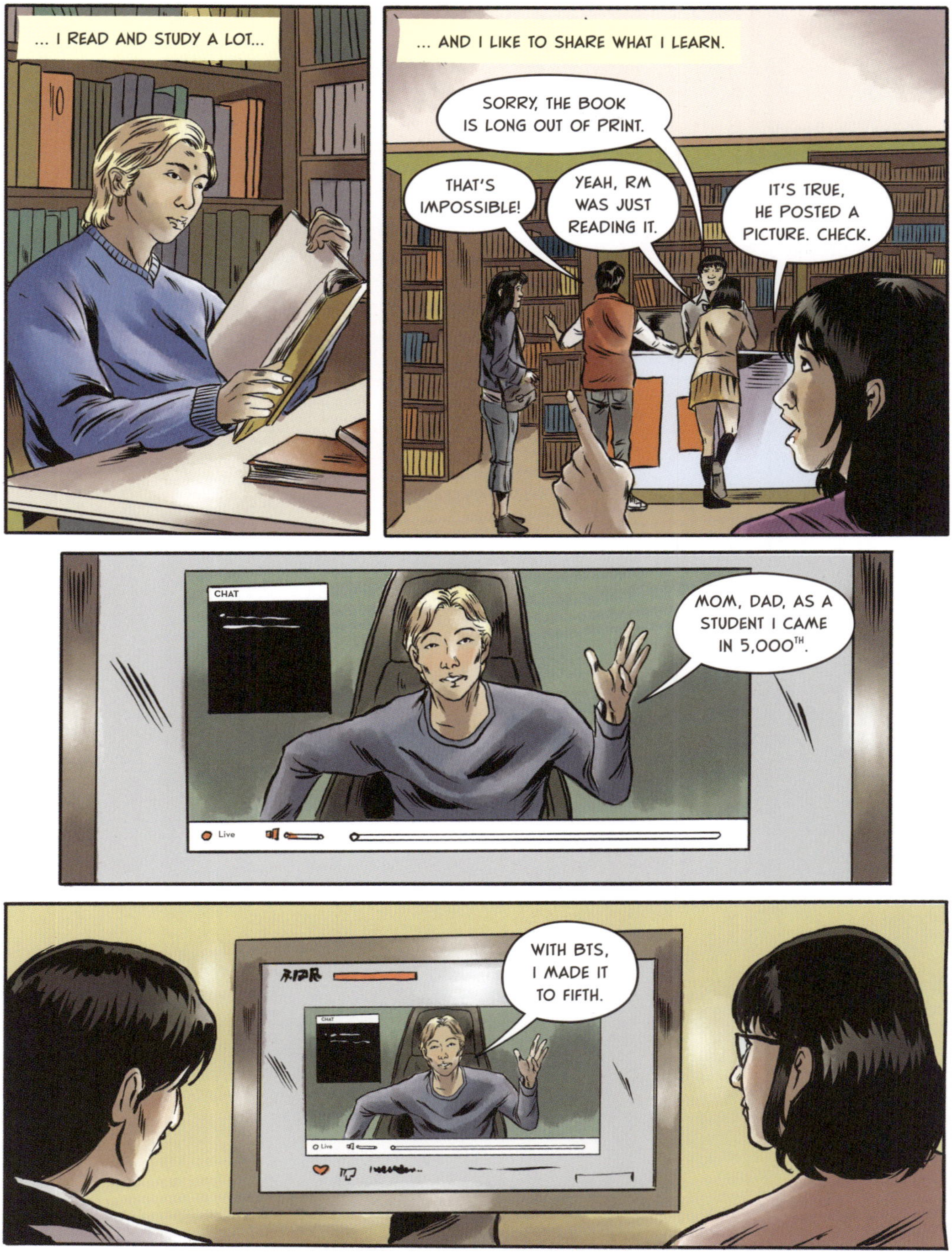
... I READ AND STUDY A LOT...
... AND I LIKE TO SHARE WHAT I LEARN.
SORRY, THE BOOK IS LONG OUT OF PRINT.
THAT'S IMPOSSIBLE!
YEAH, RM WAS JUST READING IT.
IT'S TRUE, HE POSTED A PICTURE. CHECK.
CHAT
Live
MOM, DAD, AS A STUDENT I CAME IN 5,000TH.
WITH BTS, I MADE IT TO FIFTH.

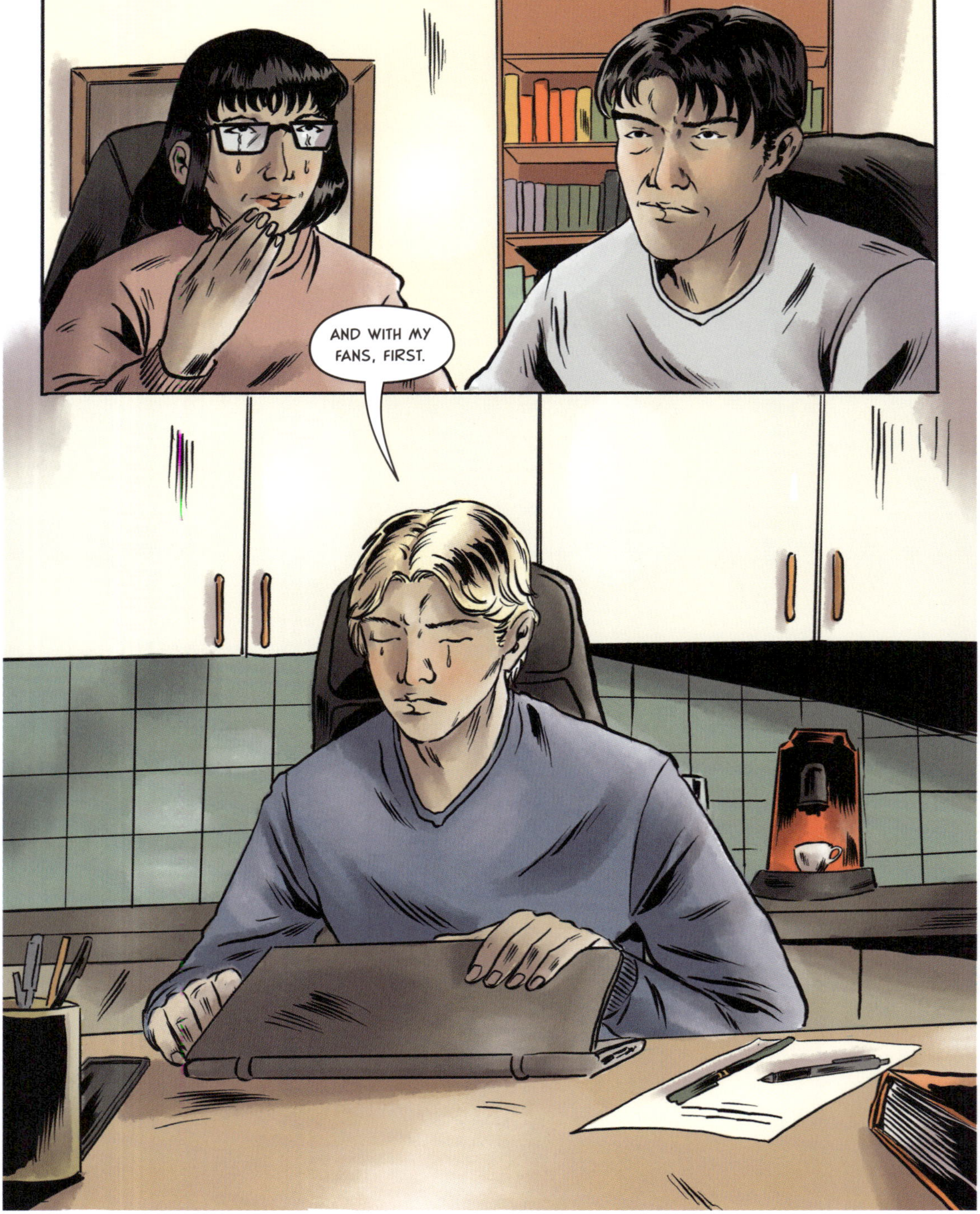
AND WITH MY FANS, FIRST.

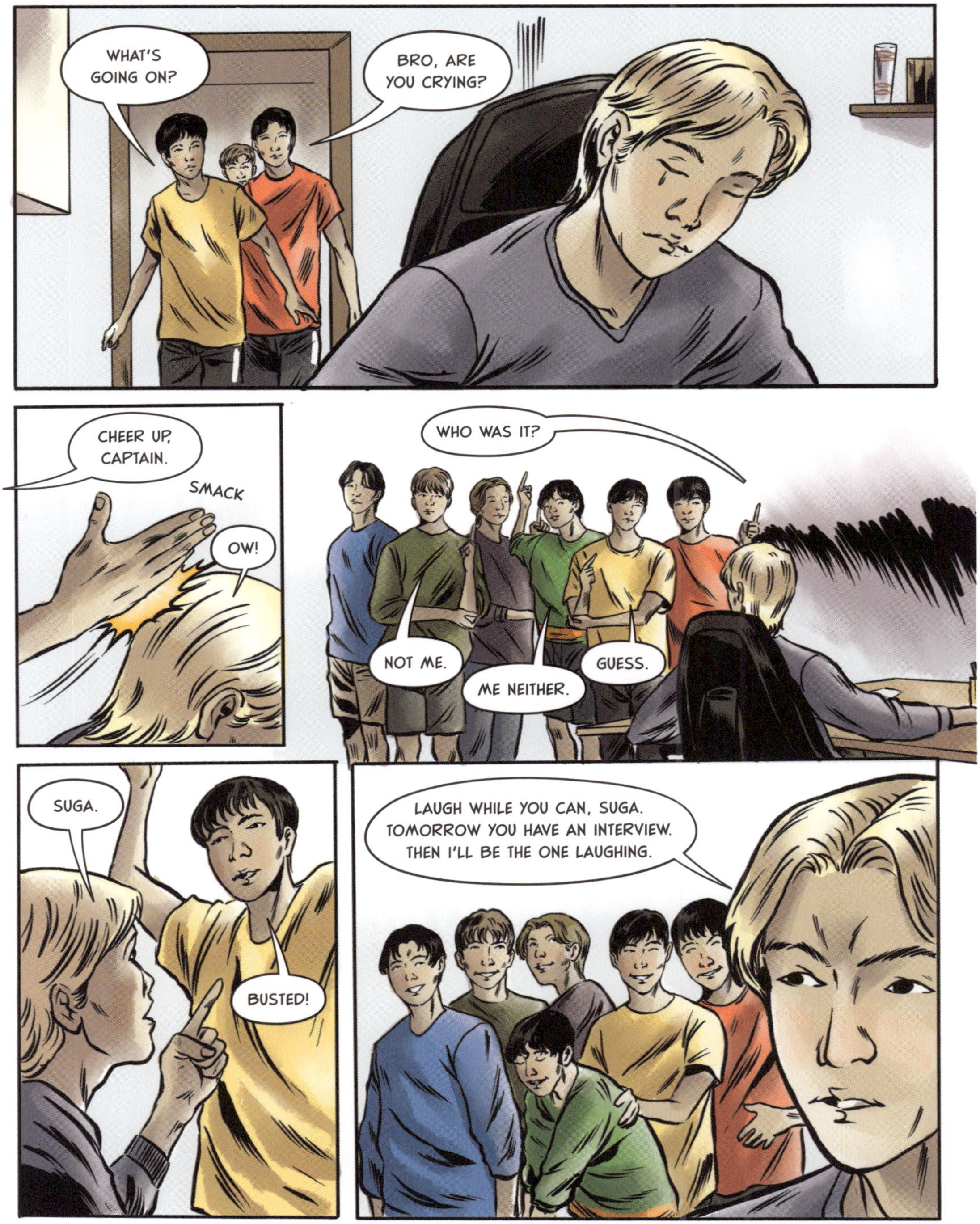
WHAT'S GOING ON?
BRO, ARE YOU CRYING?
CHEER UP, CAPTAIN.
SMACK
OW!
WHO WAS IT?
NOT ME.
ME NEITHER.
GUESS.
SUGA.
BUSTED!
LAUGH WHILE YOU CAN, SUGA. TOMORROW YOU HAVE AN INTERVIEW. THEN I'LL BE THE ONE LAUGHING.

SUGA

MIN YOON-GI

From basketball to MIDI to BTS idol.

Here is an imaginary interview, providing a glimpse into Suga's journey into music.

His memories and impressions delve into social and psychological themes, including his unwavering support for the LGBTQ+ community, continually asserting every human being's right to express their identity, because we are all equal and all different at the same time.

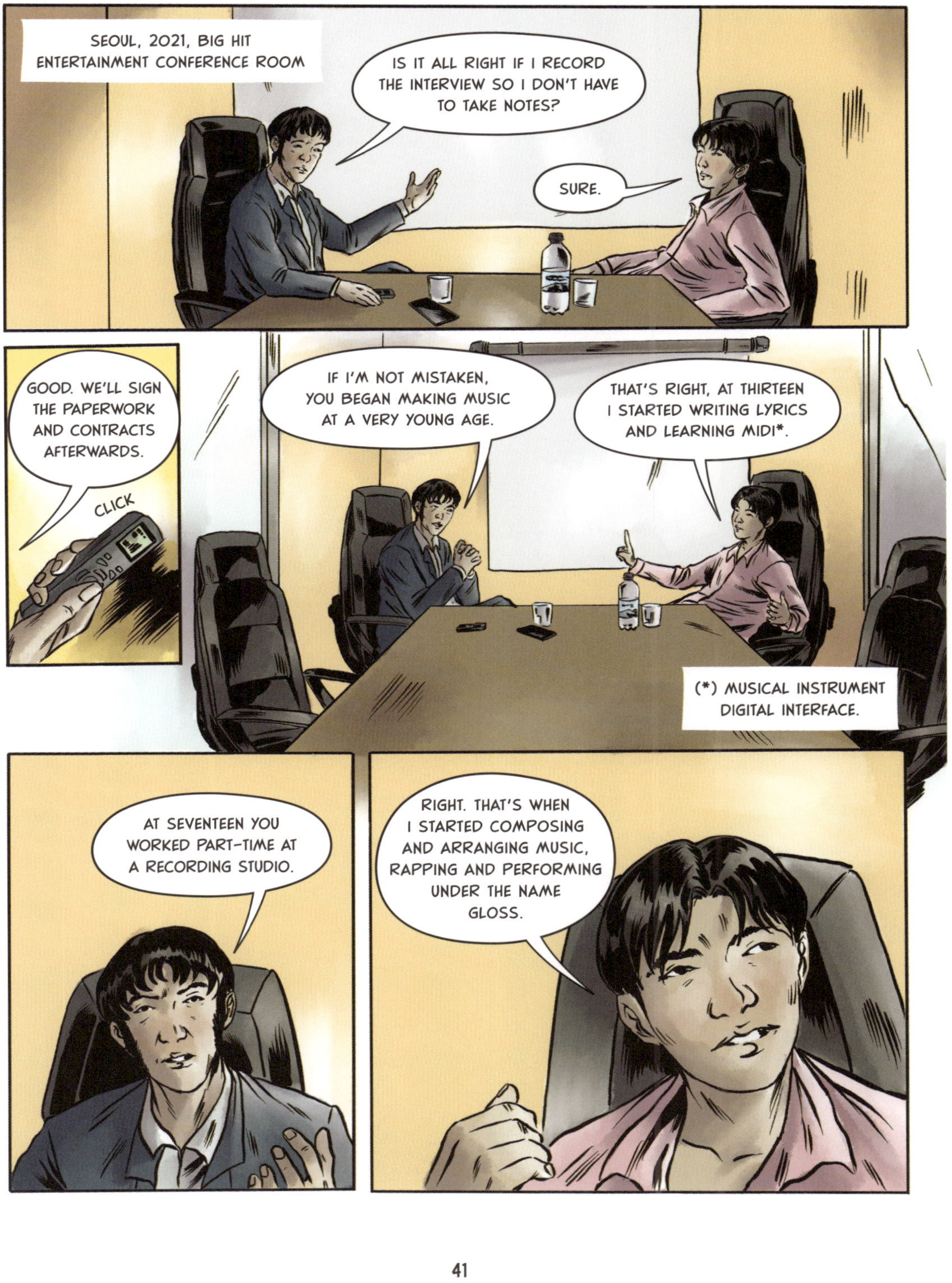
SEOUL, 2021, BIG HIT ENTERTAINMENT CONFERENCE ROOM
IS IT ALL RIGHT IF I RECORD THE INTERVIEW SO I DON'T HAVE TO TAKE NOTES?
SURE.
GOOD. WE'LL SIGN THE PAPERWORK AND CONTRACTS AFTERWARDS.
CLICK
IF I'M NOT MISTAKEN, YOU BEGAN MAKING MUSIC AT A VERY YOUNG AGE.
THAT'S RIGHT, AT THIRTEEN I STARTED WRITING LYRICS AND LEARNING MIDI*.
(*) MUSICAL INSTRUMENT DIGITAL INTERFACE.
AT SEVENTEEN YOU WORKED PART-TIME AT A RECORDING STUDIO.
RIGHT. THAT'S WHEN I STARTED COMPOSING AND ARRANGING MUSIC, RAPPING AND PERFORMING UNDER THE NAME GLOSS.

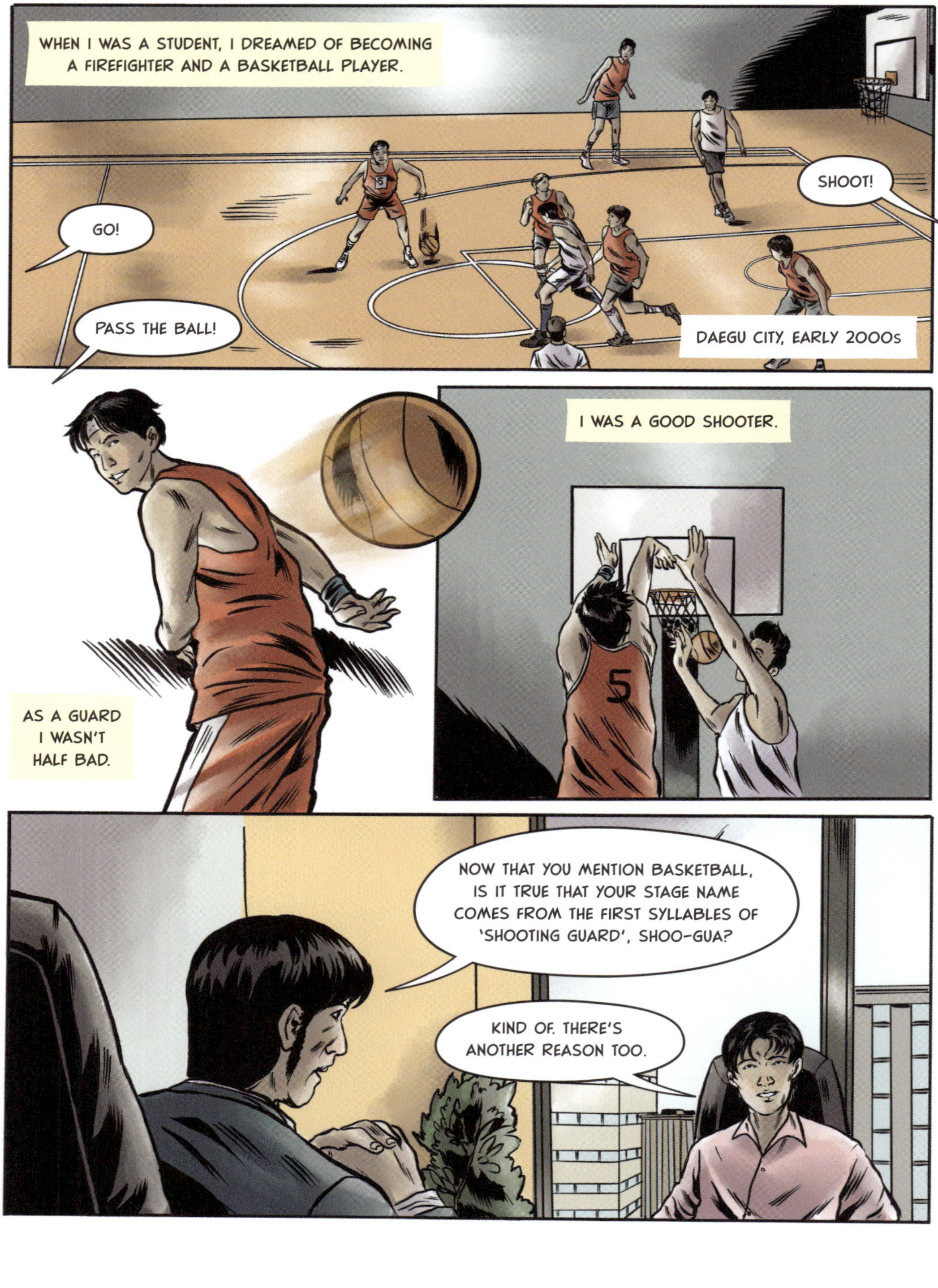
WHEN I WAS A STUDENT, I DREAMED OF BECOMING A FIREFIGHTER AND A BASKETBALL PLAYER.
GO!
PASS THE BALL!
SHOOT!
DAEGU CITY, EARLY 2000s
AS A GUARD I WASN'T HALF BAD.
I WAS A GOOD SHOOTER.
NOW THAT YOU MENTION BASKETBALL, IS IT TRUE THAT YOUR STAGE NAME COMES FROM THE FIRST SYLLABLES OF 'SHOOTING GUARD', SHOO-GUA?
KIND OF. THERE'S ANOTHER REASON TOO.

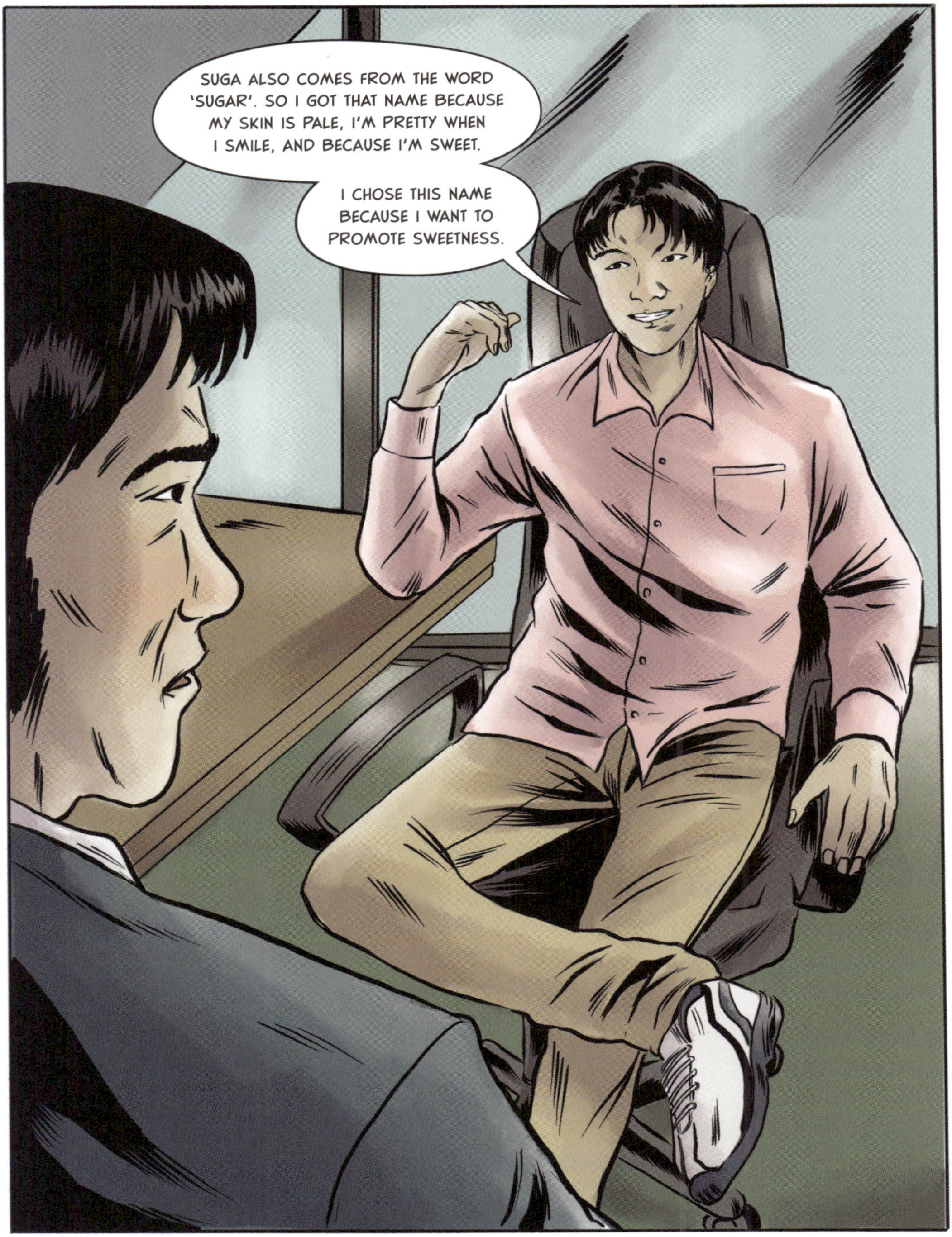
SUGA ALSO COMES FROM THE WORD 'SUGAR'. SO I GOT THAT NAME BECAUSE MY SKIN IS PALE, I'M PRETTY WHEN I SMILE, AND BECAUSE I'M SWEET.
I CHOSE THIS NAME BECAUSE I WANT TO PROMOTE SWEETNESS.

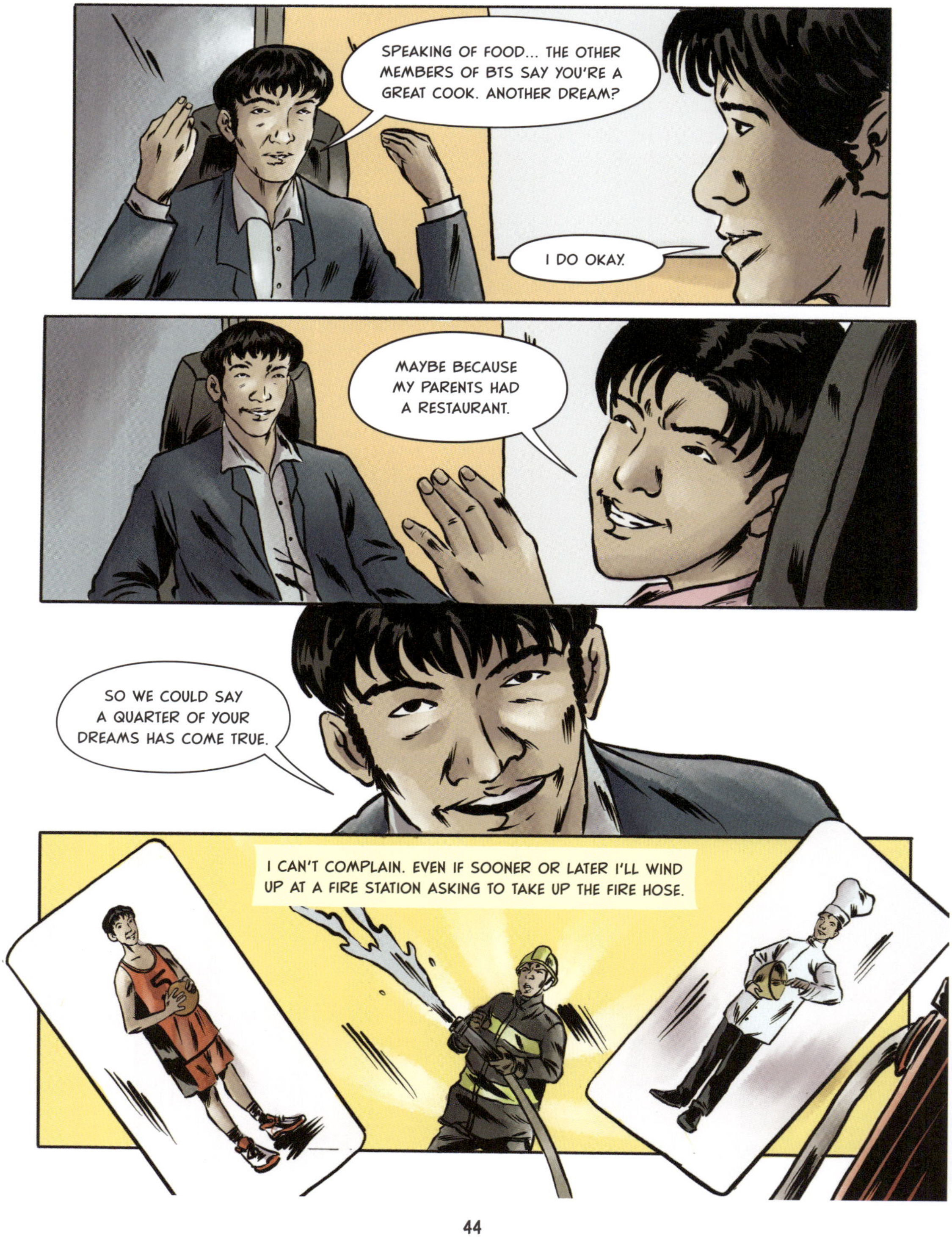
SPEAKING OF FOOD... THE OTHER MEMBERS OF BTS SAY YOU'RE A GREAT COOK. ANOTHER DREAM?
I DO OKAY.
MAYBE BECAUSE MY PARENTS HAD A RESTAURANT.
SO WE COULD SAY A QUARTER OF YOUR DREAMS HAS COME TRUE.
I CAN'T COMPLAIN. EVEN IF SOONER OR LATER I'LL WIND UP AT A FIRE STATION ASKING TO TAKE UP THE FIRE HOSE.

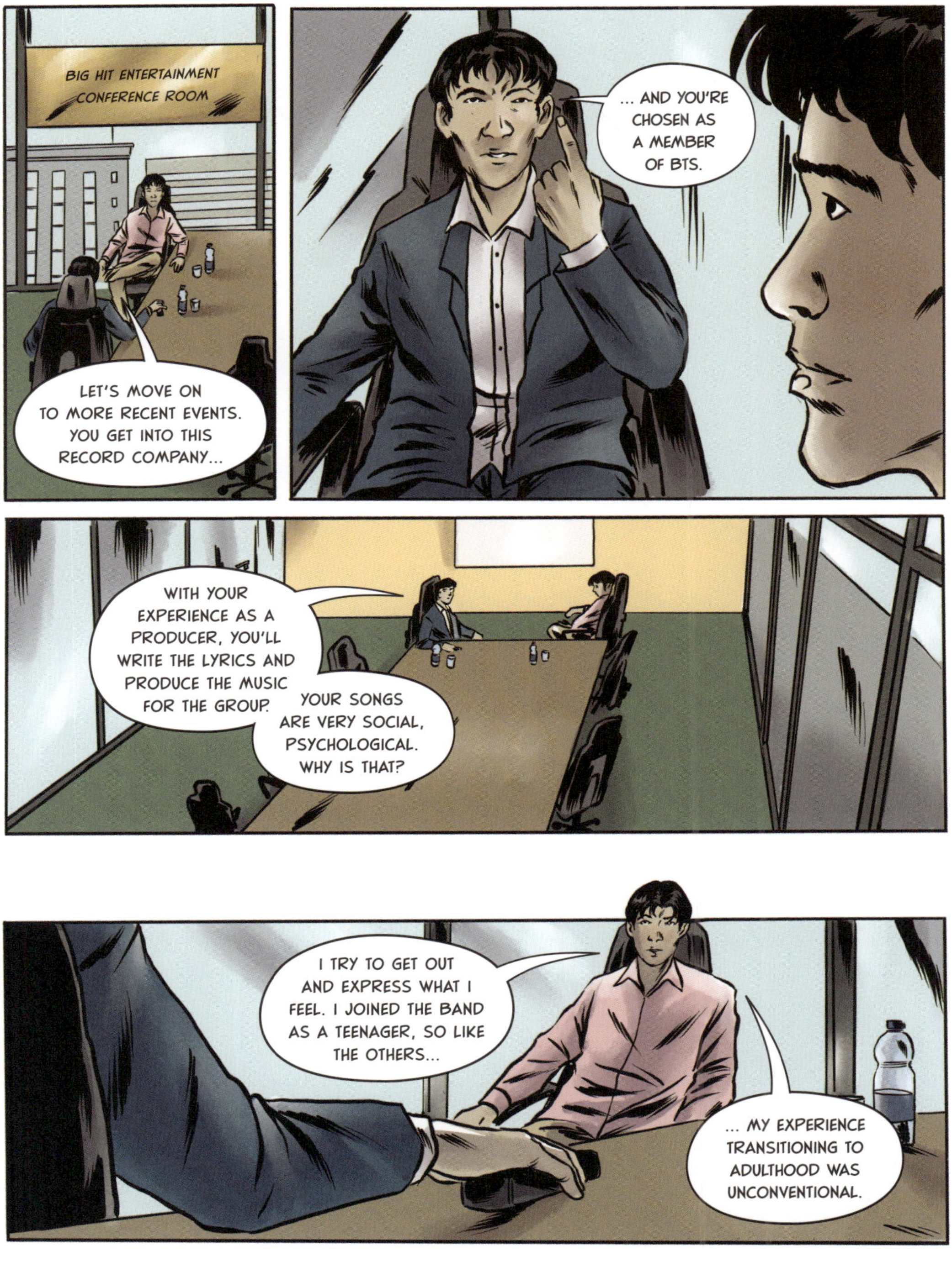
BIG HIT ENTERTAINMENT CONFERENCE ROOM
LET'S MOVE ON TO MORE RECENT EVENTS. YOU GET INTO THIS RECORD COMPANY...
... AND YOU'RE CHOSEN AS A MEMBER OF BTS.
WITH YOUR EXPERIENCE AS A PRODUCER, YOU'LL WRITE THE LYRICS AND PRODUCE THE MUSIC FOR THE GROUP.
YOUR SONGS ARE VERY SOCIAL, PSYCHOLOGICAL. WHY IS THAT?
I TRY TO GET OUT AND EXPRESS WHAT I FEEL. I JOINED THE BAND AS A TEENAGER, SO LIKE THE OTHERS...
... MY EXPERIENCE TRANSITIONING TO ADULTHOOD WAS UNCONVENTIONAL.

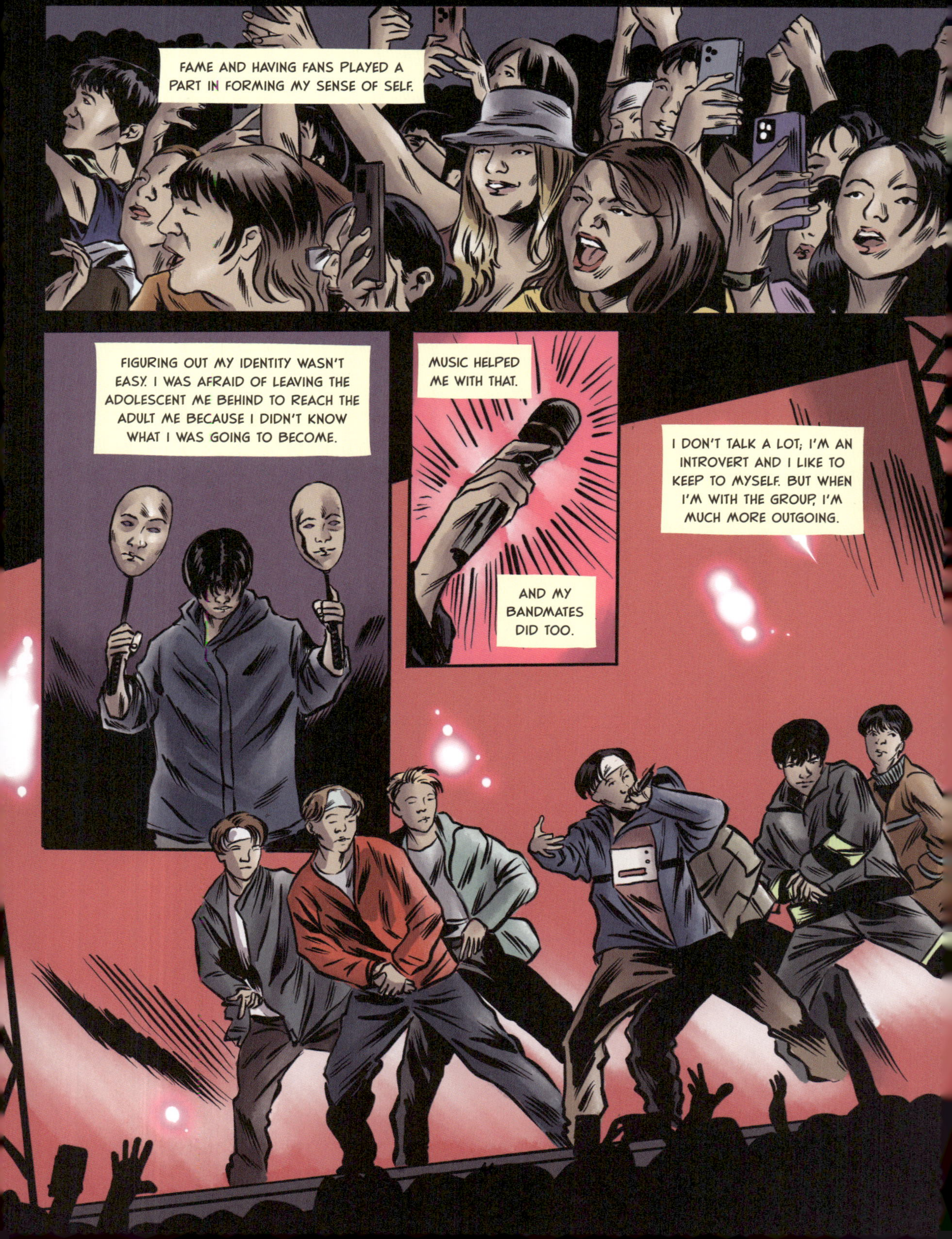
FAME AND HAVING FANS PLAYED A PART IN FORMING MY SENSE OF SELF.
FIGURING OUT MY IDENTITY WASN'T EASY. I WAS AFRAID OF LEAVING THE ADOLESCENT ME BEHIND TO REACH THE ADULT ME BECAUSE I DIDN'T KNOW WHAT I WAS GOING TO BECOME.
MUSIC HELPED ME WITH THAT.
AND MY BANDMATES DID TOO.
I DON'T TALK A LOT; I'M AN INTROVERT AND I LIKE TO KEEP TO MYSELF. BUT WHEN I'M WITH THE GROUP, I'M MUCH MORE OUTGOING.

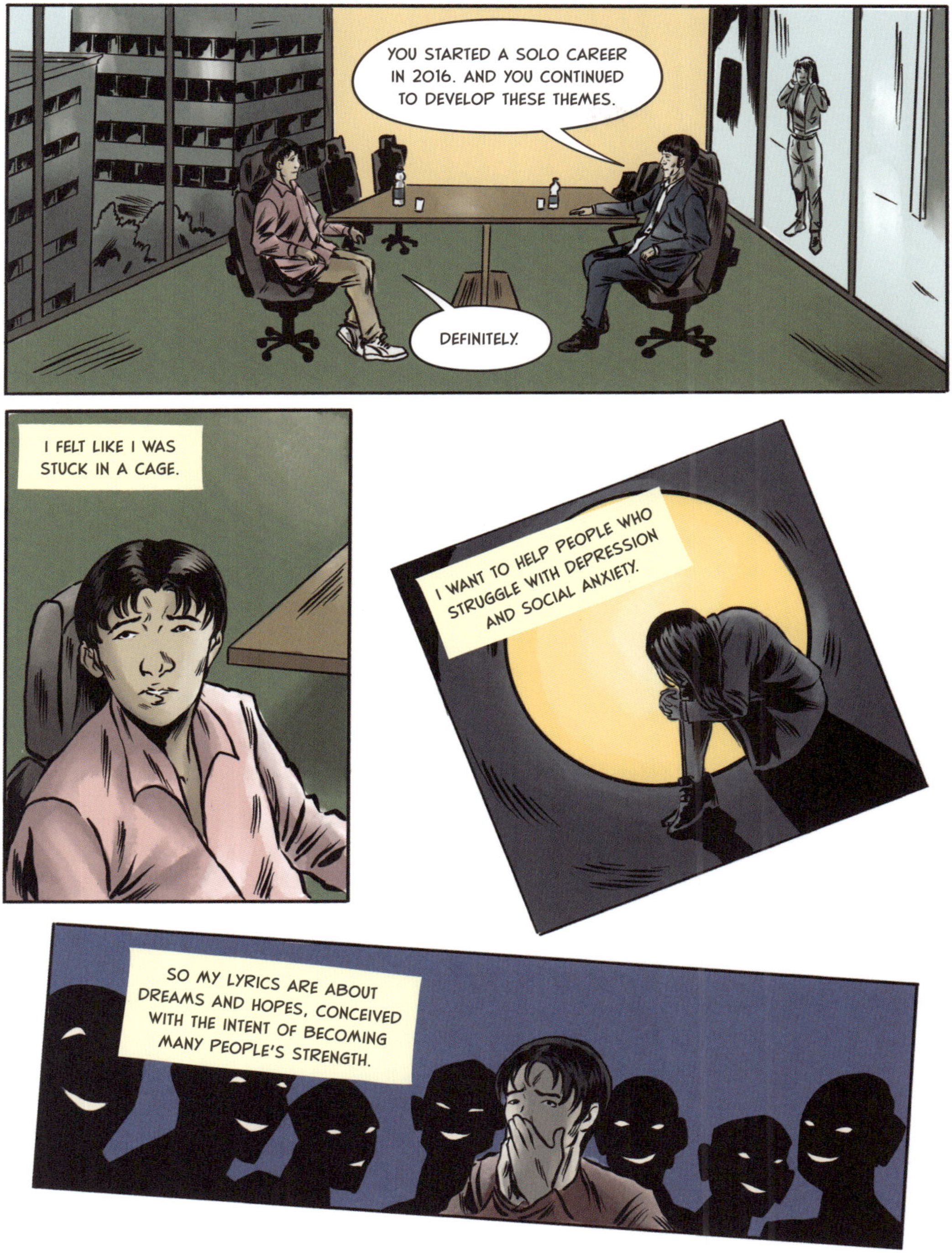
YOU STARTED A SOLO CAREER IN 2016. AND YOU CONTINUED TO DEVELOP THESE THEMES.
DEFINITELY.
I FELT LIKE I WAS STUCK IN A CAGE.
I WANT TO HELP PEOPLE WHO STRUGGLE WITH DEPRESSION AND SOCIAL ANXIETY.
SO MY LYRICS ARE ABOUT DREAMS AND HOPES, CONCEIVED WITH THE INTENT OF BECOMING MANY PEOPLE'S STRENGTH.

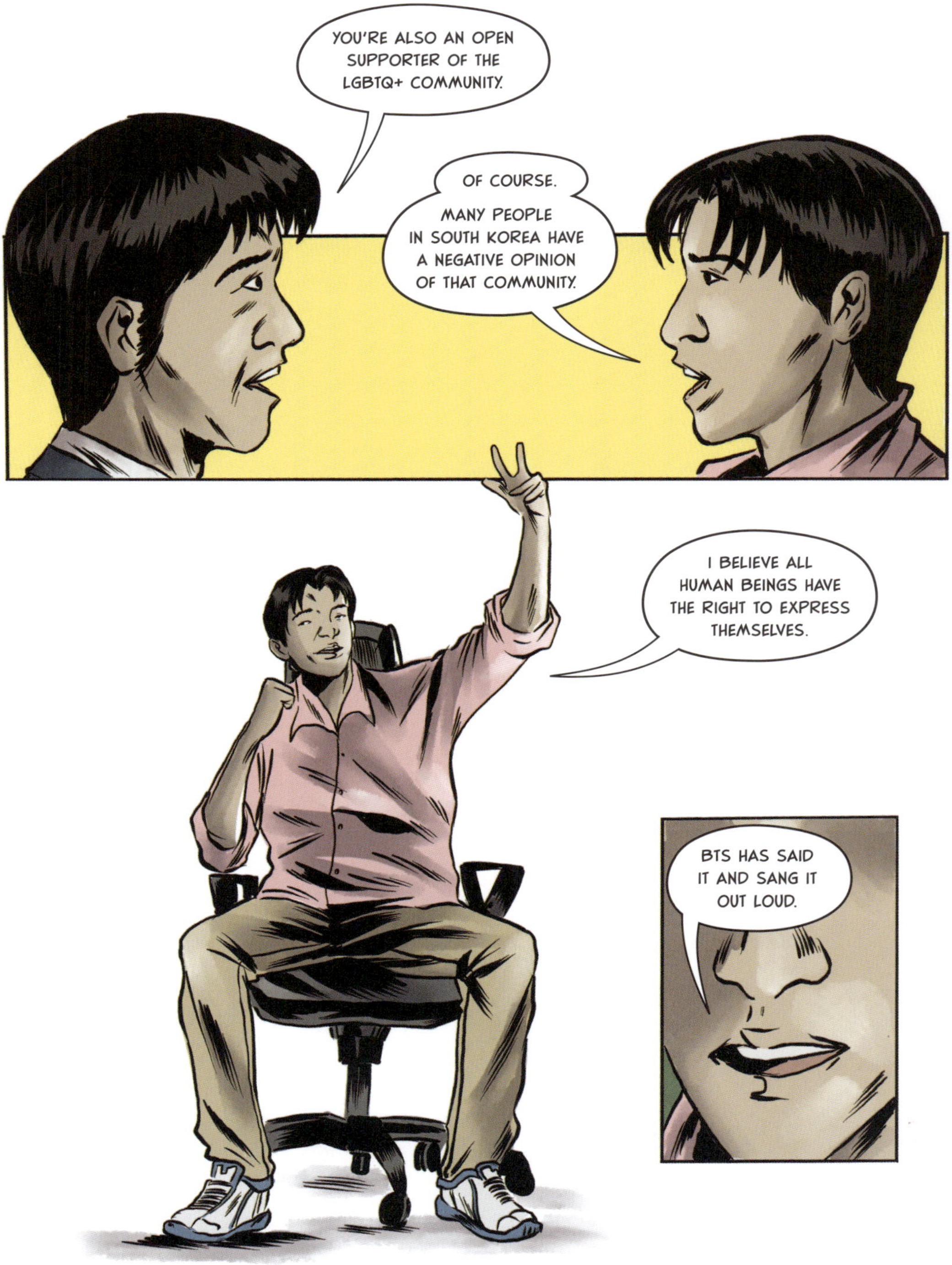
YOU'RE ALSO AN OPEN SUPPORTER OF THE LGBTQ+ COMMUNITY.
OF COURSE.
MANY PEOPLE IN SOUTH KOREA HAVE A NEGATIVE OPINION OF THAT COMMUNITY.
I BELIEVE ALL HUMAN BEINGS HAVE THE RIGHT TO EXPRESS THEMSELVES.
BTS HAS SAID IT AND SANG IT OUT LOUD.

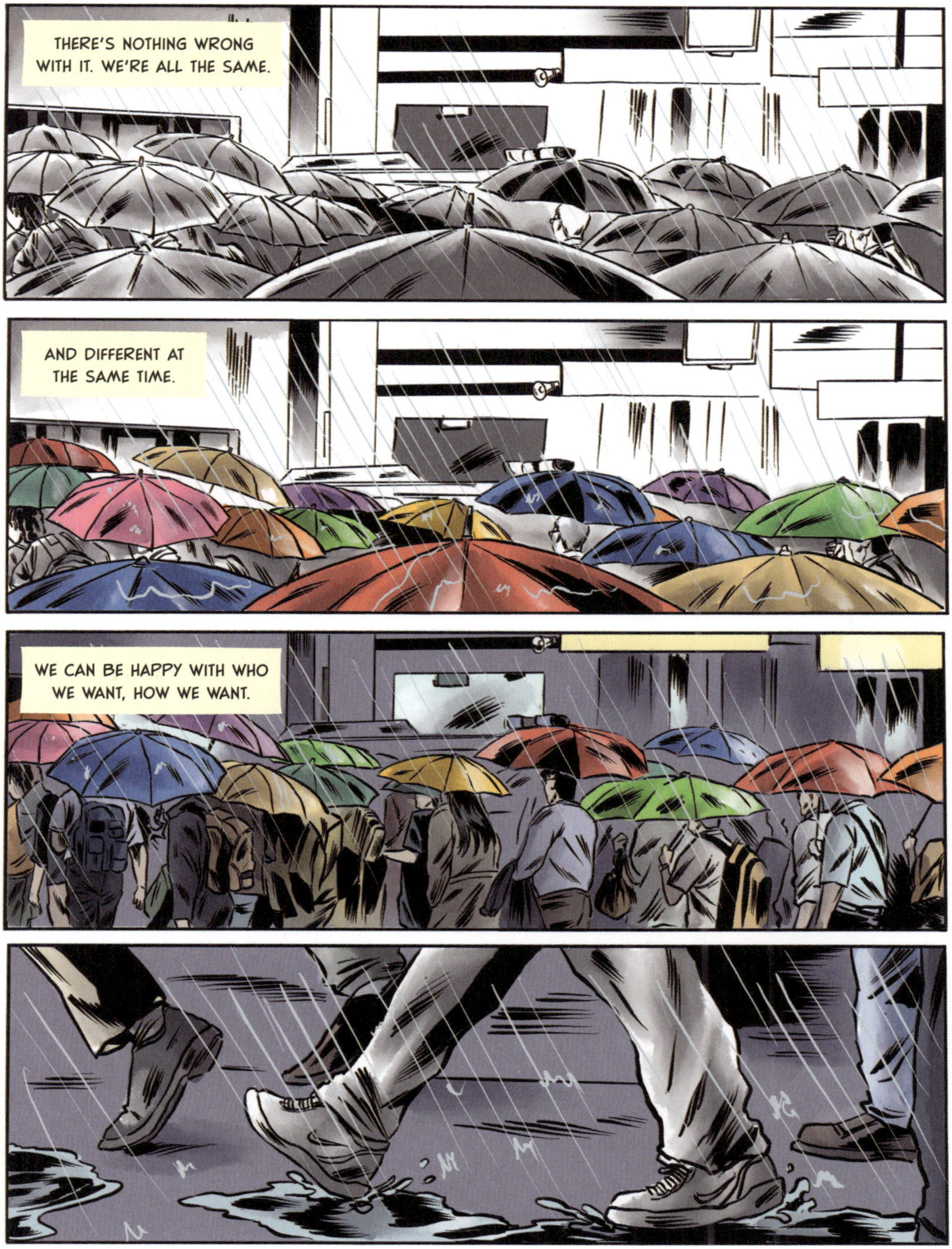
THERE'S NOTHING WRONG WITH IT. WE'RE ALL THE SAME.
AND DIFFERENT AT THE SAME TIME.
WE CAN BE HAPPY WITH WHO WE WANT, HOW WE WANT.

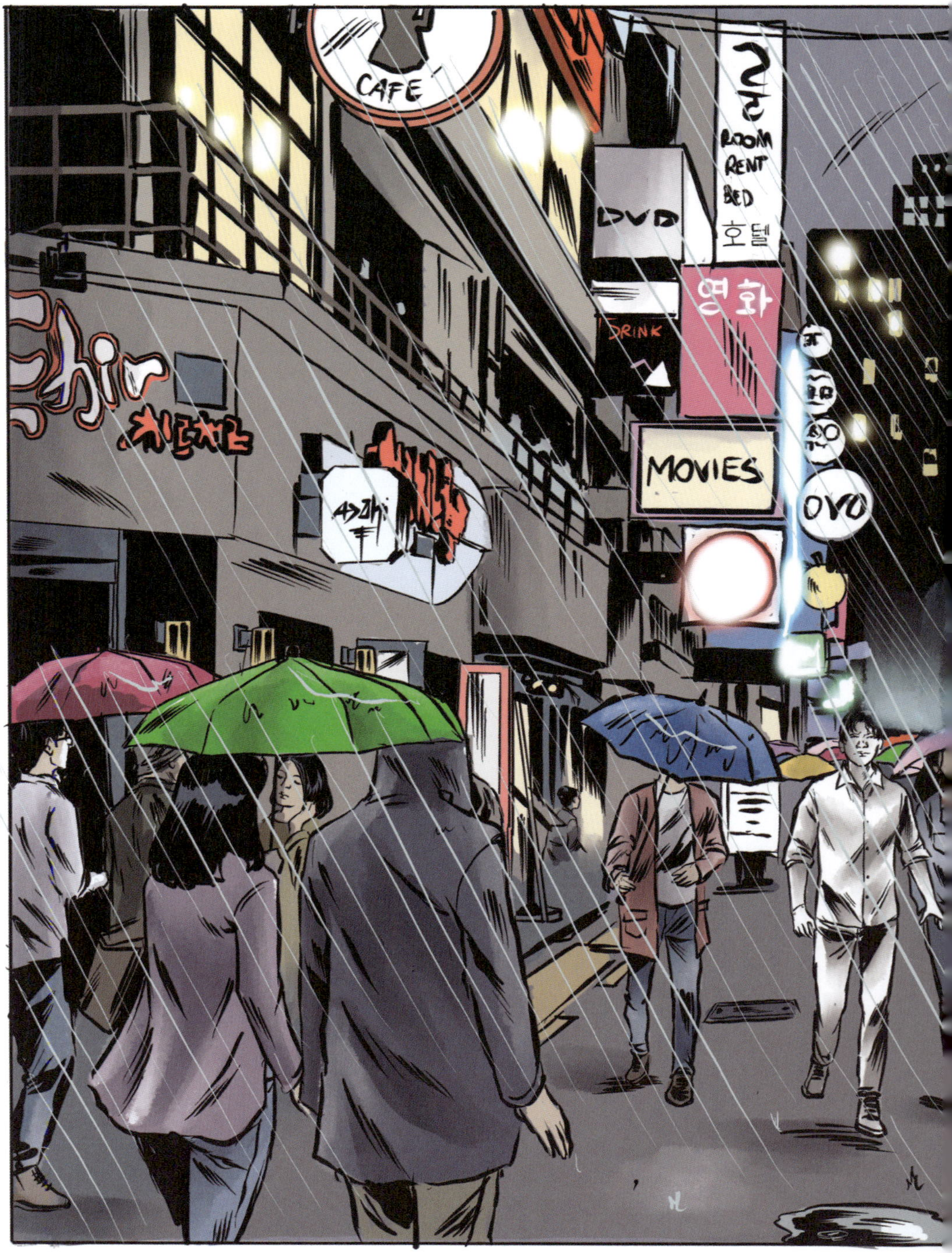
CAFE
ROOM
RENT
BED
호텔
DVD
영화
DRINK
MOVIES

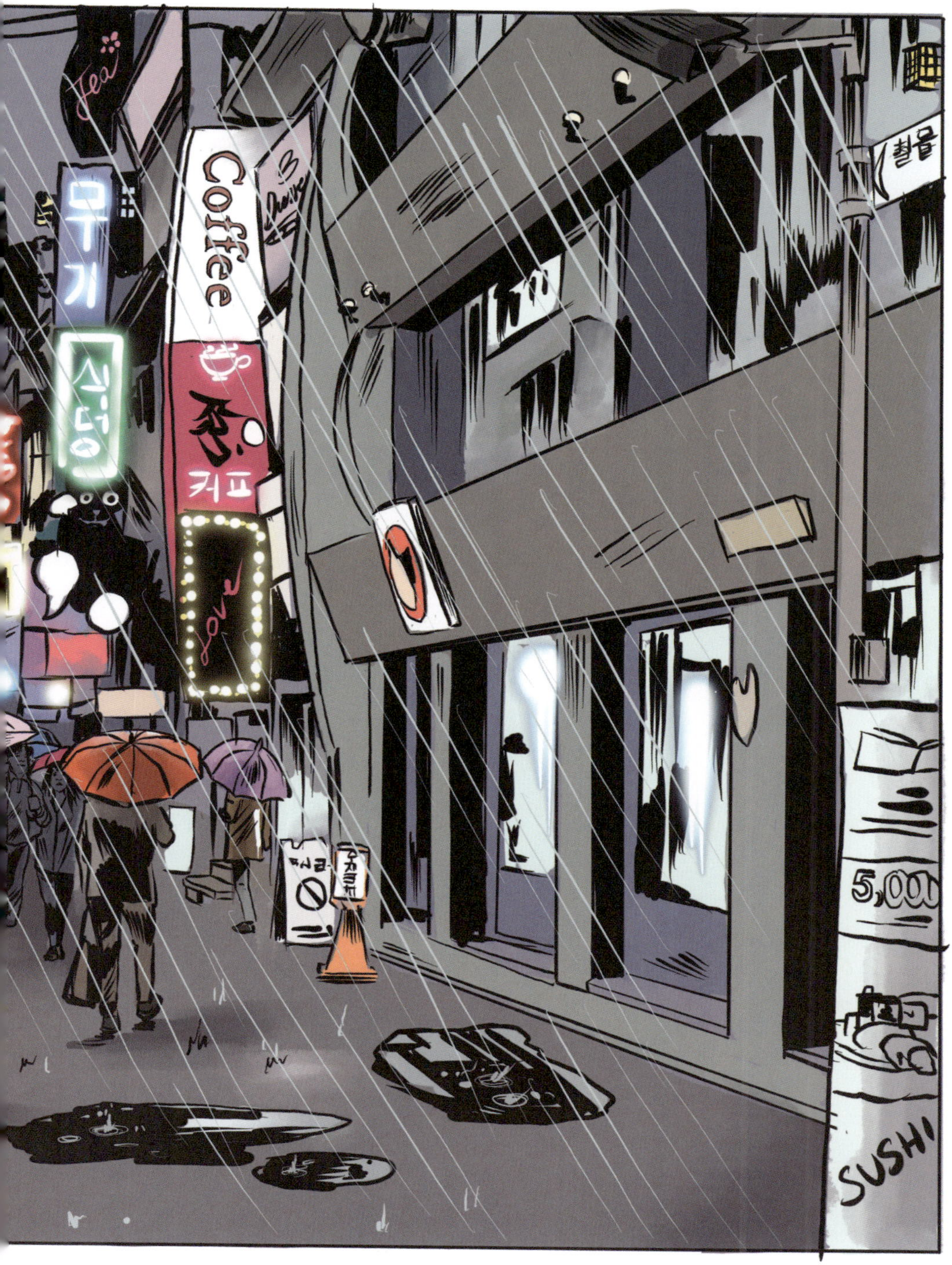
Tea
무기
식당
Coffee
커피
Love
5,000
SUSHI

J-HOPE

JUNG HO-SEOK

FROM TENNIS PLAYER TO STREET DANCER TO SINGER.

REWATCHING OLD AUDITIONS AND REVISITING THE PAST,
J-HOPE OUTLINES THE SACRIFICE, HARD WORK,
STUDIES AND FRAGILITY THAT LED HIM – ALONG
WITH HIS HYPERPRODUCTIVITY AND DEDICATION –
TO BECOME THE PERSONIFICATION OF HOPE THAT HE IS.

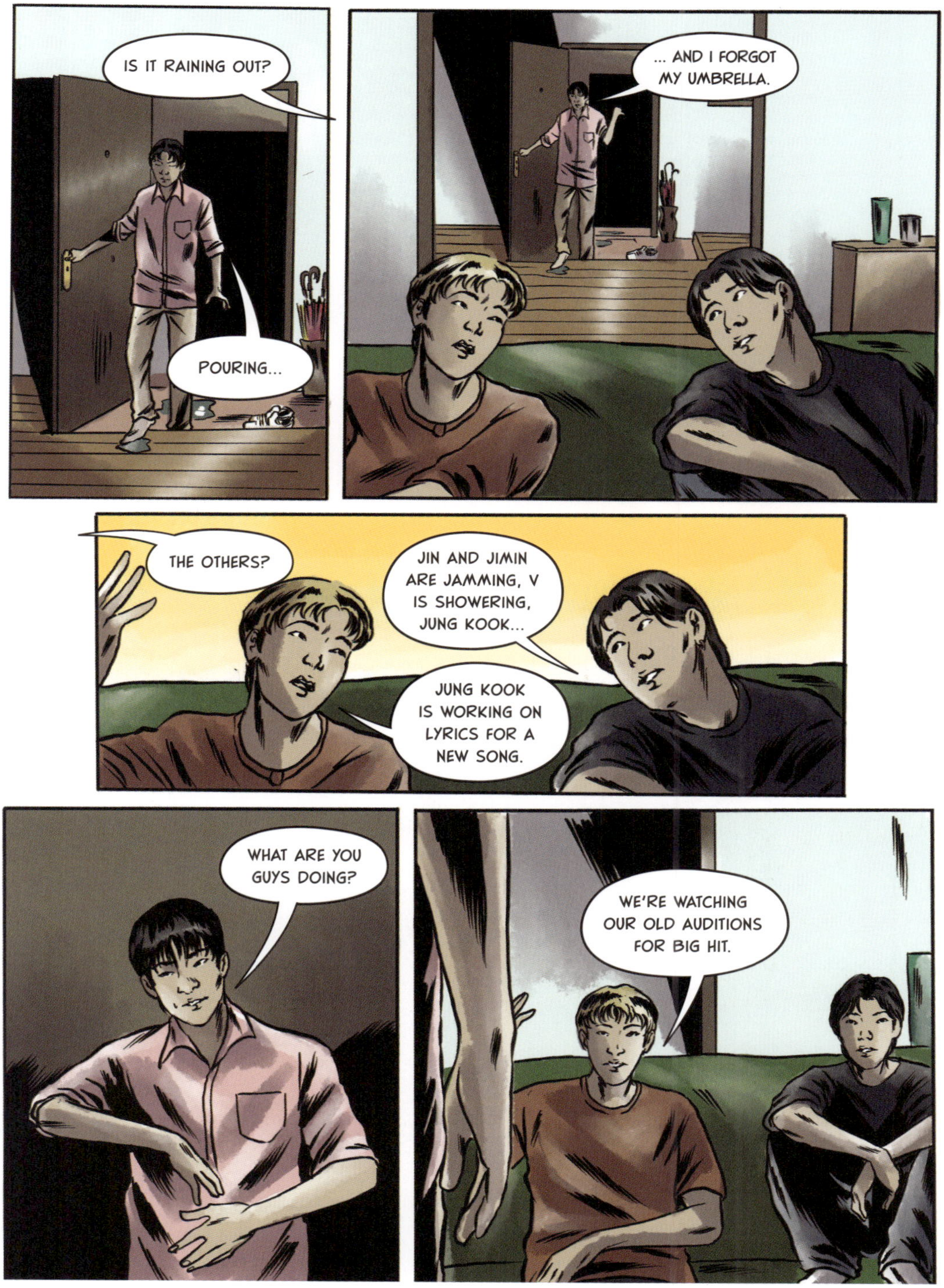
IS IT RAINING OUT?
POURING...
... AND I FORGOT MY UMBRELLA.
THE OTHERS?
JIN AND JIMIN ARE JAMMING, V IS SHOWERING, JUNG KOOK...
JUNG KOOK IS WORKING ON LYRICS FOR A NEW SONG.
WHAT ARE YOU GUYS DOING?
WE'RE WATCHING OUR OLD AUDITIONS FOR BIG HIT.

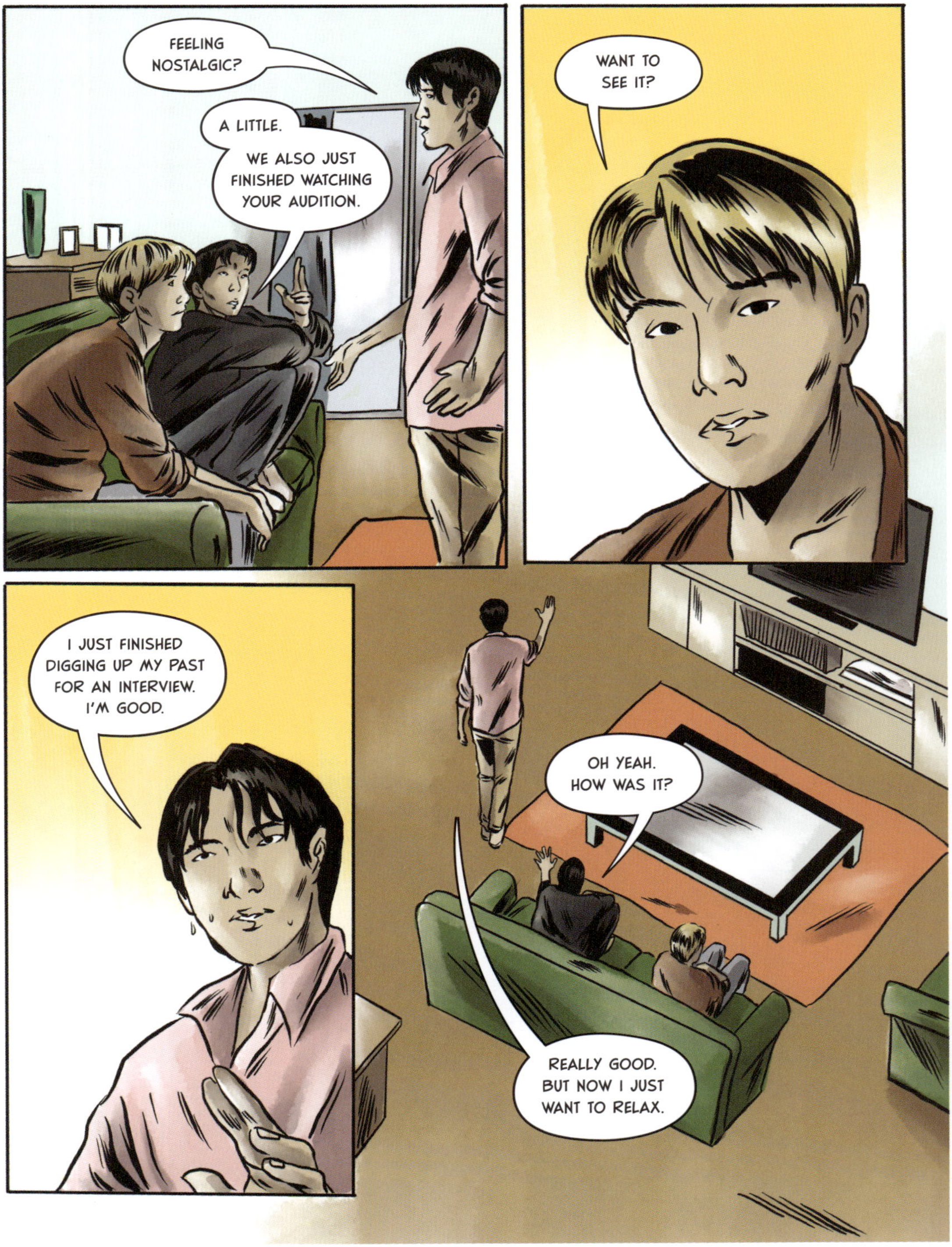
FEELING NOSTALGIC?
A LITTLE.
WE ALSO JUST FINISHED WATCHING YOUR AUDITION.
WANT TO SEE IT?
I JUST FINISHED DIGGING UP MY PAST FOR AN INTERVIEW. I'M GOOD.
OH YEAH. HOW WAS IT?
REALLY GOOD. BUT NOW I JUST WANT TO RELAX.

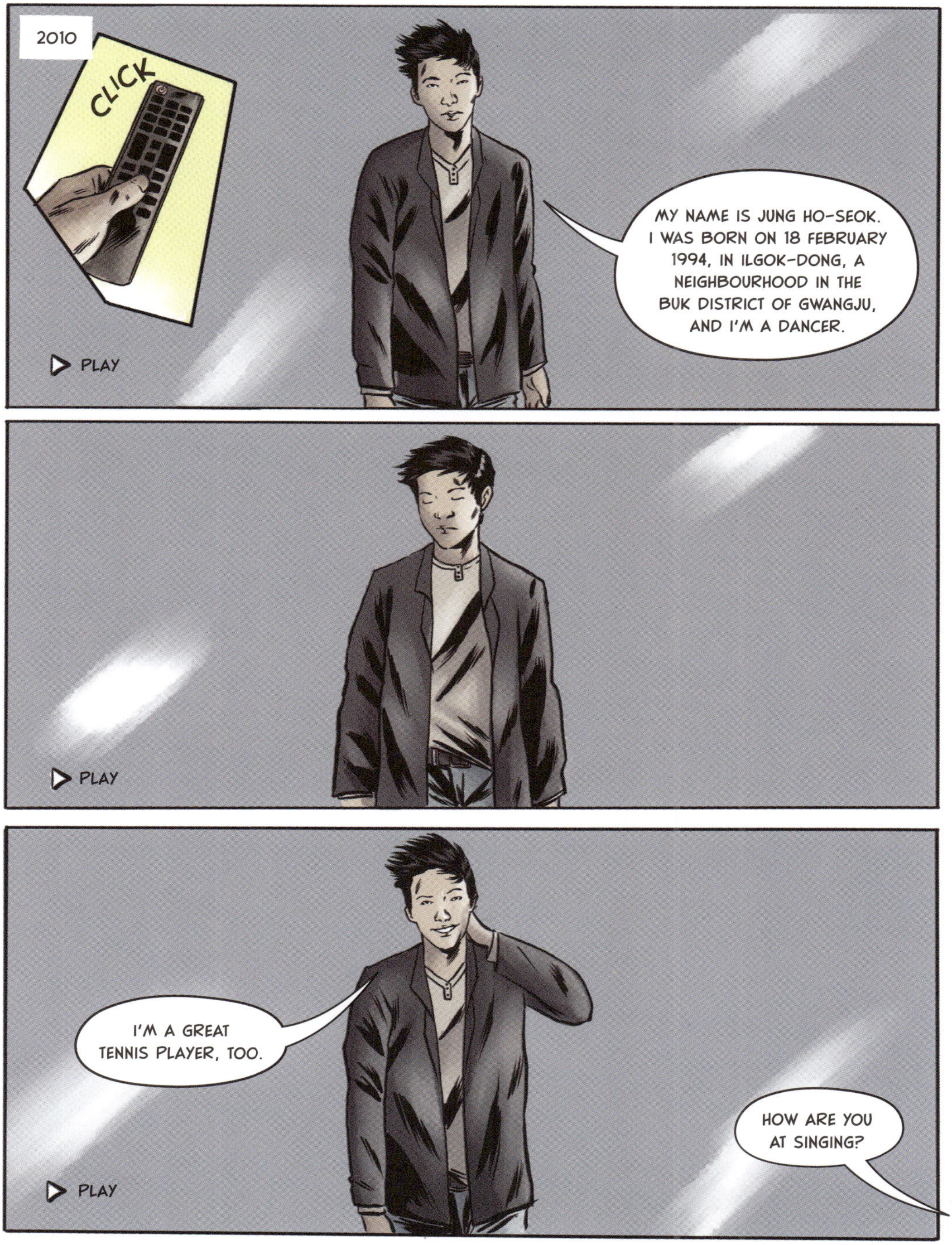
2010
CLICK
PLAY
MY NAME IS JUNG HO-SEOK. I WAS BORN ON 18 FEBRUARY 1994, IN ILGOK-DONG, A NEIGHBOURHOOD IN THE BUK DISTRICT OF GWANGJU, AND I'M A DANCER.
PLAY
I'M A GREAT TENNIS PLAYER, TOO.
HOW ARE YOU AT SINGING?
PLAY

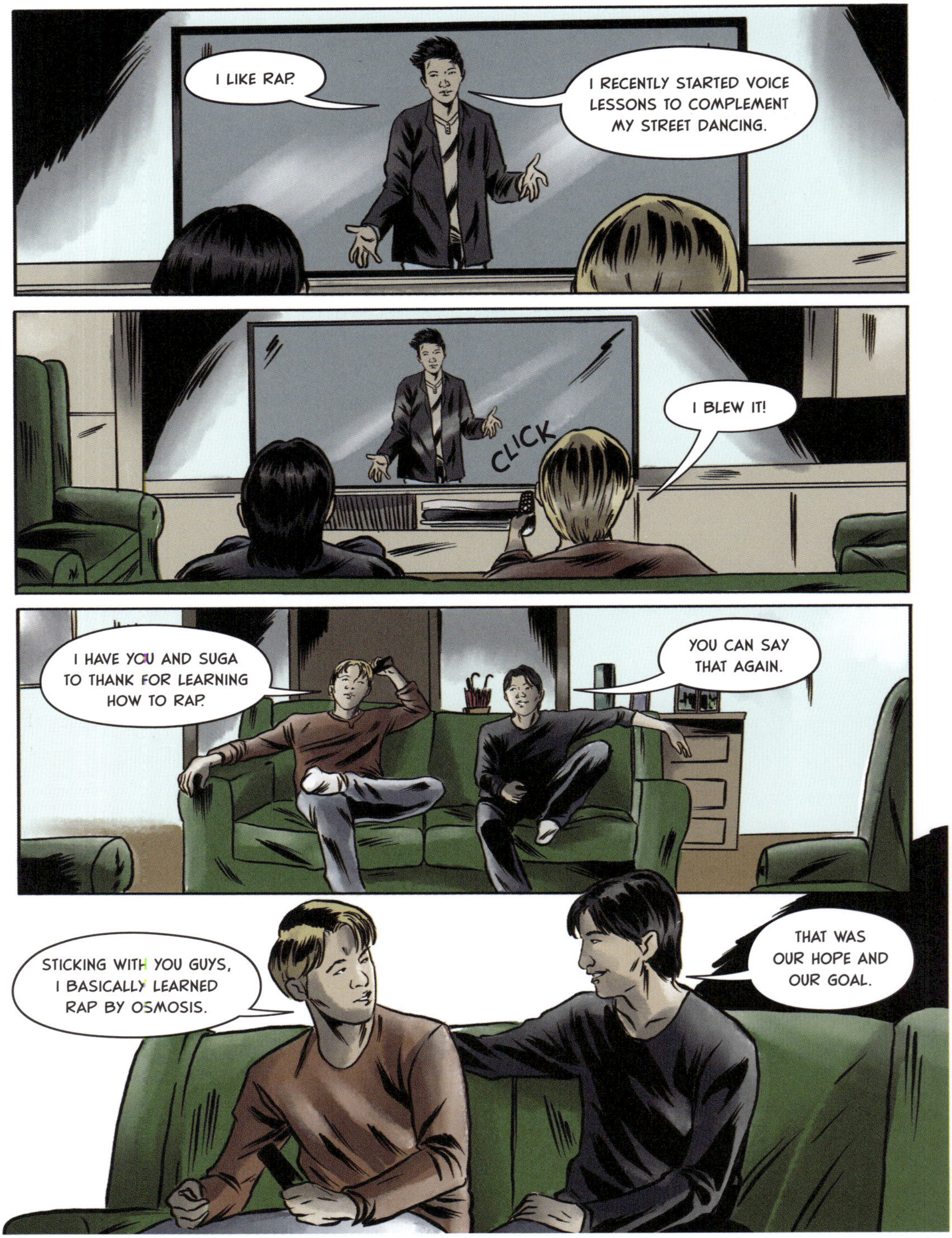
I LIKE RAP.
I RECENTLY STARTED VOICE LESSONS TO COMPLEMENT MY STREET DANCING.
CLICK
I BLEW IT!
I HAVE YOU AND SUGA TO THANK FOR LEARNING HOW TO RAP.
YOU CAN SAY THAT AGAIN.
STICKING WITH YOU GUYS, I BASICALLY LEARNED RAP BY OSMOSIS.
THAT WAS OUR HOPE AND OUR GOAL.

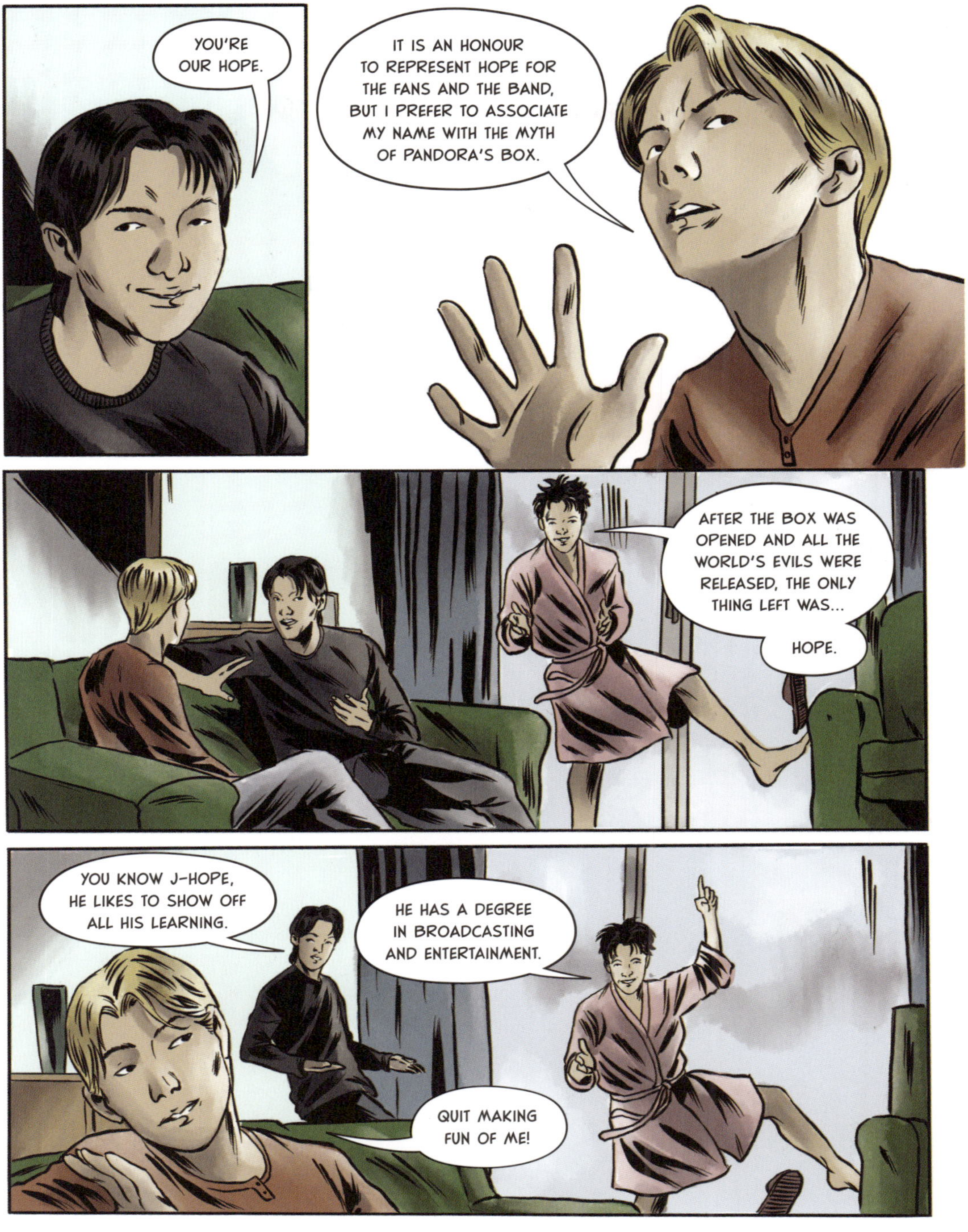
YOU'RE OUR HOPE.
IT IS AN HONOUR TO REPRESENT HOPE FOR THE FANS AND THE BAND, BUT I PREFER TO ASSOCIATE MY NAME WITH THE MYTH OF PANDORA'S BOX.
AFTER THE BOX WAS OPENED AND ALL THE WORLD'S EVILS WERE RELEASED, THE ONLY THING LEFT WAS...
HOPE.
YOU KNOW J-HOPE, HE LIKES TO SHOW OFF ALL HIS LEARNING.
HE HAS A DEGREE IN BROADCASTING AND ENTERTAINMENT.
QUIT MAKING FUN OF ME!

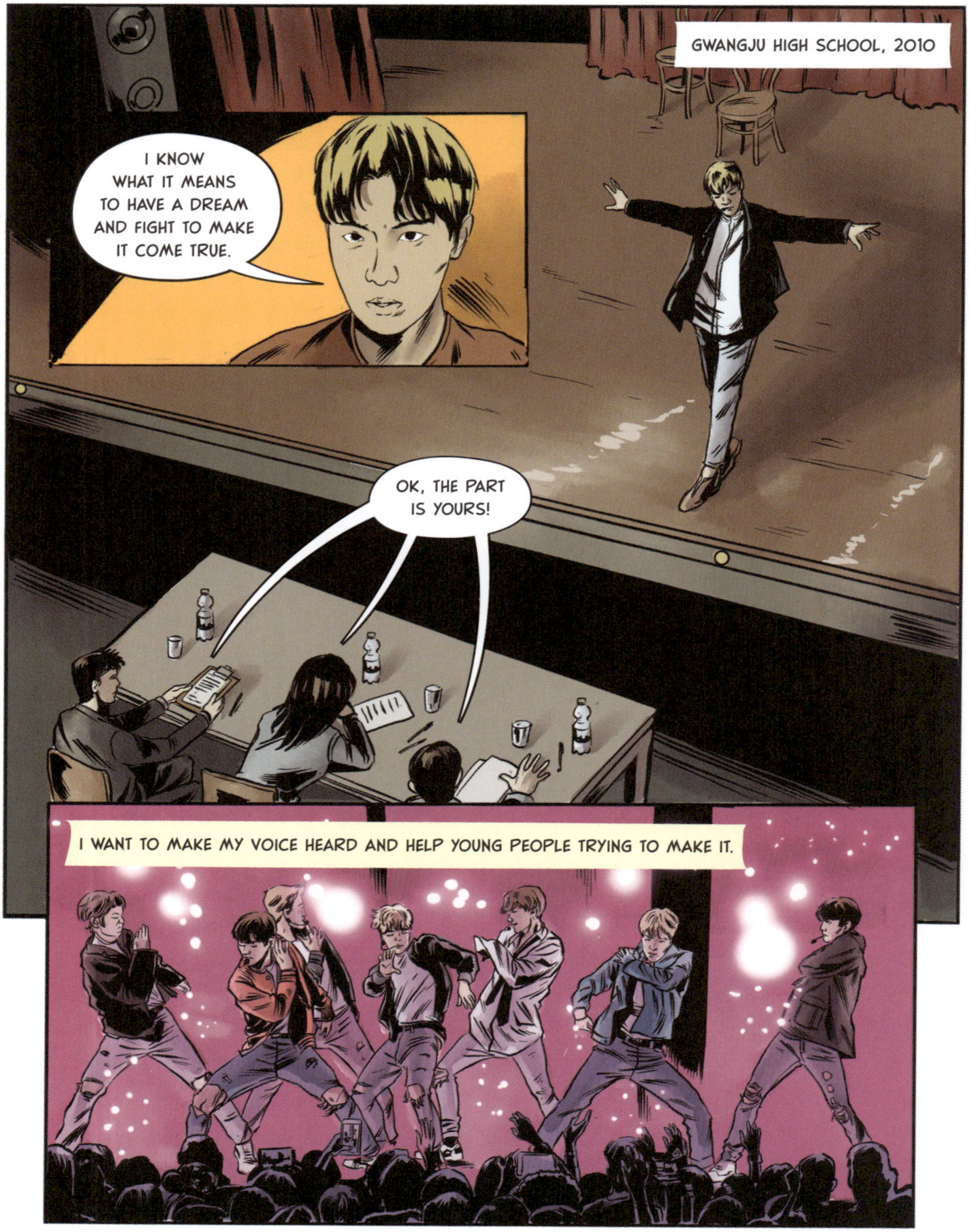
GWANGJU HIGH SCHOOL, 2010
I KNOW WHAT IT MEANS TO HAVE A DREAM AND FIGHT TO MAKE IT COME TRUE.
OK, THE PART IS YOURS!
I WANT TO MAKE MY VOICE HEARD AND HELP YOUNG PEOPLE TRYING TO MAKE IT.

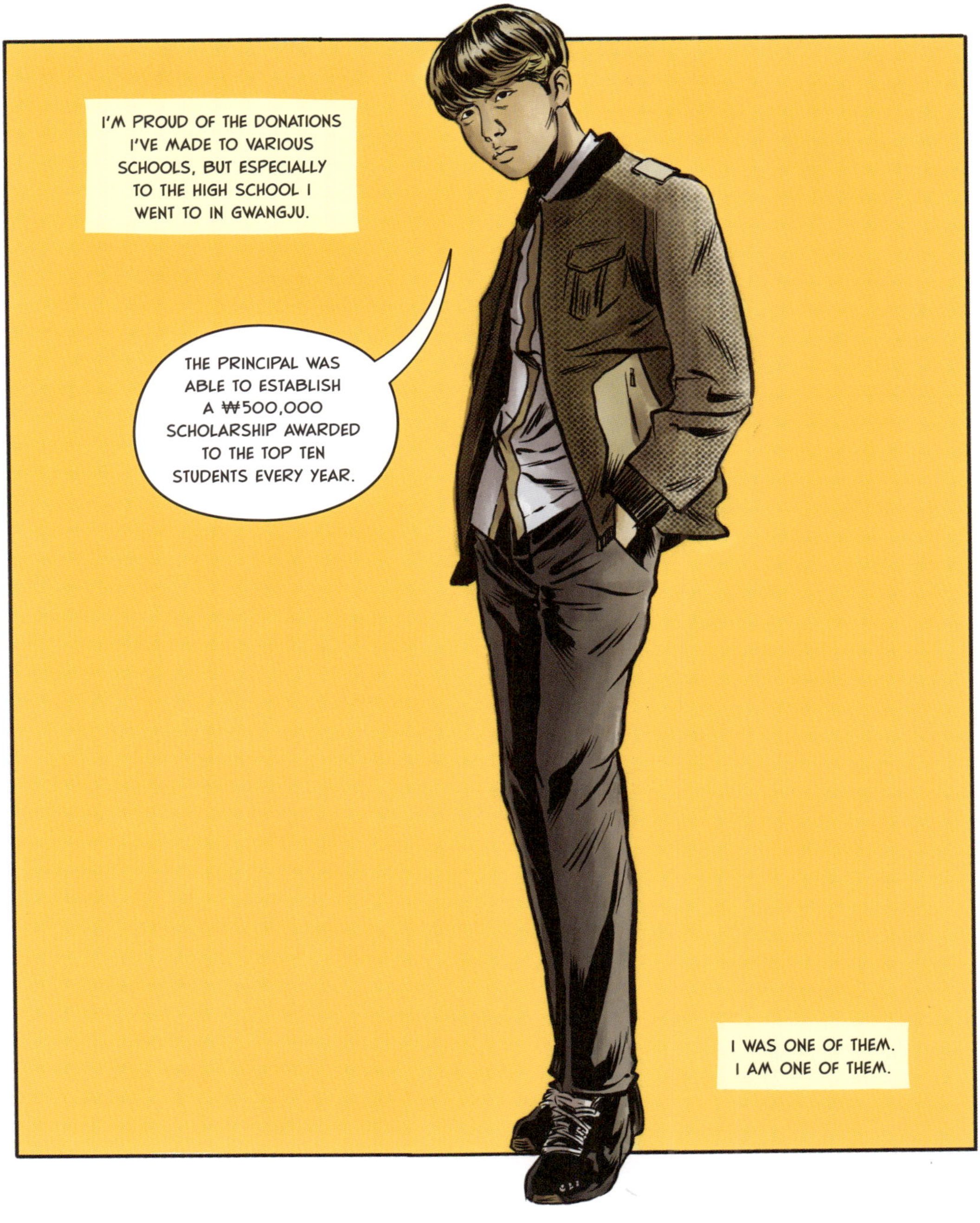
I'M PROUD OF THE DONATIONS I'VE MADE TO VARIOUS SCHOOLS, BUT ESPECIALLY TO THE HIGH SCHOOL I WENT TO IN GWANGJU.
THE PRINCIPAL WAS ABLE TO ESTABLISH A ₩500,000 SCHOLARSHIP AWARDED TO THE TOP TEN STUDENTS EVERY YEAR.
I WAS ONE OF THEM. I AM ONE OF THEM.

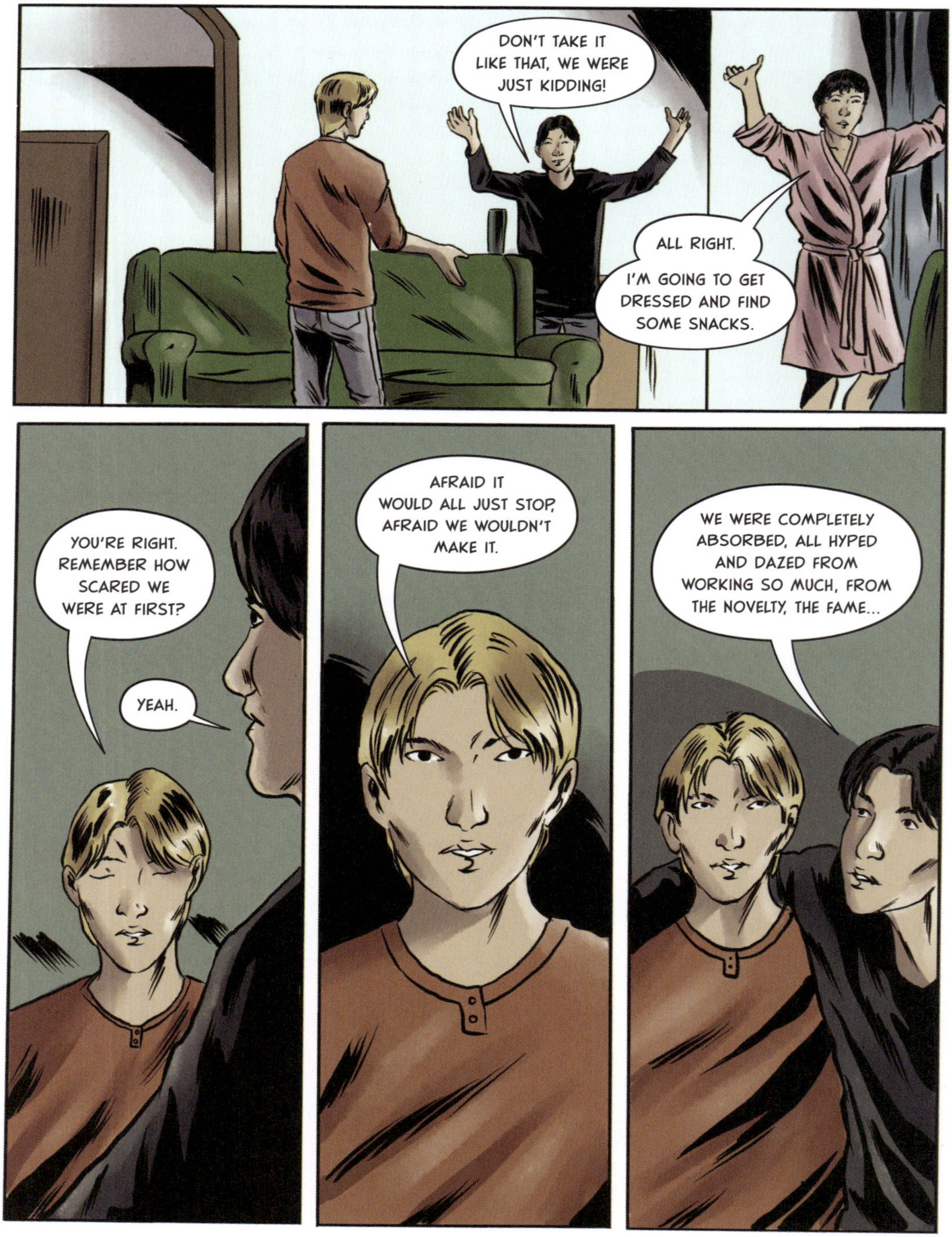
DON'T TAKE IT LIKE THAT, WE WERE JUST KIDDING!
ALL RIGHT.
I'M GOING TO GET DRESSED AND FIND SOME SNACKS.
YOU'RE RIGHT. REMEMBER HOW SCARED WE WERE AT FIRST?
YEAH.
AFRAID IT WOULD ALL JUST STOP, AFRAID WE WOULDN'T MAKE IT.
WE WERE COMPLETELY ABSORBED, ALL HYPED AND DAZED FROM WORKING SO MUCH, FROM THE NOVELTY, THE FAME...

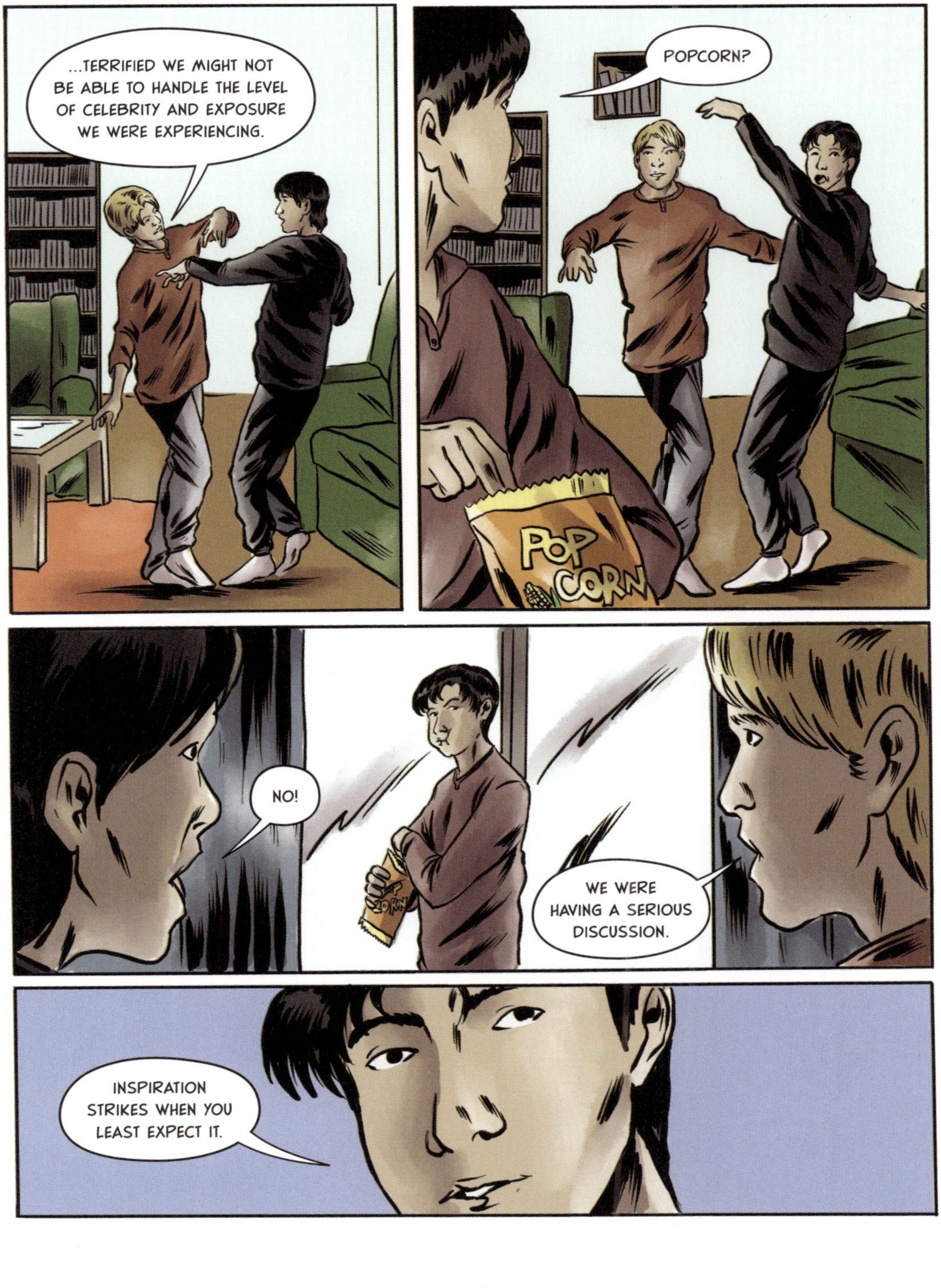
...TERRIFIED WE MIGHT NOT BE ABLE TO HANDLE THE LEVEL OF CELEBRITY AND EXPOSURE WE WERE EXPERIENCING.
POPCORN?
POP CORN
NO!
WE WERE HAVING A SERIOUS DISCUSSION.
INSPIRATION STRIKES WHEN YOU LEAST EXPECT IT.

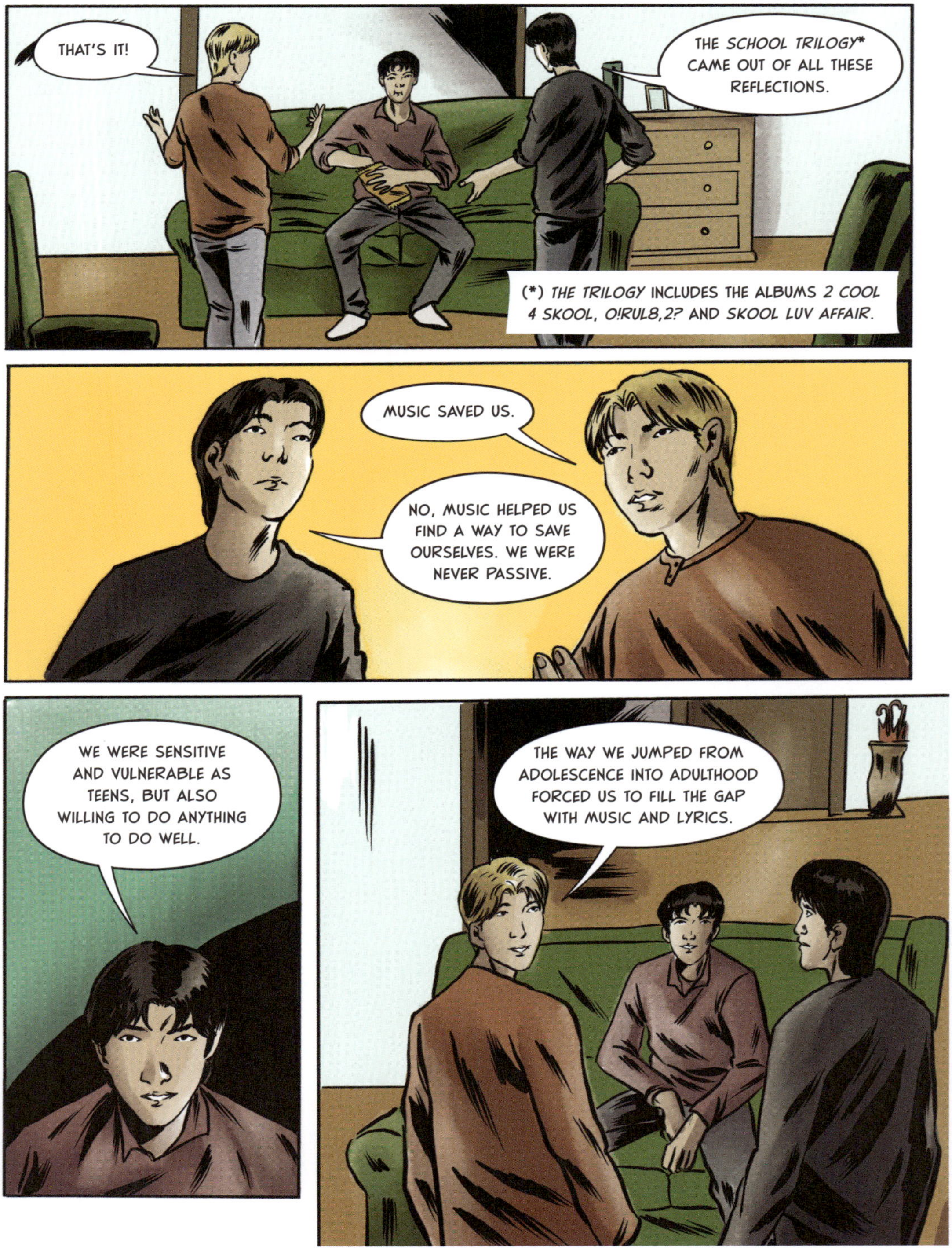
THAT'S IT!
THE *SCHOOL TRILOGY** CAME OUT OF ALL THESE REFLECTIONS.
(*) *THE TRILOGY* INCLUDES THE ALBUMS *2 COOL 4 SKOOL*, *O!RUL8,2?* AND *SKOOL LUV AFFAIR*.
MUSIC SAVED US.
NO, MUSIC HELPED US FIND A WAY TO SAVE OURSELVES. WE WERE NEVER PASSIVE.
WE WERE SENSITIVE AND VULNERABLE AS TEENS, BUT ALSO WILLING TO DO ANYTHING TO DO WELL.
THE WAY WE JUMPED FROM ADOLESCENCE INTO ADULTHOOD FORCED US TO FILL THE GAP WITH MUSIC AND LYRICS.

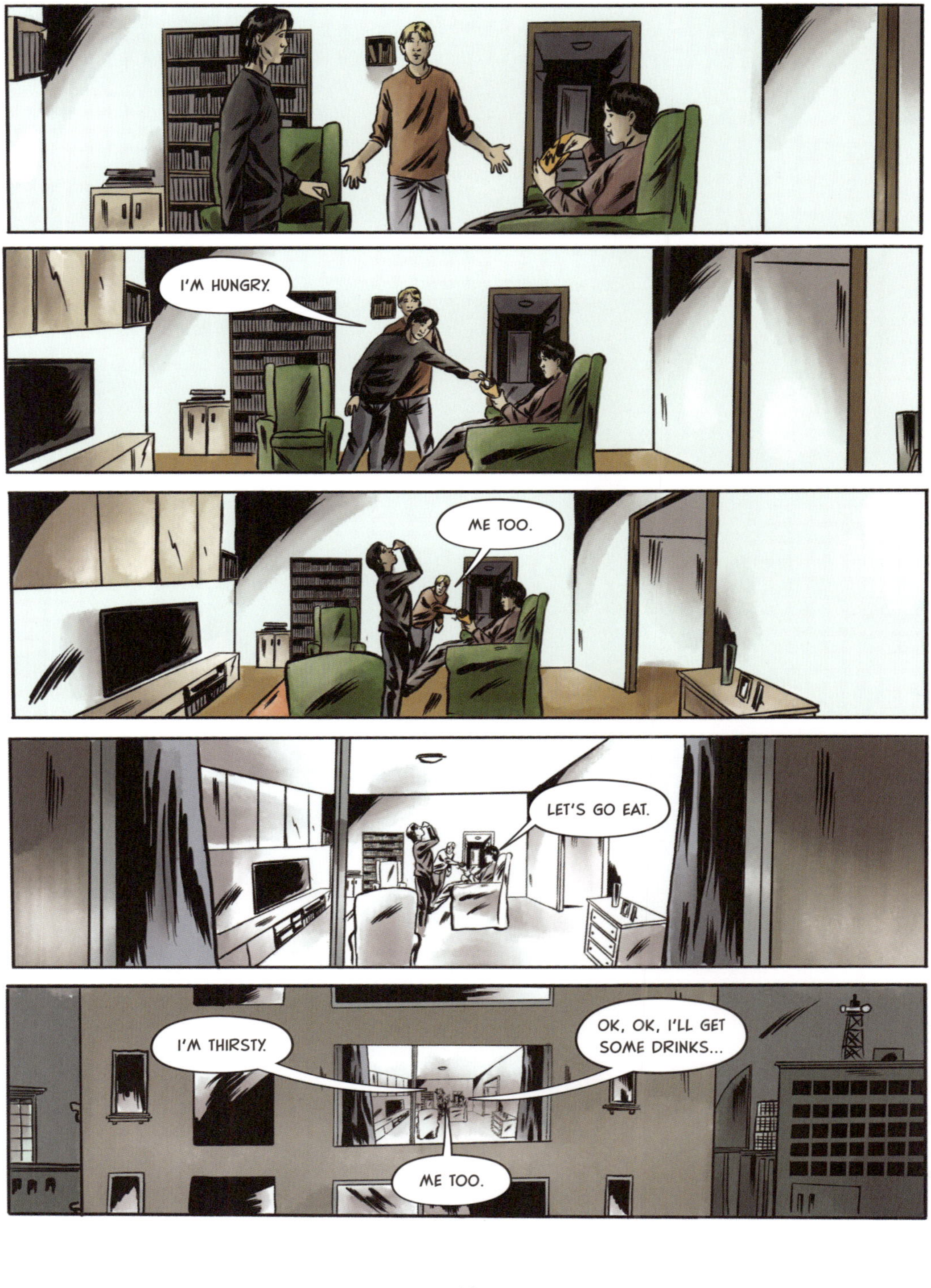
I'M HUNGRY.
ME TOO.
LET'S GO EAT.
I'M THIRSTY.
OK, OK, I'LL GET SOME DRINKS...
ME TOO.

JUNG KOOK

JEON JUNG-KOOK

FROM TIRELESS ATHLETE TO HEARTBREAKER TO HONEST WORKER.

JUNG KOOK, A SMALL FIFTEEN-YEAR-OLD IN THE ENORMOUS CITY OF SEOUL, IS A DREAMER, FILLED WITH AMBITIONS AND WISHES. WHEN THEY COME TO FRUITION, HE SAVOURS THEM, KNOWING THAT WHAT COUNTS IS THE PRESENT MOMENT HE'S LIVING IN, NOT WHAT HE HAS BEEN OR WILL BECOME.

WITH BTS AND AS A SOLO ARTIST HE SUPPORTS LOCAL TRADITIONS AND CULTURES, ESPECIALLY THOSE OF KOREA, SHARING THEM, SPREADING THEM, MODERNISING THEM, MAKING THEM KNOWN AND PRACTISED BY FANS IN A GLOBALISED WORLD.

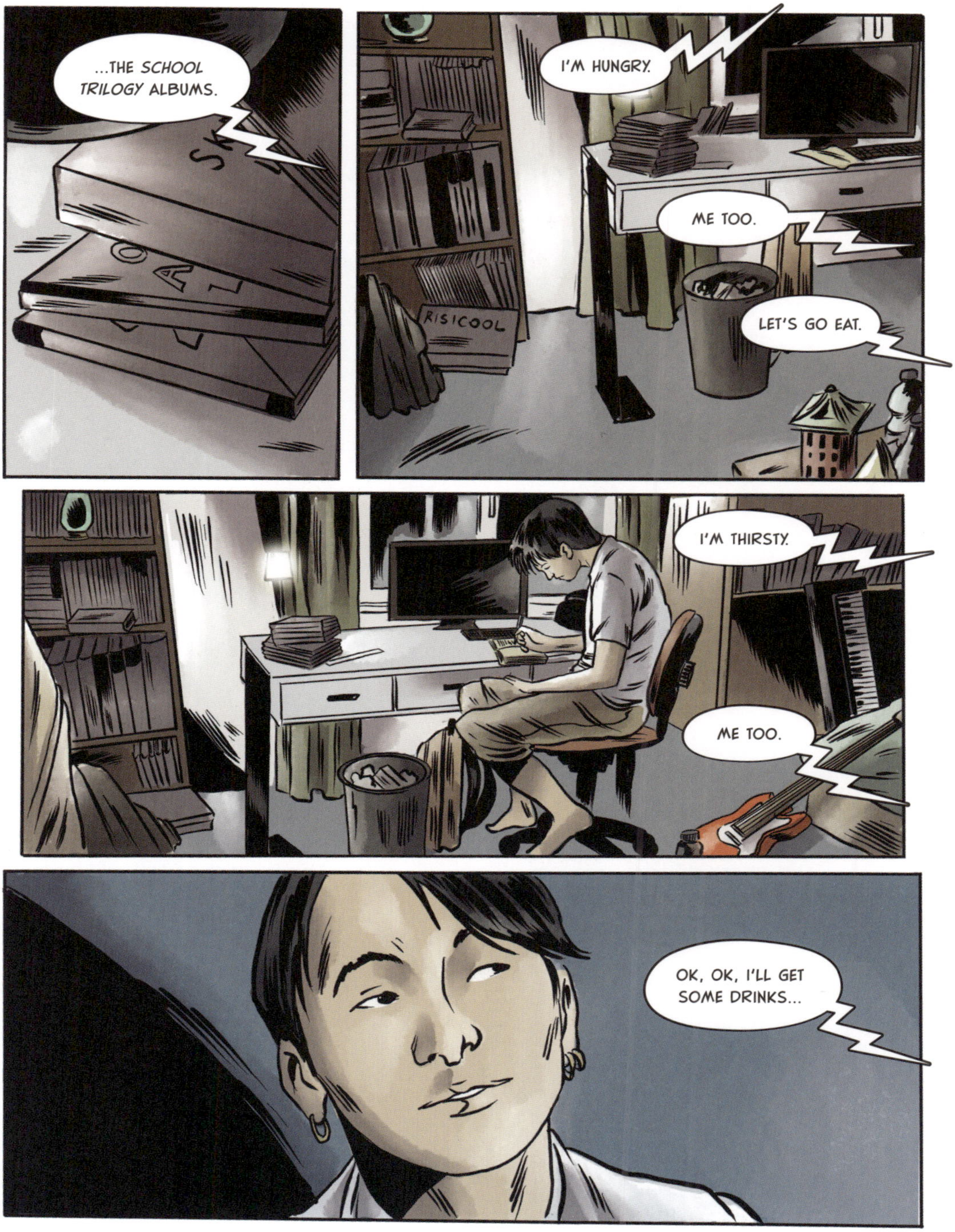
...THE *SCHOOL TRILOGY* ALBUMS.
I'M HUNGRY.
ME TOO.
RISICOOL
LET'S GO EAT.
I'M THIRSTY.
ME TOO.
OK, OK, I'LL GET SOME DRINKS...

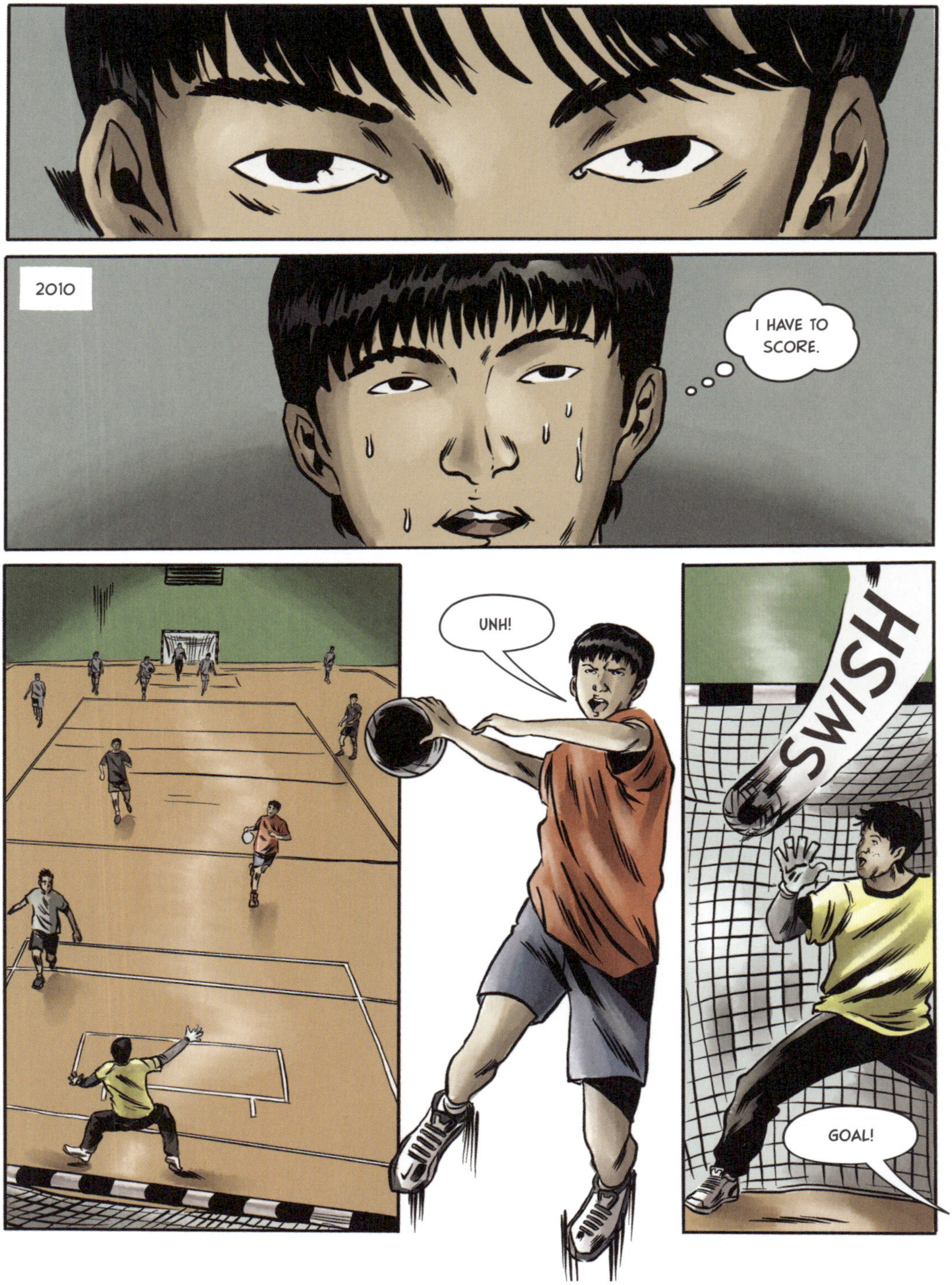
2010
I HAVE TO SCORE.
UNH!
SWISH
GOAL!

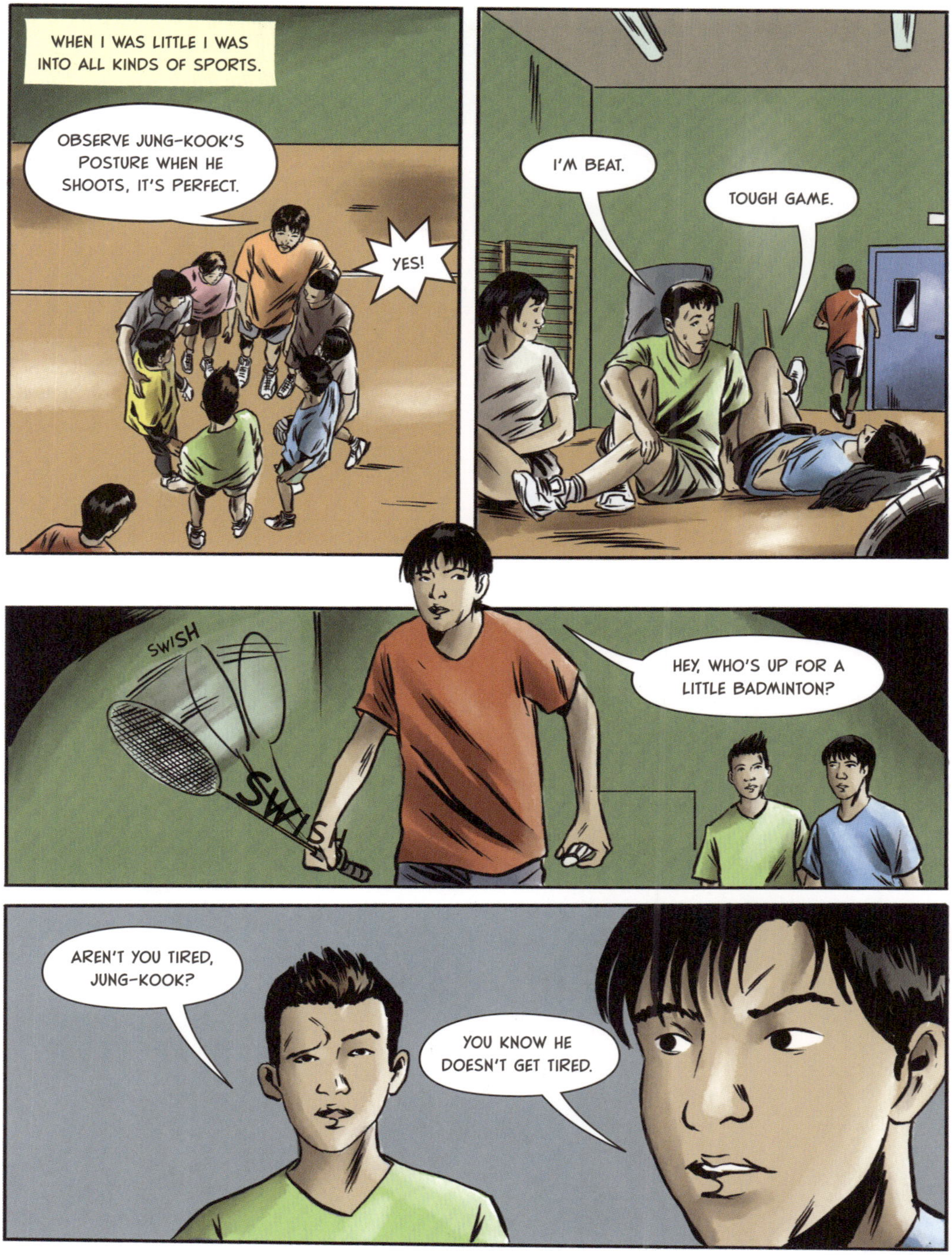
WHEN I WAS LITTLE I WAS INTO ALL KINDS OF SPORTS.
OBSERVE JUNG-KOOK'S POSTURE WHEN HE SHOOTS, IT'S PERFECT.
YES!
I'M BEAT.
TOUGH GAME.
SWISH
SWISH
HEY, WHO'S UP FOR A LITTLE BADMINTON?
AREN'T YOU TIRED, JUNG-KOOK?
YOU KNOW HE DOESN'T GET TIRED.

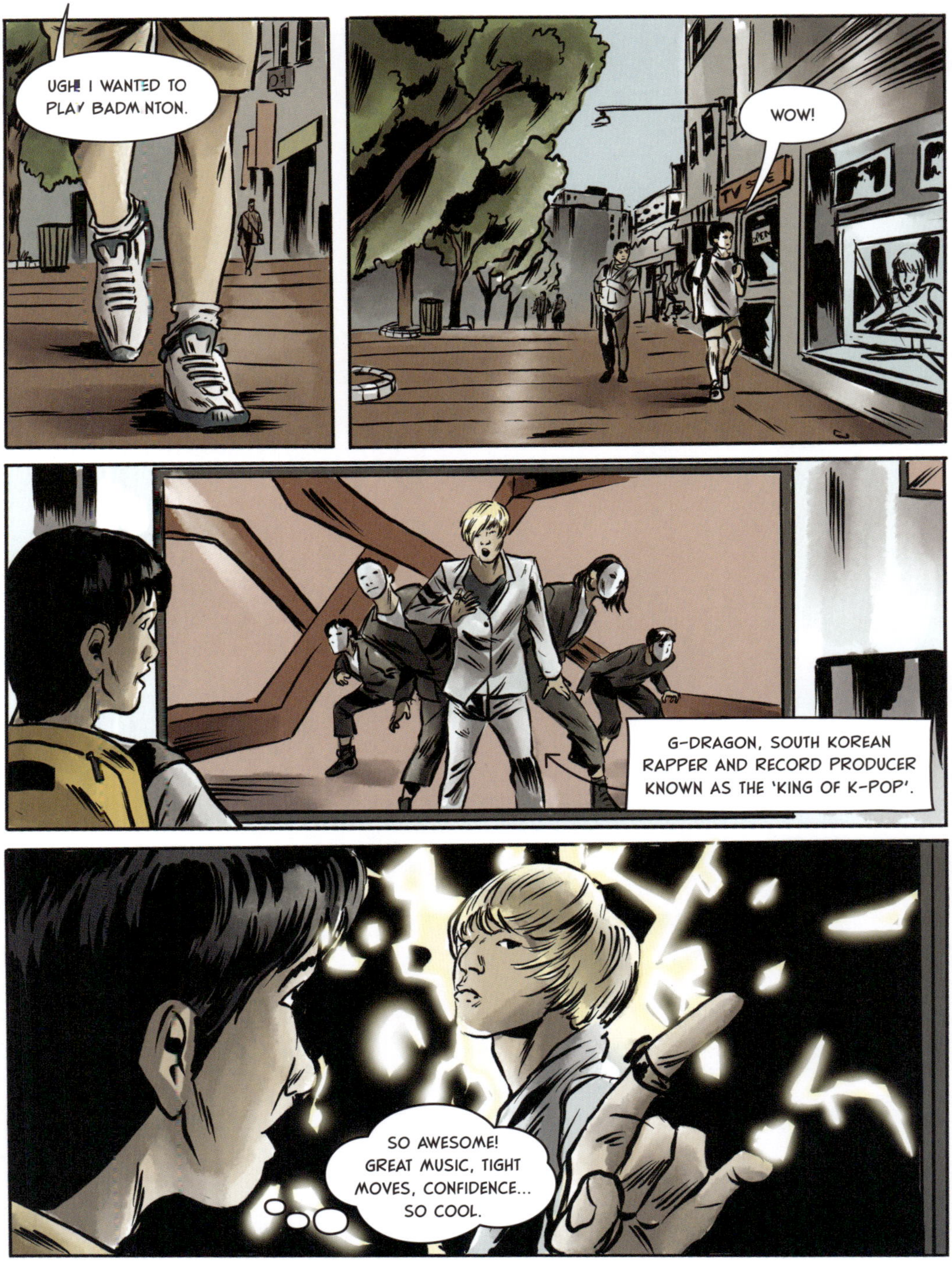
UGH! I WANTED TO PLAY BADMINTON.
WOW!
G-DRAGON, SOUTH KOREAN RAPPER AND RECORD PRODUCER KNOWN AS THE 'KING OF K-POP'.
SO AWESOME! GREAT MUSIC, TIGHT MOVES, CONFIDENCE... SO COOL.

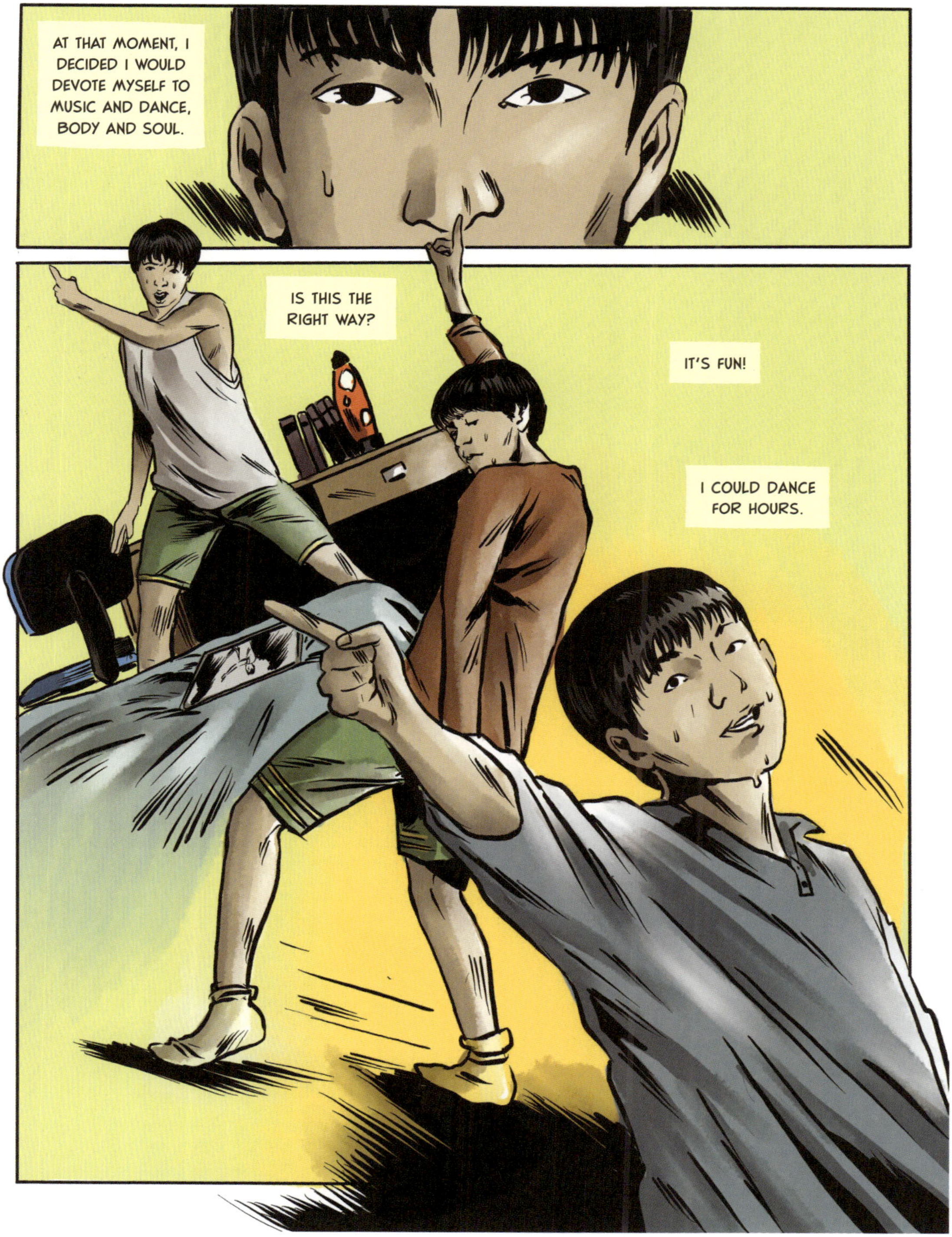
AT THAT MOMENT, I DECIDED I WOULD DEVOTE MYSELF TO MUSIC AND DANCE, BODY AND SOUL.
IS THIS THE RIGHT WAY?
IT'S FUN!
I COULD DANCE FOR HOURS.

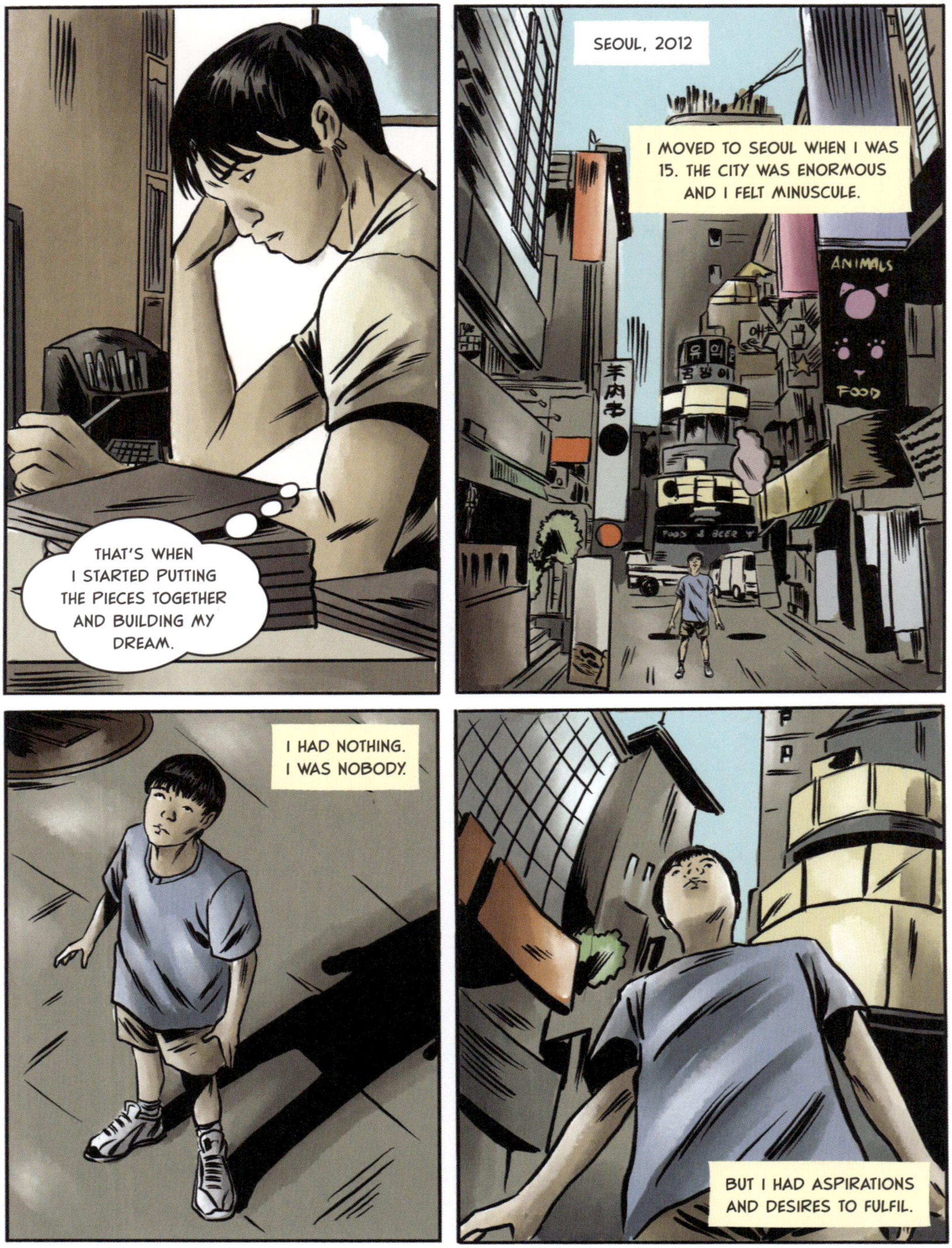
THAT'S WHEN I STARTED PUTTING THE PIECES TOGETHER AND BUILDING MY DREAM.
SEOUL, 2012
I MOVED TO SEOUL WHEN I WAS 15. THE CITY WAS ENORMOUS AND I FELT MINUSCULE.
ANIMALS
FOOD
I HAD NOTHING. I WAS NOBODY.
BUT I HAD ASPIRATIONS AND DESIRES TO FULFIL.

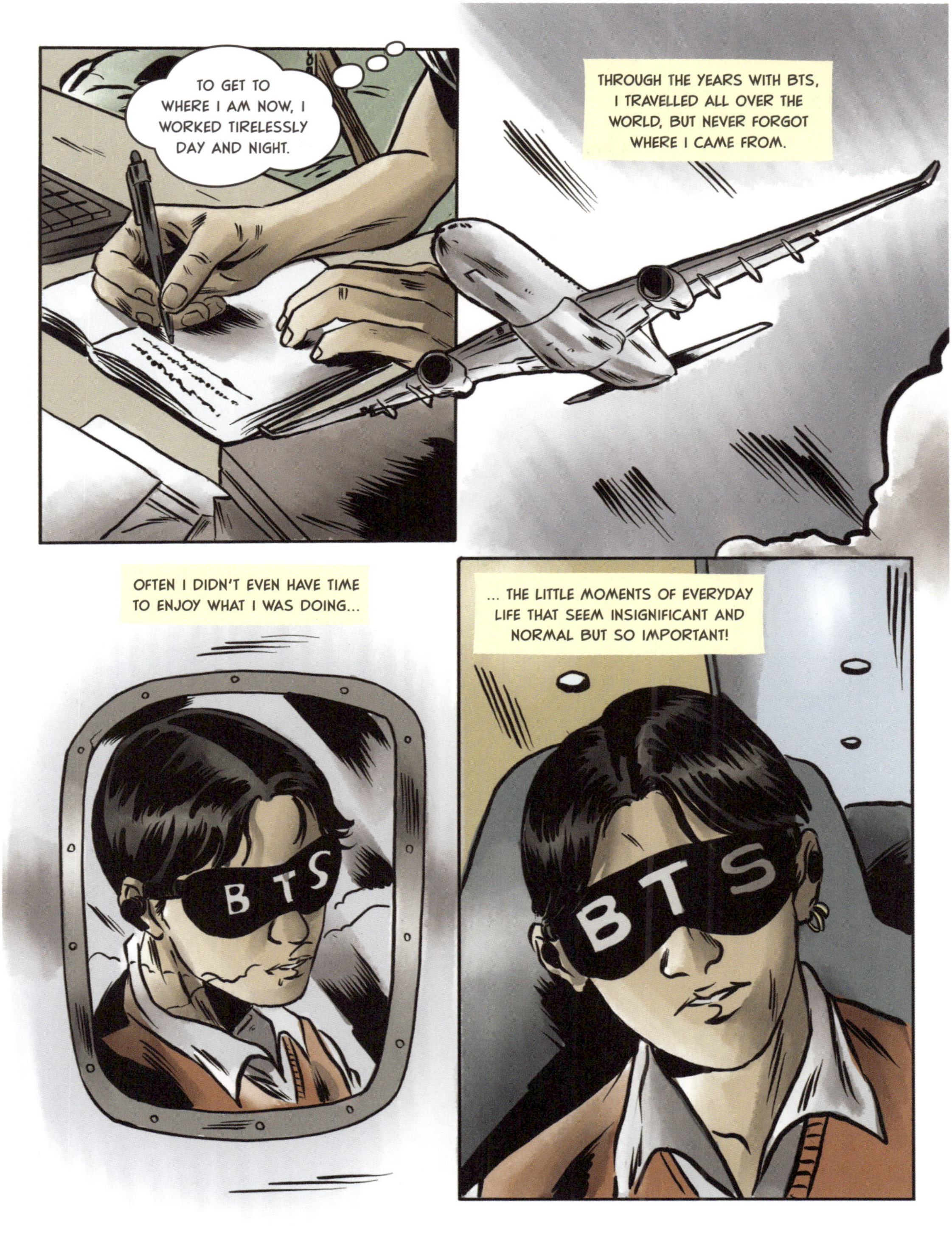

TO GET TO WHERE I AM NOW, I WORKED TIRELESSLY DAY AND NIGHT.
THROUGH THE YEARS WITH BTS, I TRAVELLED ALL OVER THE WORLD, BUT NEVER FORGOT WHERE I CAME FROM.
OFTEN I DIDN'T EVEN HAVE TIME TO ENJOY WHAT I WAS DOING...
BTS
... THE LITTLE MOMENTS OF EVERYDAY LIFE THAT SEEM INSIGNIFICANT AND NORMAL BUT SO IMPORTANT!
BTS

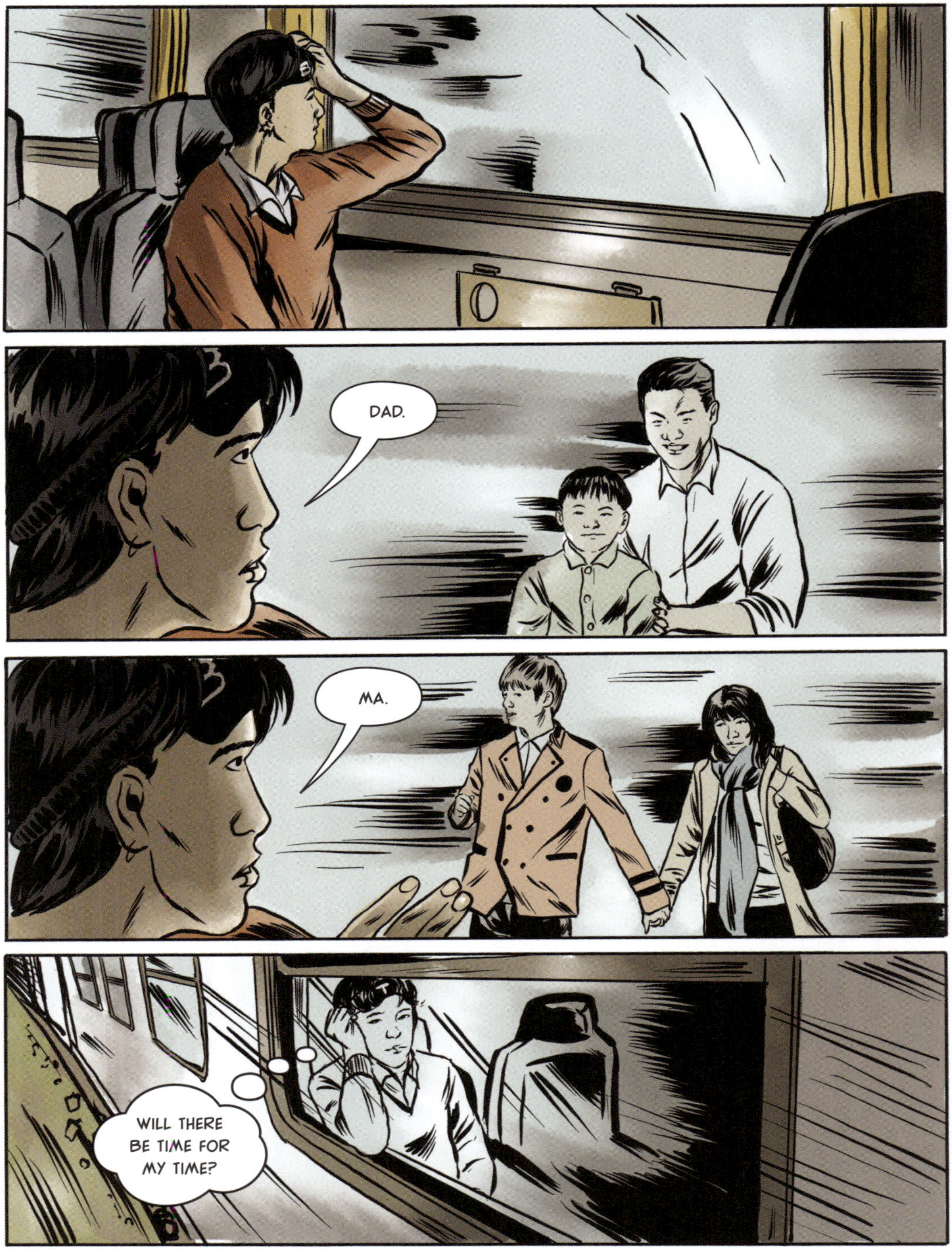
DAD.
MA.
WILL THERE BE TIME FOR MY TIME?

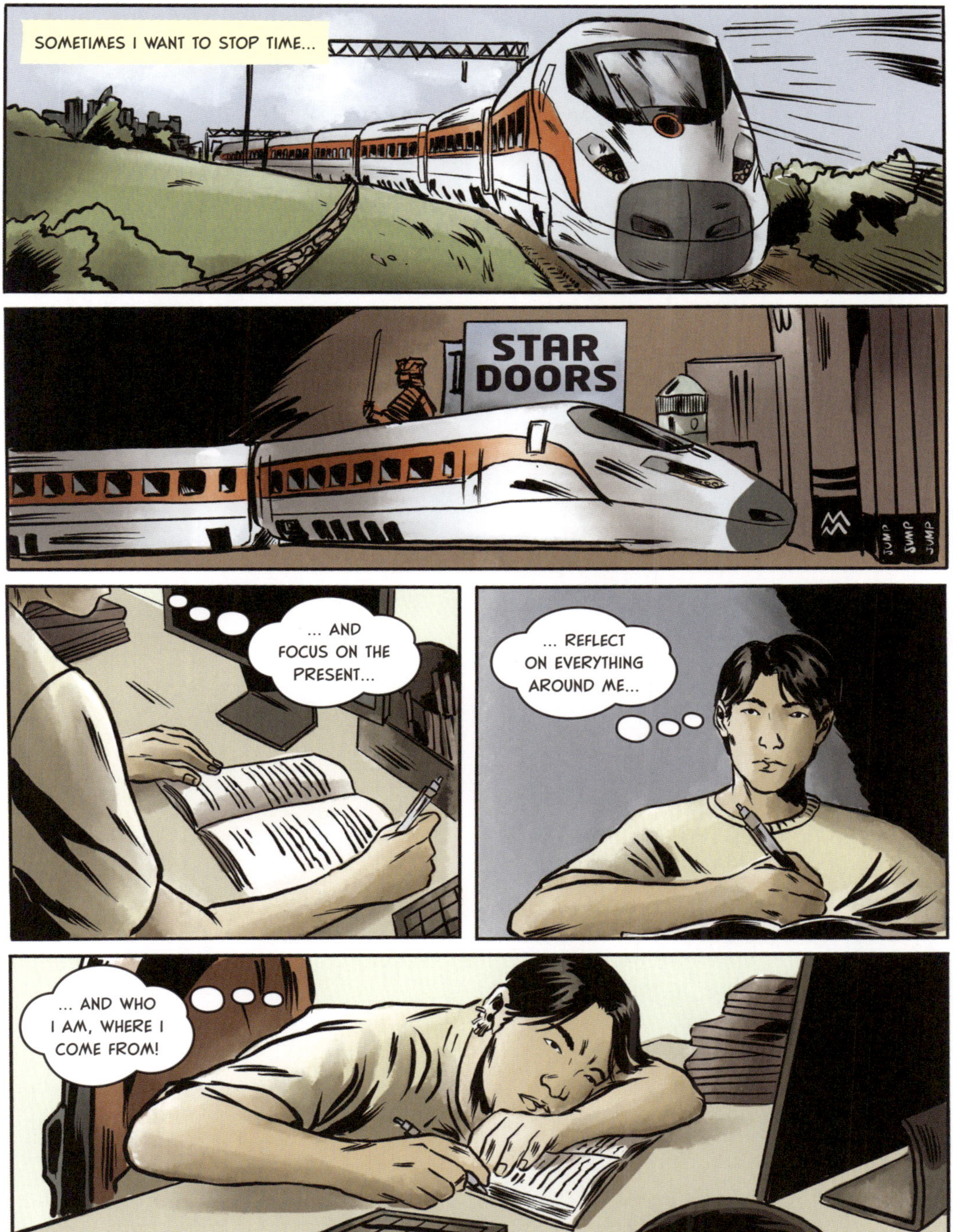
SOMETIMES I WANT TO STOP TIME...
STAR DOORS
... AND FOCUS ON THE PRESENT...
... REFLECT ON EVERYTHING AROUND ME...
... AND WHO I AM, WHERE I COME FROM!

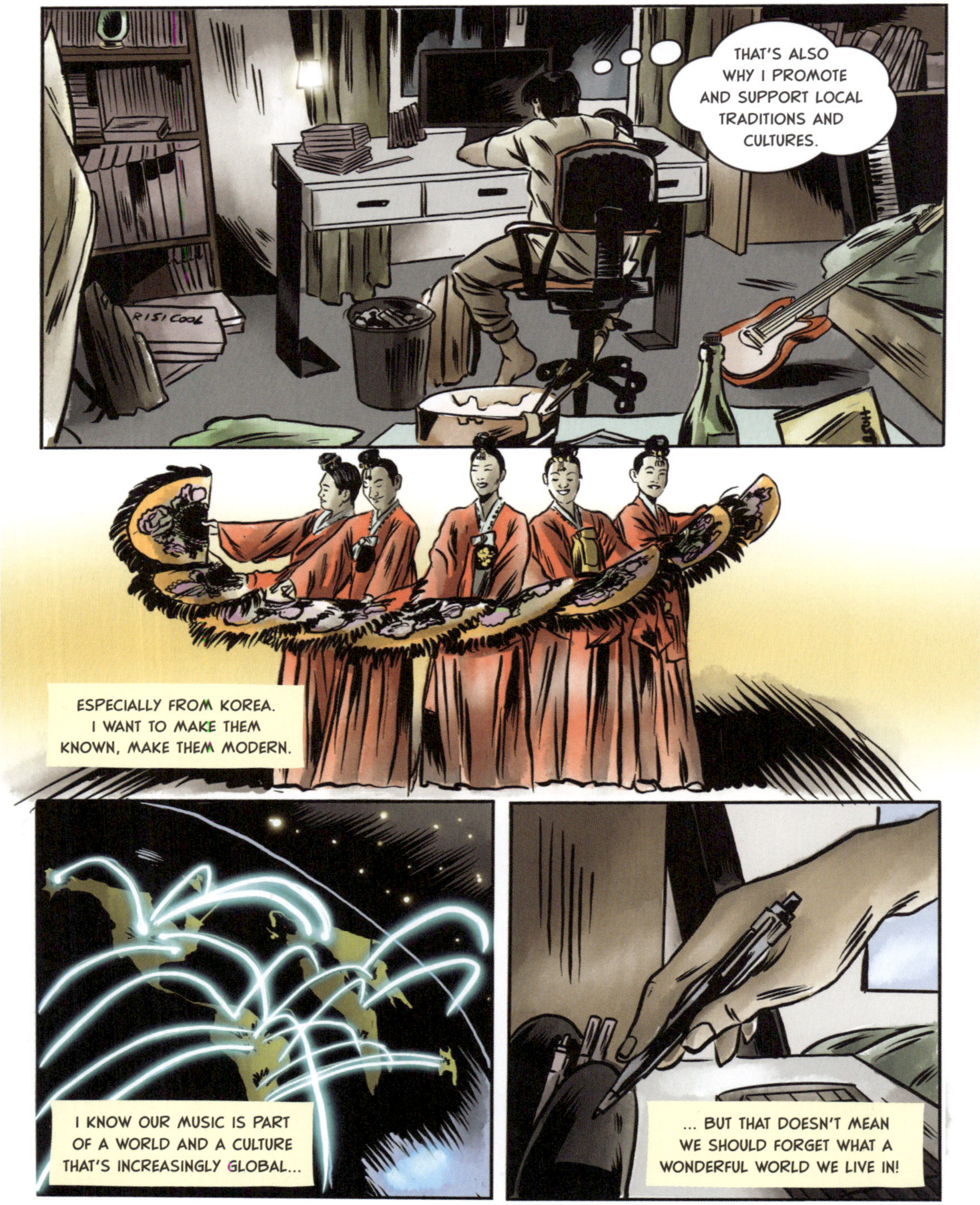
THAT'S ALSO WHY I PROMOTE AND SUPPORT LOCAL TRADITIONS AND CULTURES.
ESPECIALLY FROM KOREA. I WANT TO MAKE THEM KNOWN, MAKE THEM MODERN.
I KNOW OUR MUSIC IS PART OF A WORLD AND A CULTURE THAT'S INCREASINGLY GLOBAL...
... BUT THAT DOESN'T MEAN WE SHOULD FORGET WHAT A WONDERFUL WORLD WE LIVE IN!

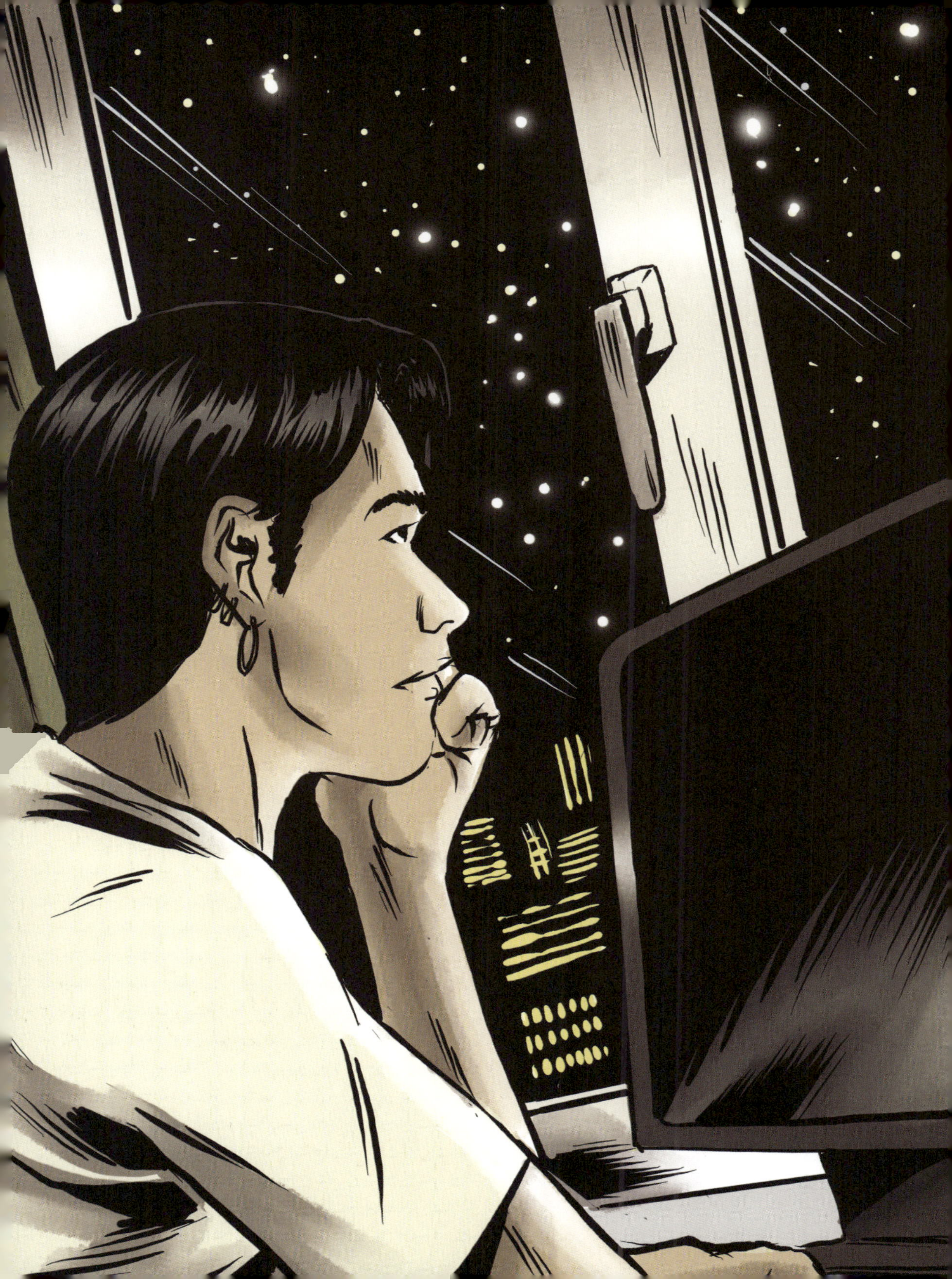

V

KIM TAE-HYUNG

FROM THE SAXOPHONE TO SINGING TO BTS.

SEEING VAN GOGH'S *STARRY NIGHT* SPARKS V'S MEMORIES OF CHILDHOOD AT HIS GRANDMOTHER'S HOUSE IN THE COUNTRY, BRINGING HIM A MIX OF NOSTALGIA, ANXIETY AND STRESS SO POTENT HE BREAKS OUT IN HIVES – A CHRONIC ALLERGY.

V AND BTS HAVE CHANGED THE WAY PEOPLE SEE AND TALK ABOUT MENTAL HEALTH THROUGH THEIR MUSIC. THEY SUGGEST THAT EVERYONE IS PERFECT AS THEY ARE, THAT NO ONE SHOULD CHANGE THEMSELVES TO FIT SOMEONE ELSE'S STANDARDS. THEY SPREAD THE COMMANDMENT 'EMBRACE YOUR FLAWS AND SHINE'.

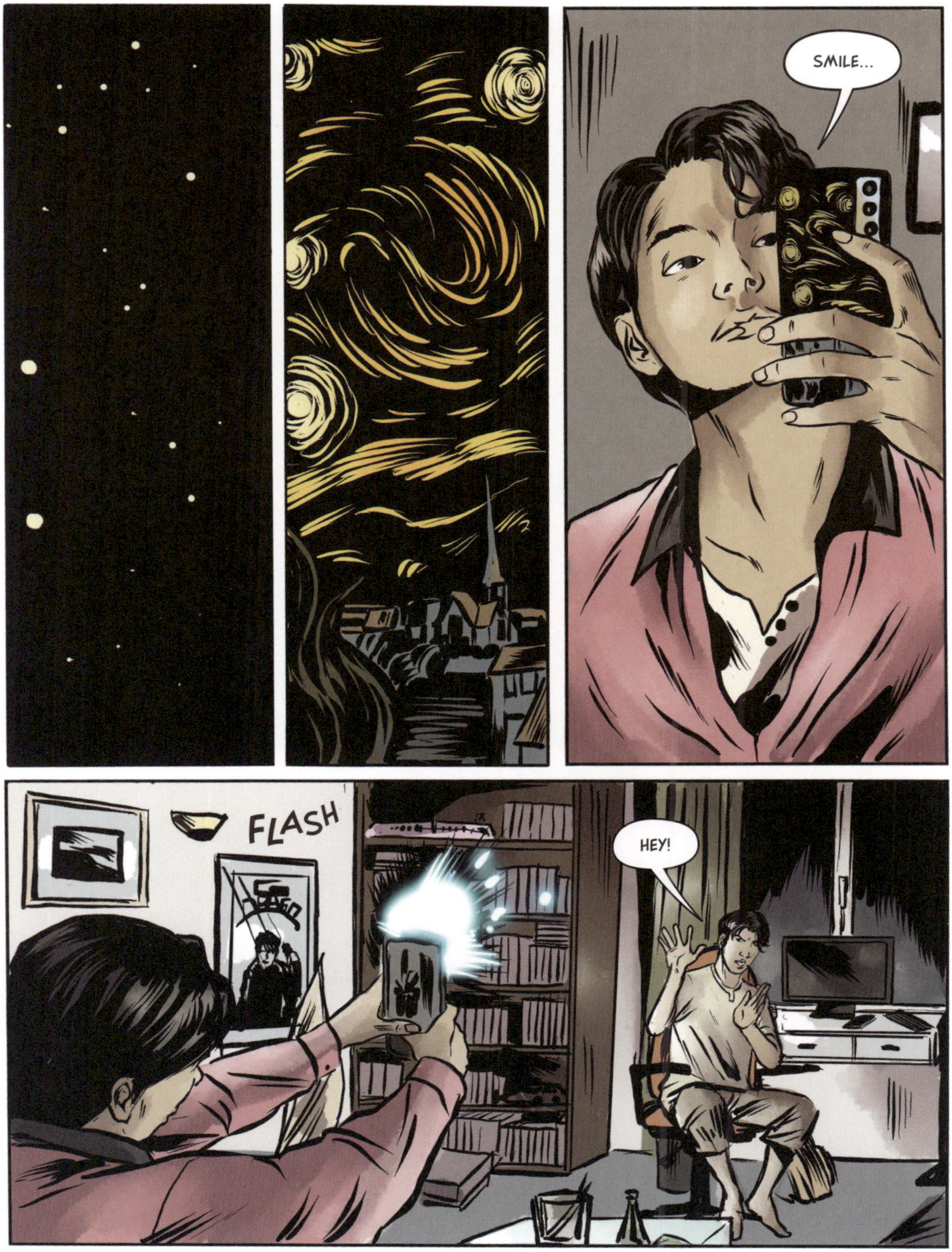
SMILE...
FLASH
HEY!

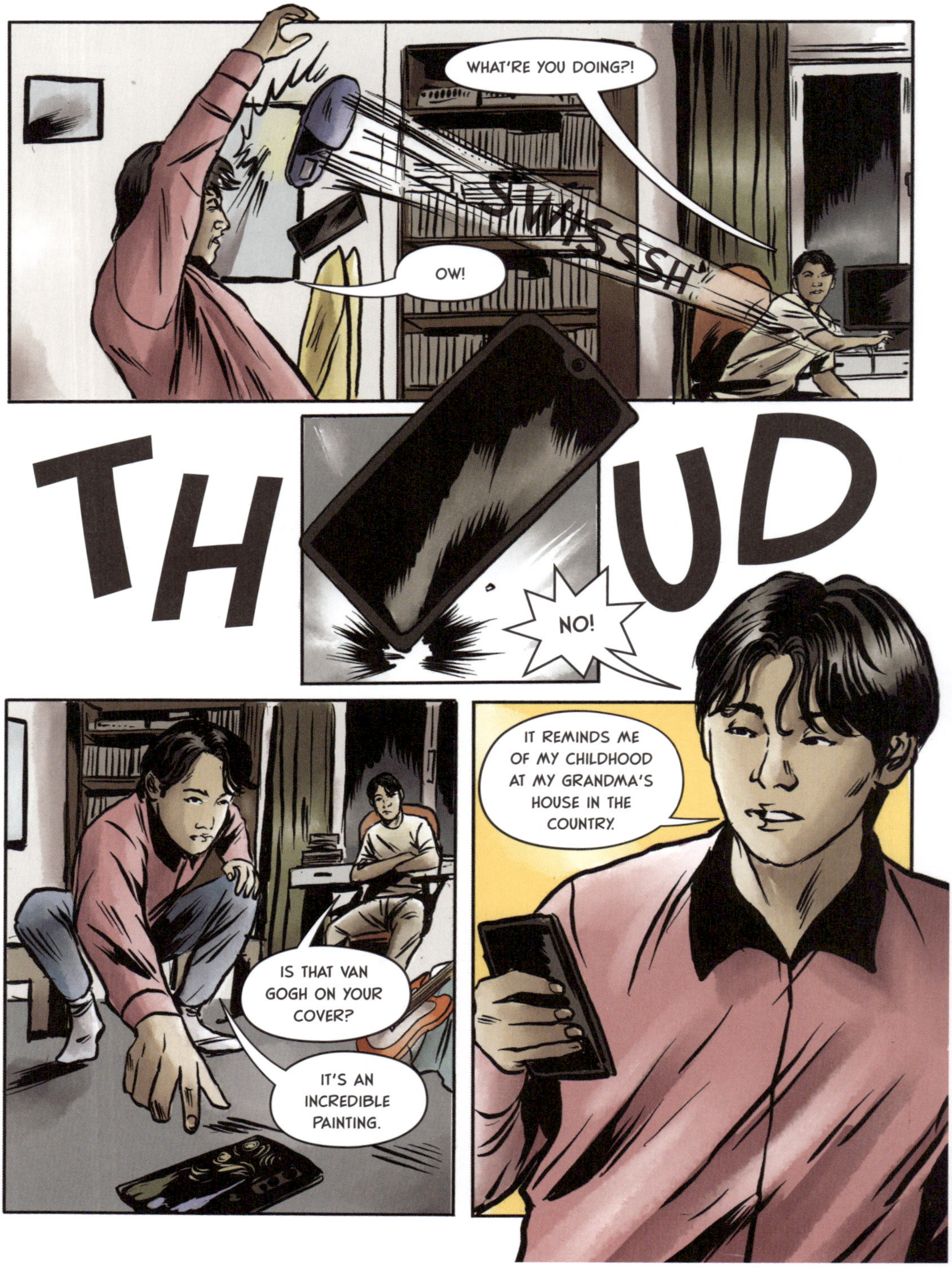
WHAT'RE YOU DOING?!
SWISSSH
OW!
THUD
NO!
IS THAT VAN GOGH ON YOUR COVER?
IT'S AN INCREDIBLE PAINTING.
IT REMINDS ME OF MY CHILDHOOD AT MY GRANDMA'S HOUSE IN THE COUNTRY.

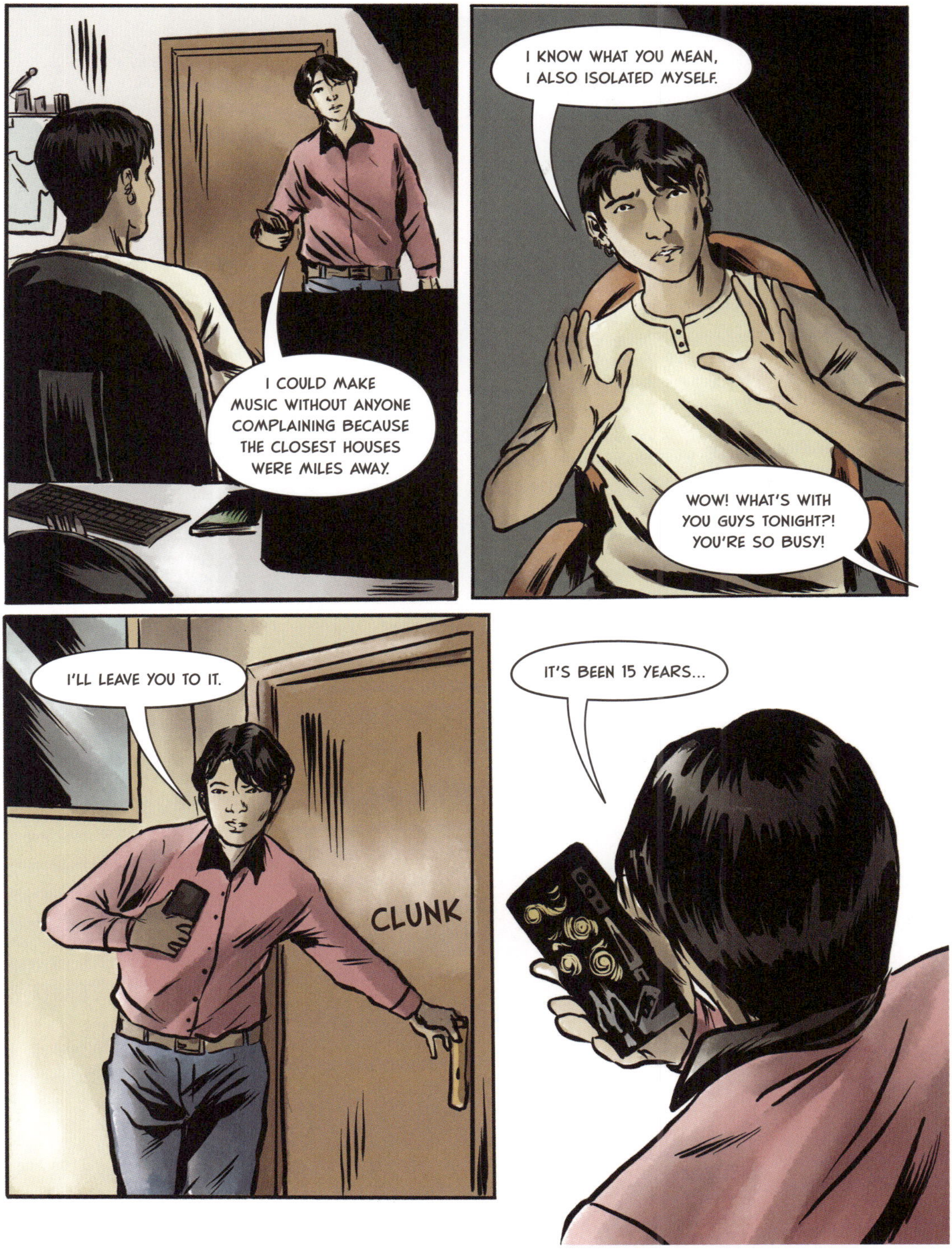
I COULD MAKE MUSIC WITHOUT ANYONE COMPLAINING BECAUSE THE CLOSEST HOUSES WERE MILES AWAY.
I KNOW WHAT YOU MEAN, I ALSO ISOLATED MYSELF.
WOW! WHAT'S WITH YOU GUYS TONIGHT?! YOU'RE SO BUSY!
I'LL LEAVE YOU TO IT.
CLUNK
IT'S BEEN 15 YEARS...

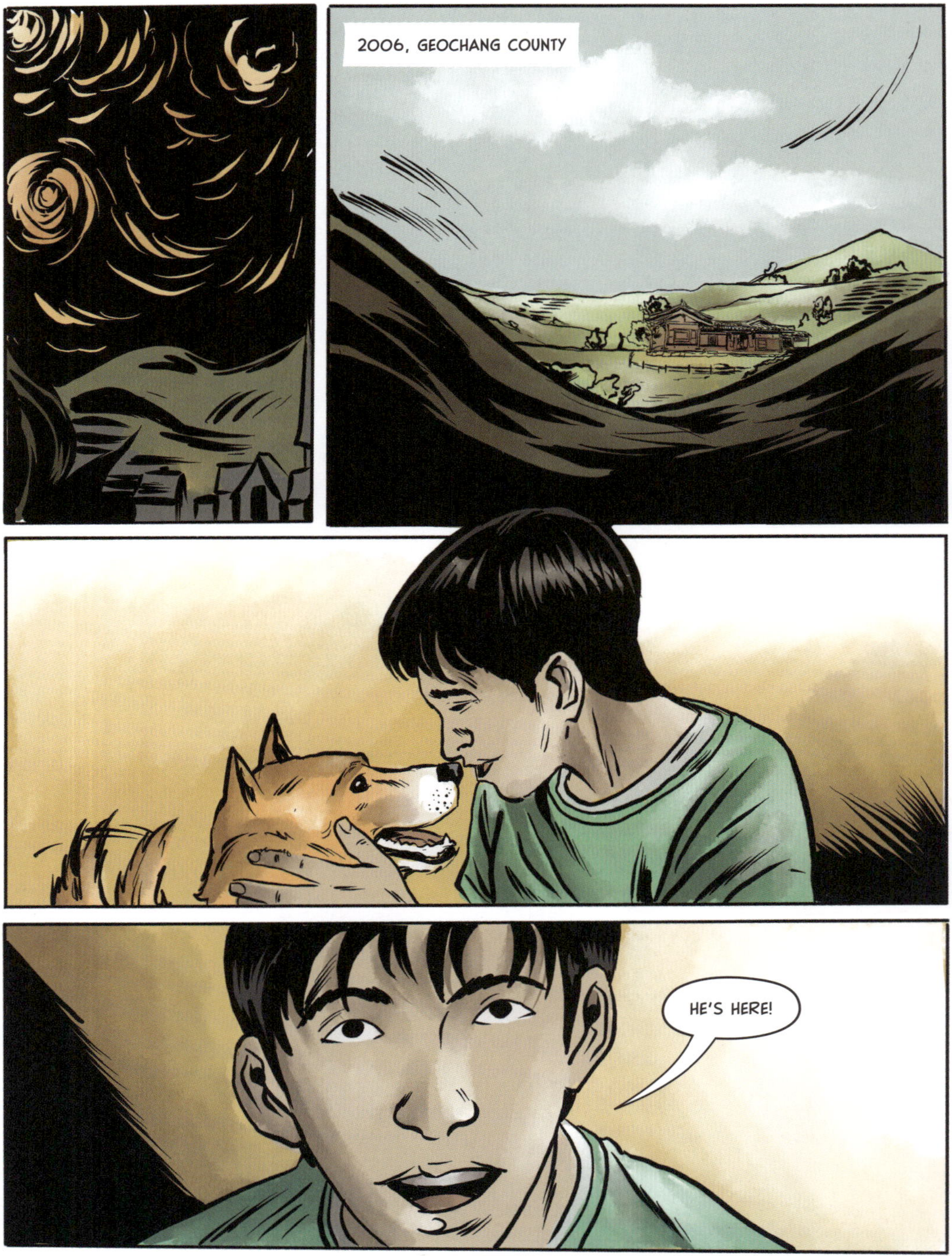
2006, GEOCHANG COUNTY
HE'S HERE!

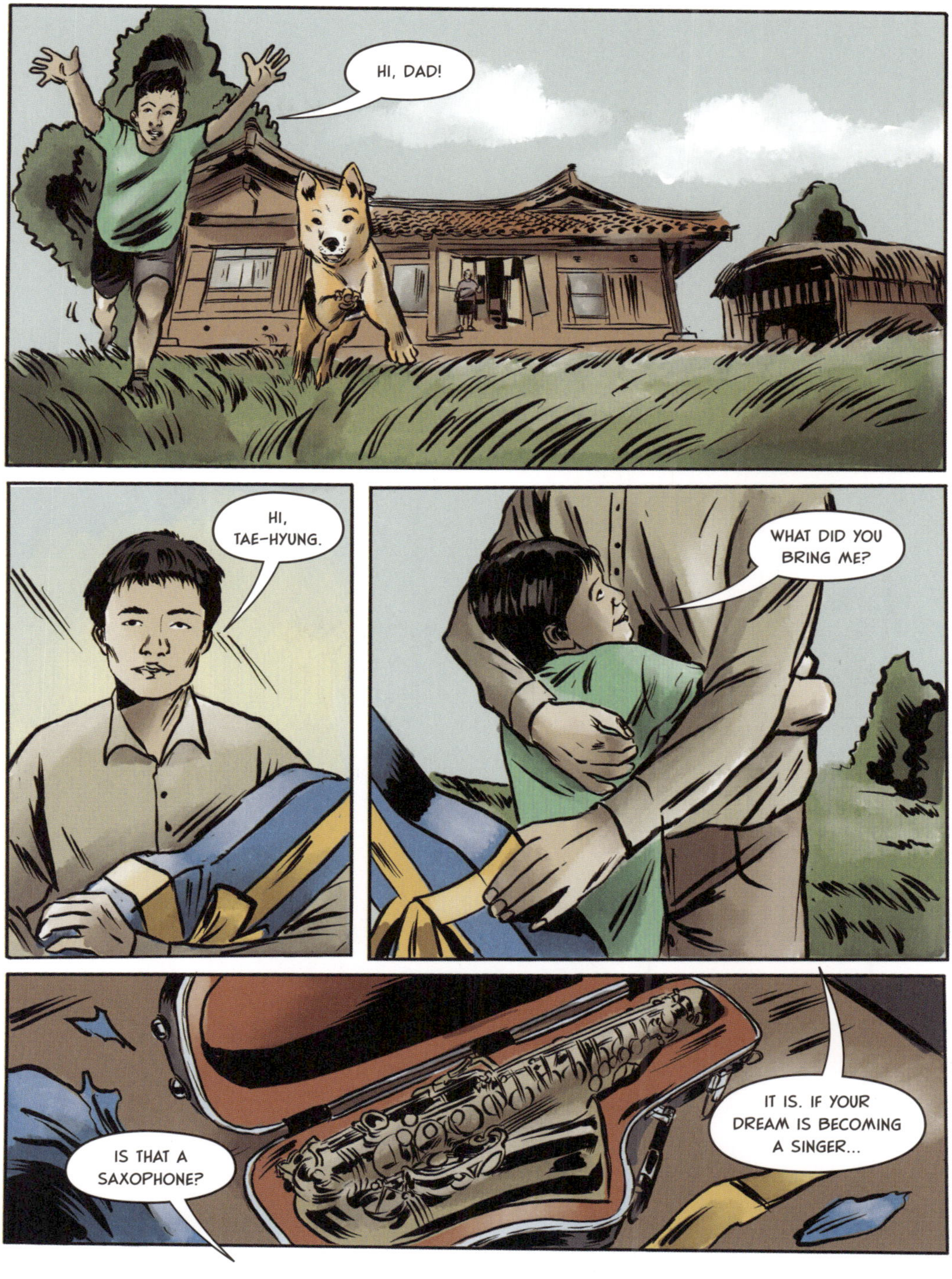
HI, DAD!
HI, TAE-HYUNG.
WHAT DID YOU BRING ME?
IS THAT A SAXOPHONE?
IT IS. IF YOUR DREAM IS BECOMING A SINGER...

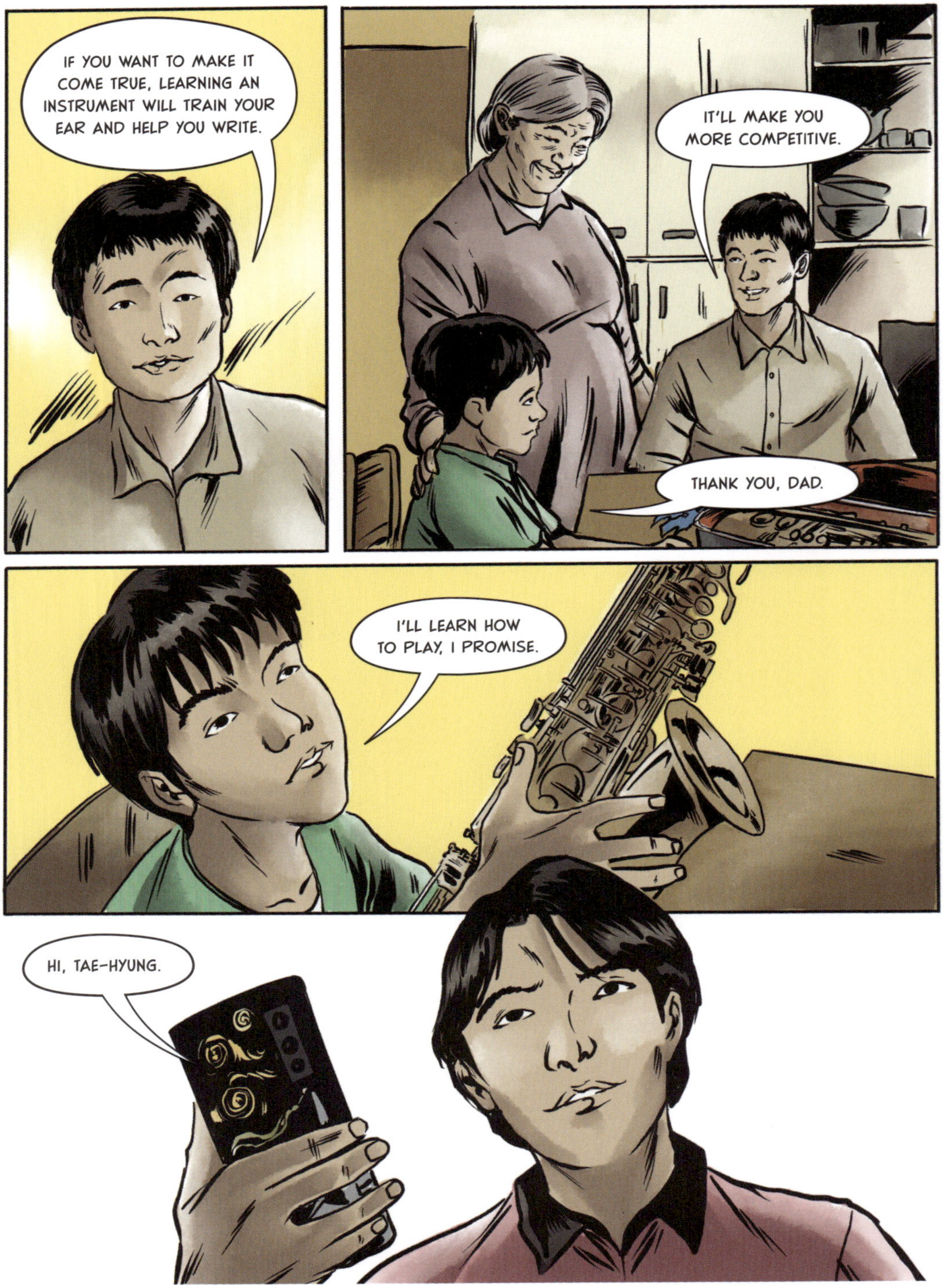
IF YOU WANT TO MAKE IT COME TRUE, LEARNING AN INSTRUMENT WILL TRAIN YOUR EAR AND HELP YOU WRITE.
IT'LL MAKE YOU MORE COMPETITIVE.
THANK YOU, DAD.
I'LL LEARN HOW TO PLAY, I PROMISE.
HI, TAE-HYUNG.

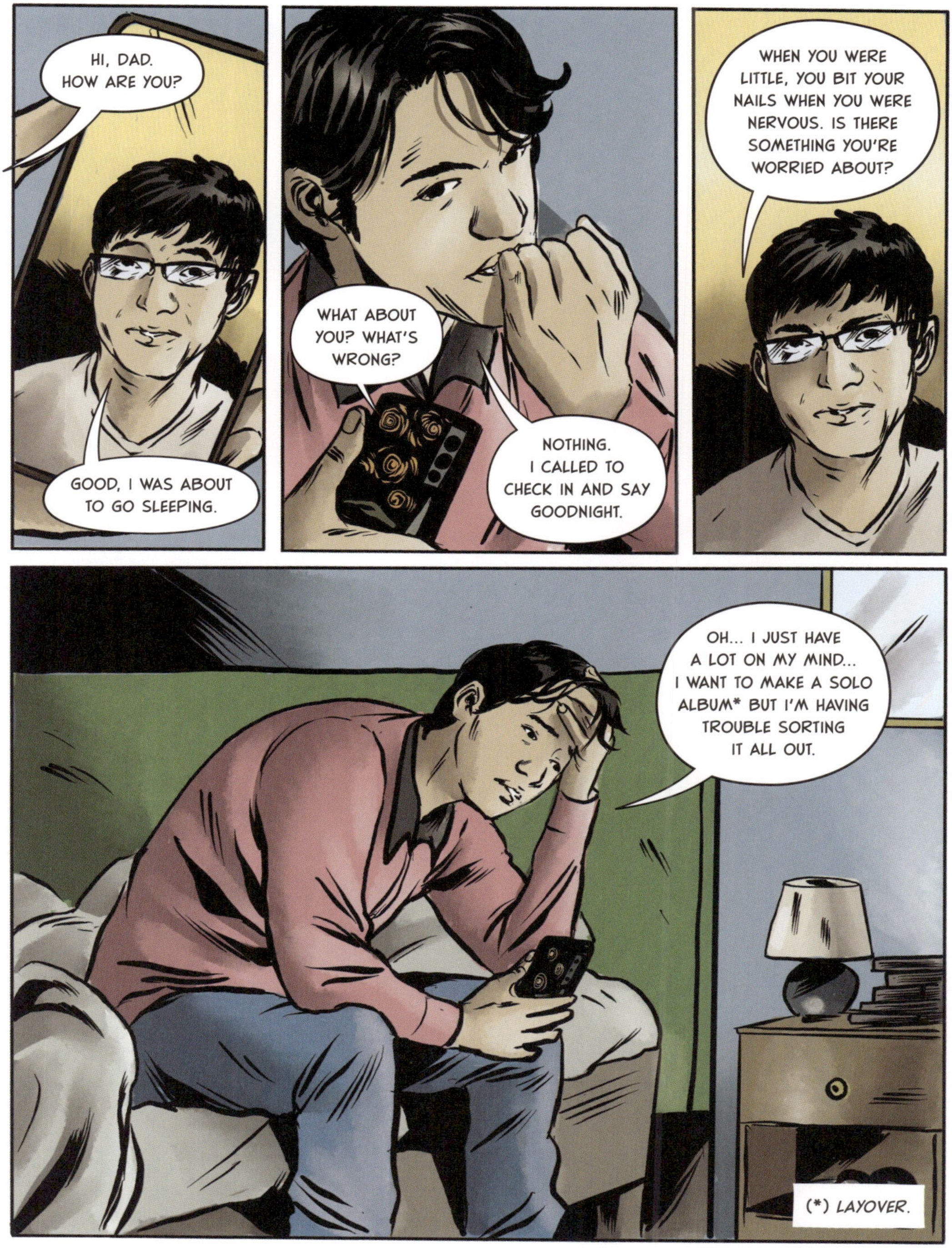
HI, DAD. HOW ARE YOU?
GOOD, I WAS ABOUT TO GO SLEEPING.
WHAT ABOUT YOU? WHAT'S WRONG?
NOTHING. I CALLED TO CHECK IN AND SAY GOODNIGHT.
WHEN YOU WERE LITTLE, YOU BIT YOUR NAILS WHEN YOU WERE NERVOUS. IS THERE SOMETHING YOU'RE WORRIED ABOUT?
OH... I JUST HAVE A LOT ON MY MIND... I WANT TO MAKE A SOLO ALBUM* BUT I'M HAVING TROUBLE SORTING IT ALL OUT.
(*) LAYOVER.

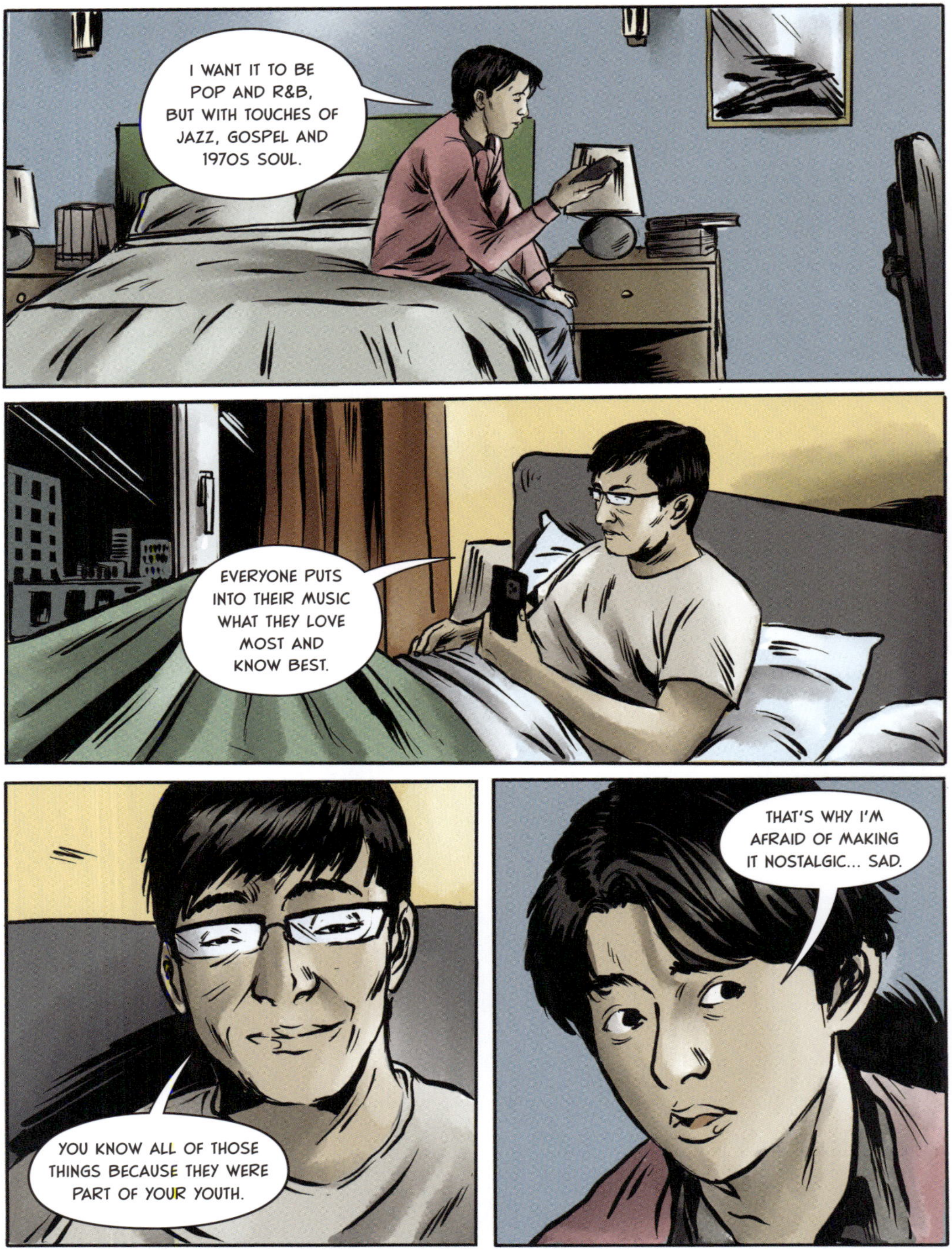
I WANT IT TO BE POP AND R&B, BUT WITH TOUCHES OF JAZZ, GOSPEL AND 1970S SOUL.
EVERYONE PUTS INTO THEIR MUSIC WHAT THEY LOVE MOST AND KNOW BEST.
YOU KNOW ALL OF THOSE THINGS BECAUSE THEY WERE PART OF YOUR YOUTH.
THAT'S WHY I'M AFRAID OF MAKING IT NOSTALGIC... SAD.

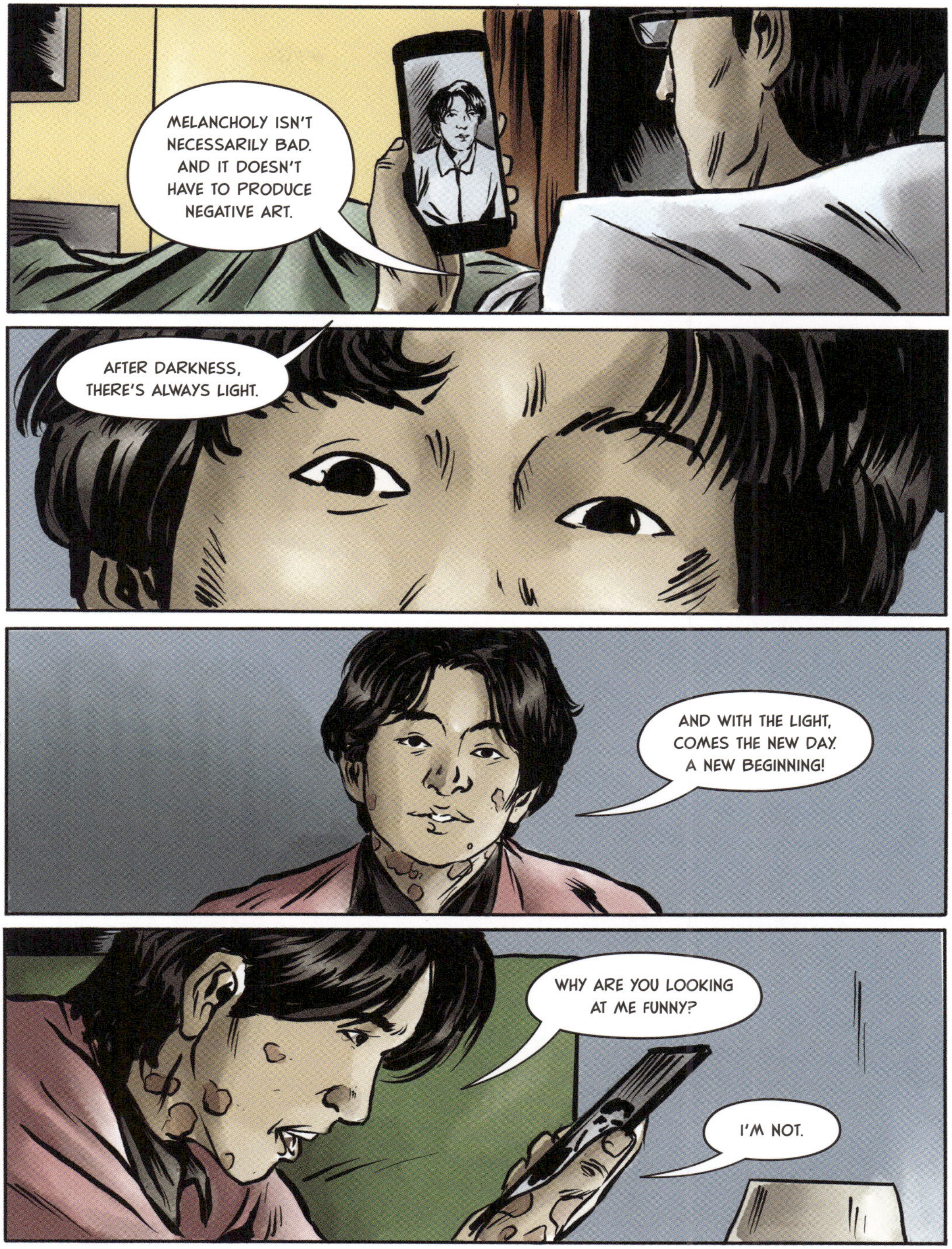
MELANCHOLY ISN'T NECESSARILY BAD. AND IT DOESN'T HAVE TO PRODUCE NEGATIVE ART.
AFTER DARKNESS, THERE'S ALWAYS LIGHT.
AND WITH THE LIGHT, COMES THE NEW DAY. A NEW BEGINNING!
WHY ARE YOU LOOKING AT ME FUNNY?
I'M NOT.

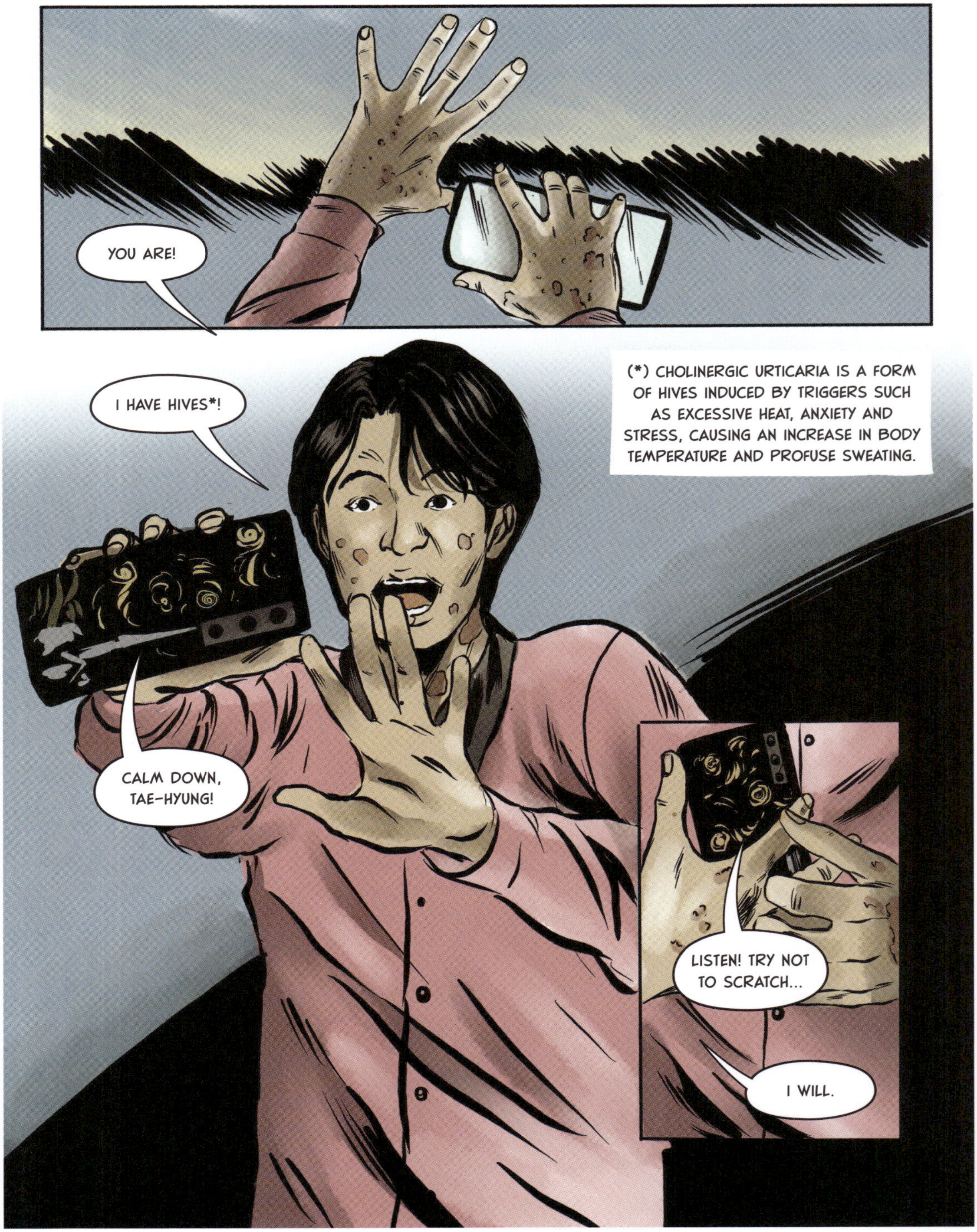
YOU ARE!
I HAVE HIVES*!
(*) CHOLINERGIC URTICARIA IS A FORM OF HIVES INDUCED BY TRIGGERS SUCH AS EXCESSIVE HEAT, ANXIETY AND STRESS, CAUSING AN INCREASE IN BODY TEMPERATURE AND PROFUSE SWEATING.
CALM DOWN, TAE-HYUNG!
LISTEN! TRY NOT TO SCRATCH...
I WILL.

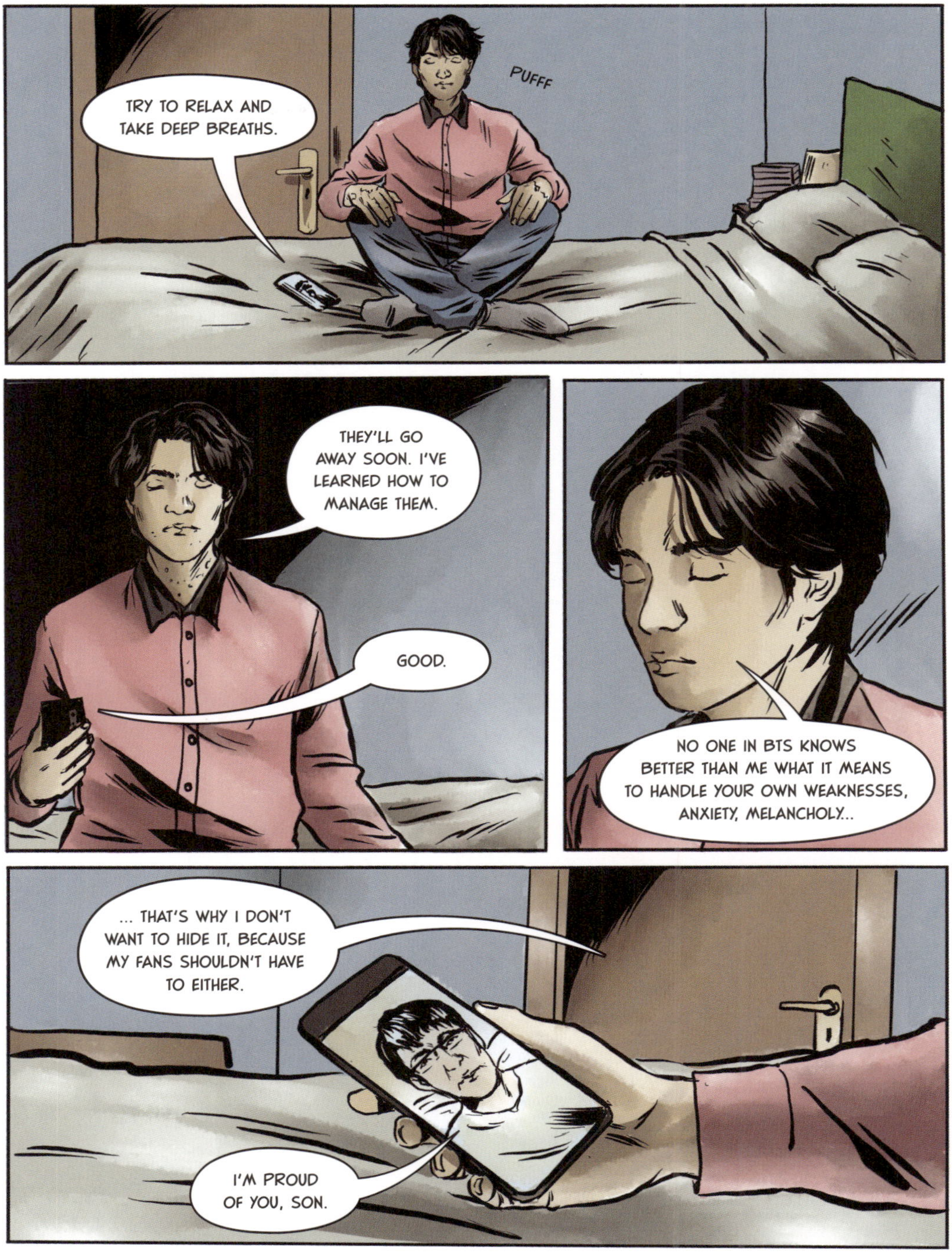
TRY TO RELAX AND TAKE DEEP BREATHS.
PUFFF
THEY'LL GO AWAY SOON. I'VE LEARNED HOW TO MANAGE THEM.
GOOD.
NO ONE IN BTS KNOWS BETTER THAN ME WHAT IT MEANS TO HANDLE YOUR OWN WEAKNESSES, ANXIETY, MELANCHOLY...
... THAT'S WHY I DON'T WANT TO HIDE IT, BECAUSE MY FANS SHOULDN'T HAVE TO EITHER.
I'M PROUD OF YOU, SON.

JIN

KIM SEOK-JIN

From aspiring actor to celebrity, crossing the catwalk.

During the night, Jin relives his dreams from when he was 15, his beloved animal companions by his side.

Animal rights is an issue dear to his heart. He donates food, dishes, blankets and other supplies to various charities for the care of stray animals, and supports numerous organisations that save dogs from animal testing.

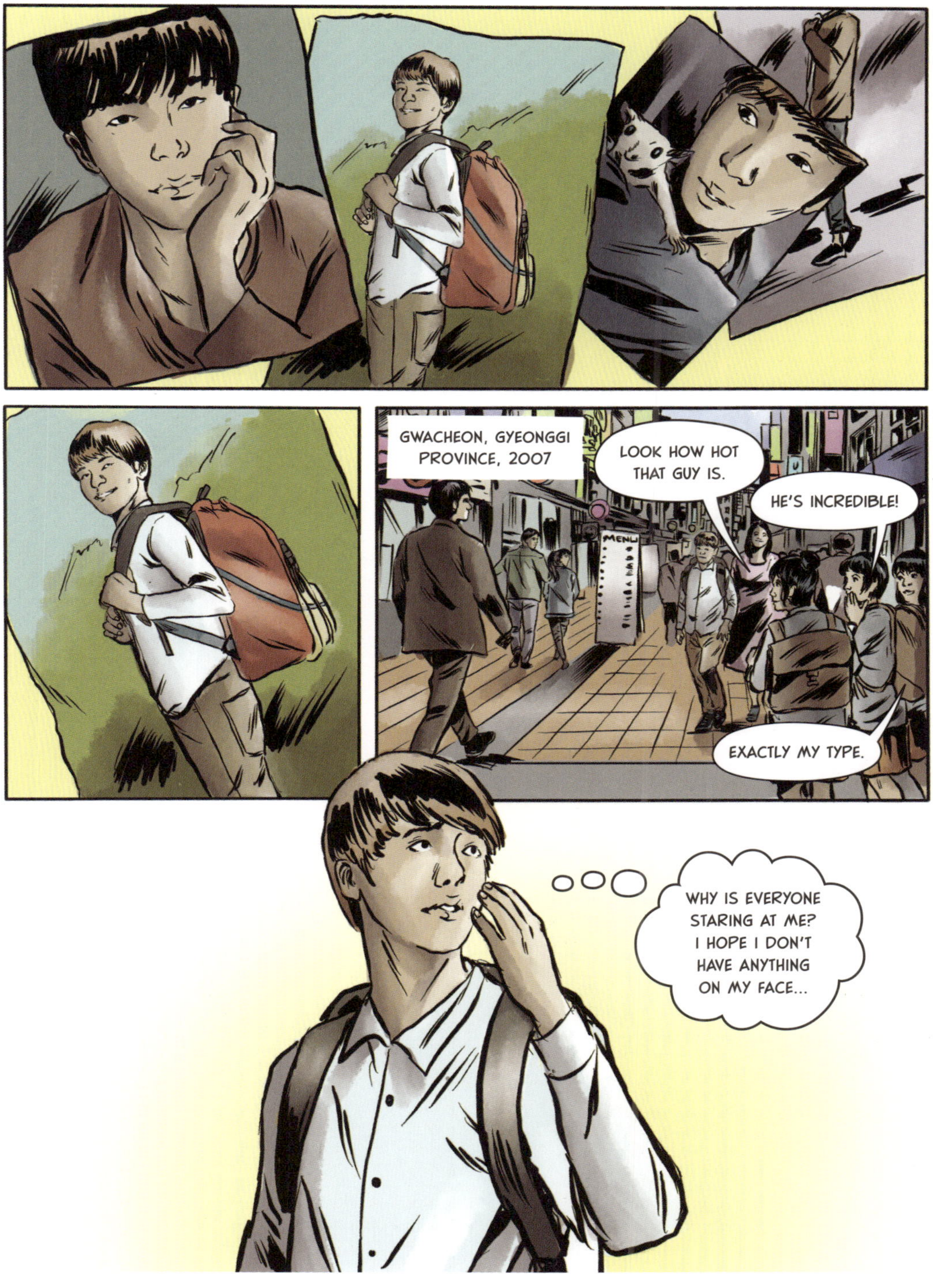
GWACHEON, GYEONGGI PROVINCE, 2007
LOOK HOW HOT THAT GUY IS.
HE'S INCREDIBLE!
EXACTLY MY TYPE.
WHY IS EVERYONE STARING AT ME? I HOPE I DON'T HAVE ANYTHING ON MY FACE...

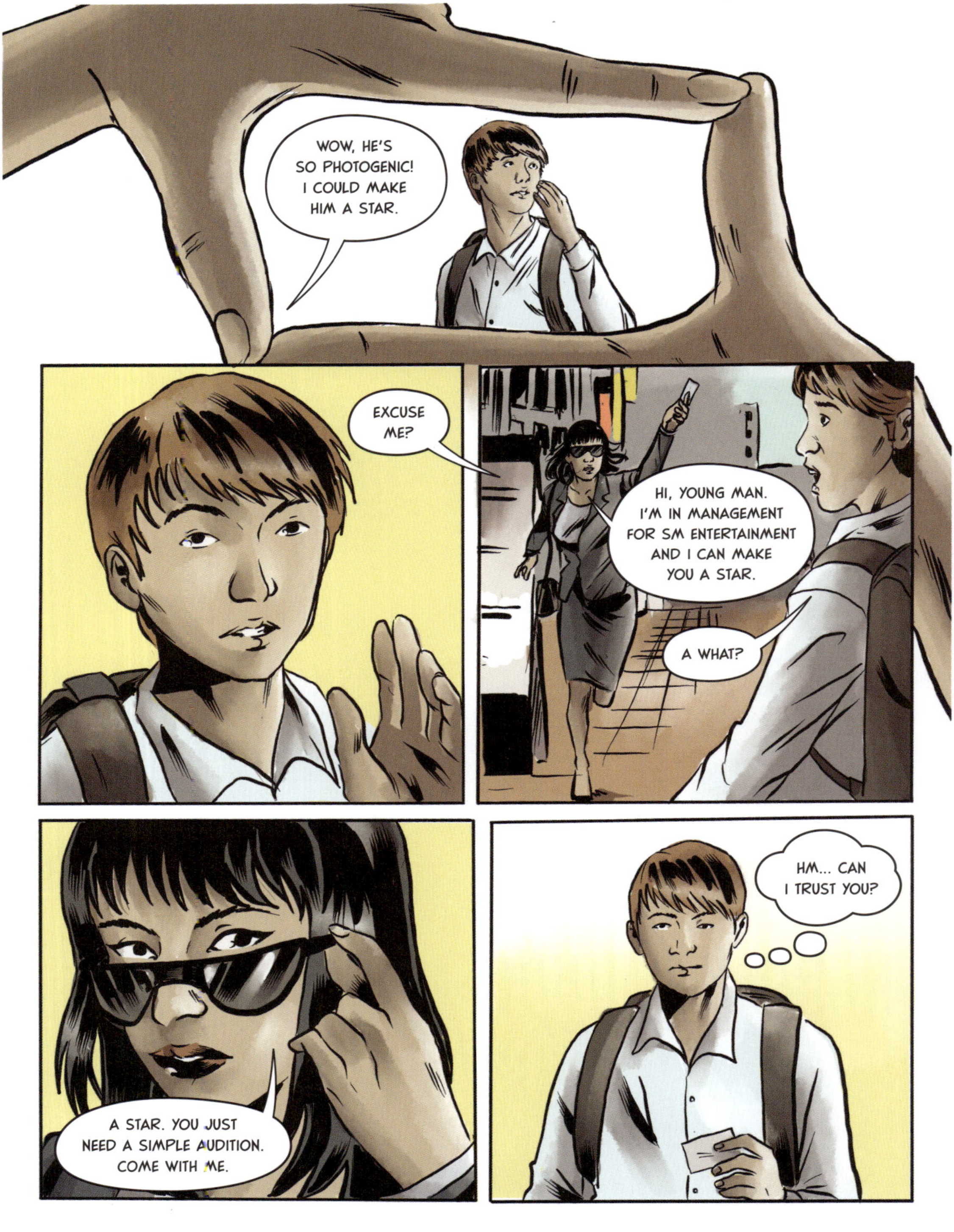
WOW, HE'S SO PHOTOGENIC! I COULD MAKE HIM A STAR.
EXCUSE ME?
HI, YOUNG MAN. I'M IN MANAGEMENT FOR SM ENTERTAINMENT AND I CAN MAKE YOU A STAR.
A WHAT?
A STAR. YOU JUST NEED A SIMPLE AUDITION. COME WITH ME.
HM... CAN I TRUST YOU?

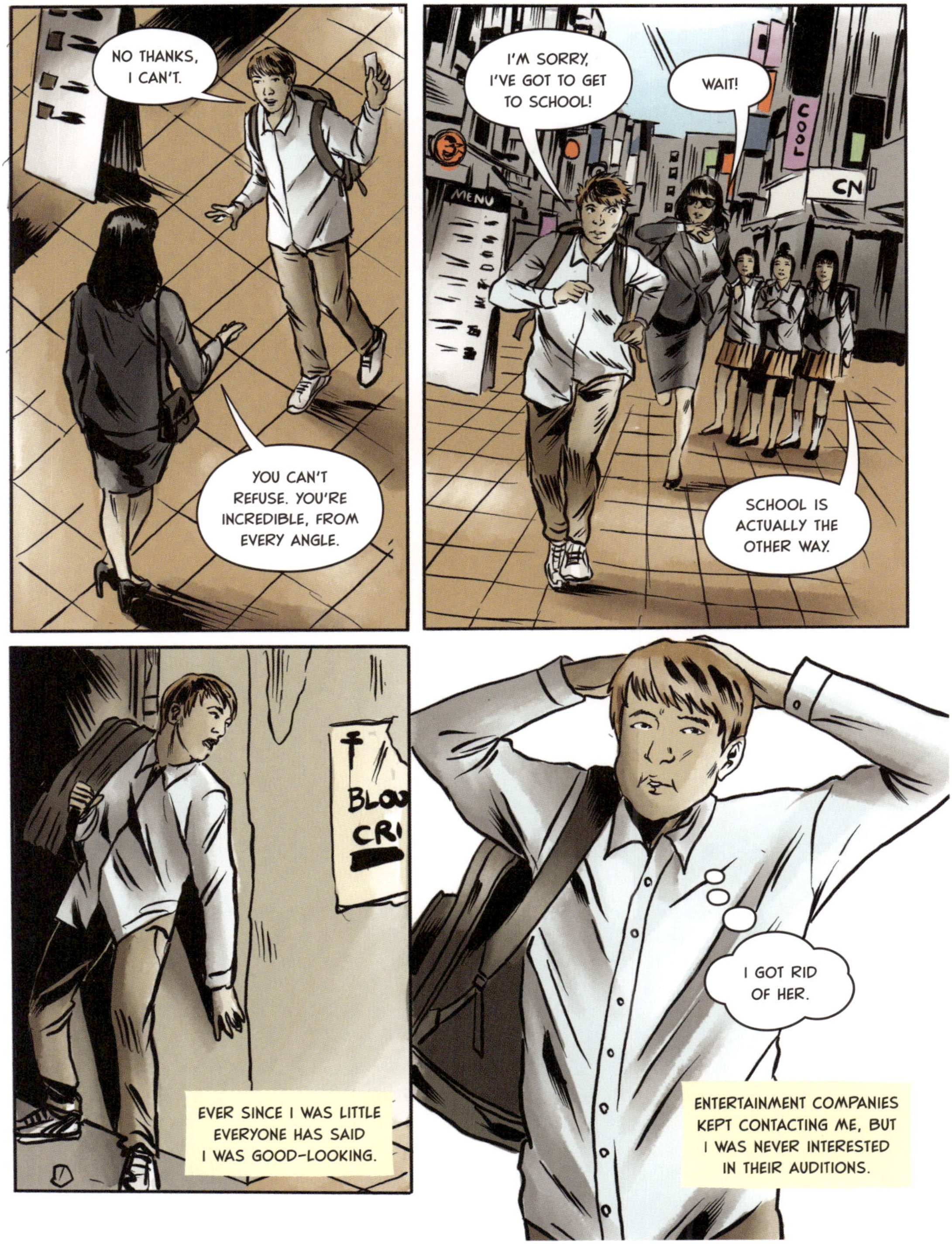
NO THANKS, I CAN'T.
YOU CAN'T REFUSE. YOU'RE INCREDIBLE, FROM EVERY ANGLE.
MENU
COOL
CN
I'M SORRY, I'VE GOT TO GET TO SCHOOL!
WAIT!
SCHOOL IS ACTUALLY THE OTHER WAY.
EVER SINCE I WAS LITTLE EVERYONE HAS SAID I WAS GOOD-LOOKING.
I GOT RID OF HER.
ENTERTAINMENT COMPANIES KEPT CONTACTING ME, BUT I WAS NEVER INTERESTED IN THEIR AUDITIONS.

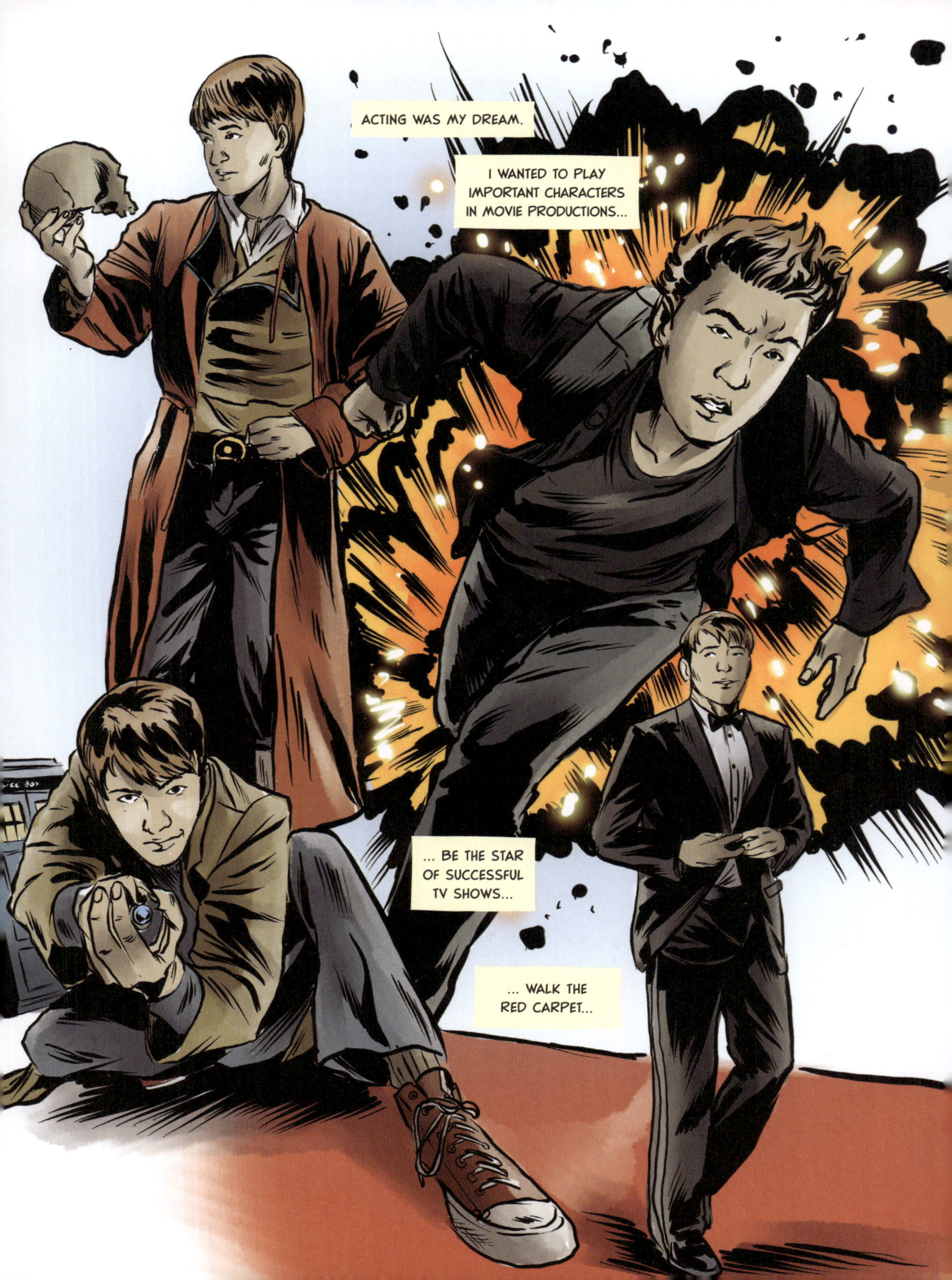
ACTING WAS MY DREAM.
I WANTED TO PLAY IMPORTANT CHARACTERS IN MOVIE PRODUCTIONS...
... BE THE STAR OF SUCCESSFUL TV SHOWS...
... WALK THE RED CARPET...

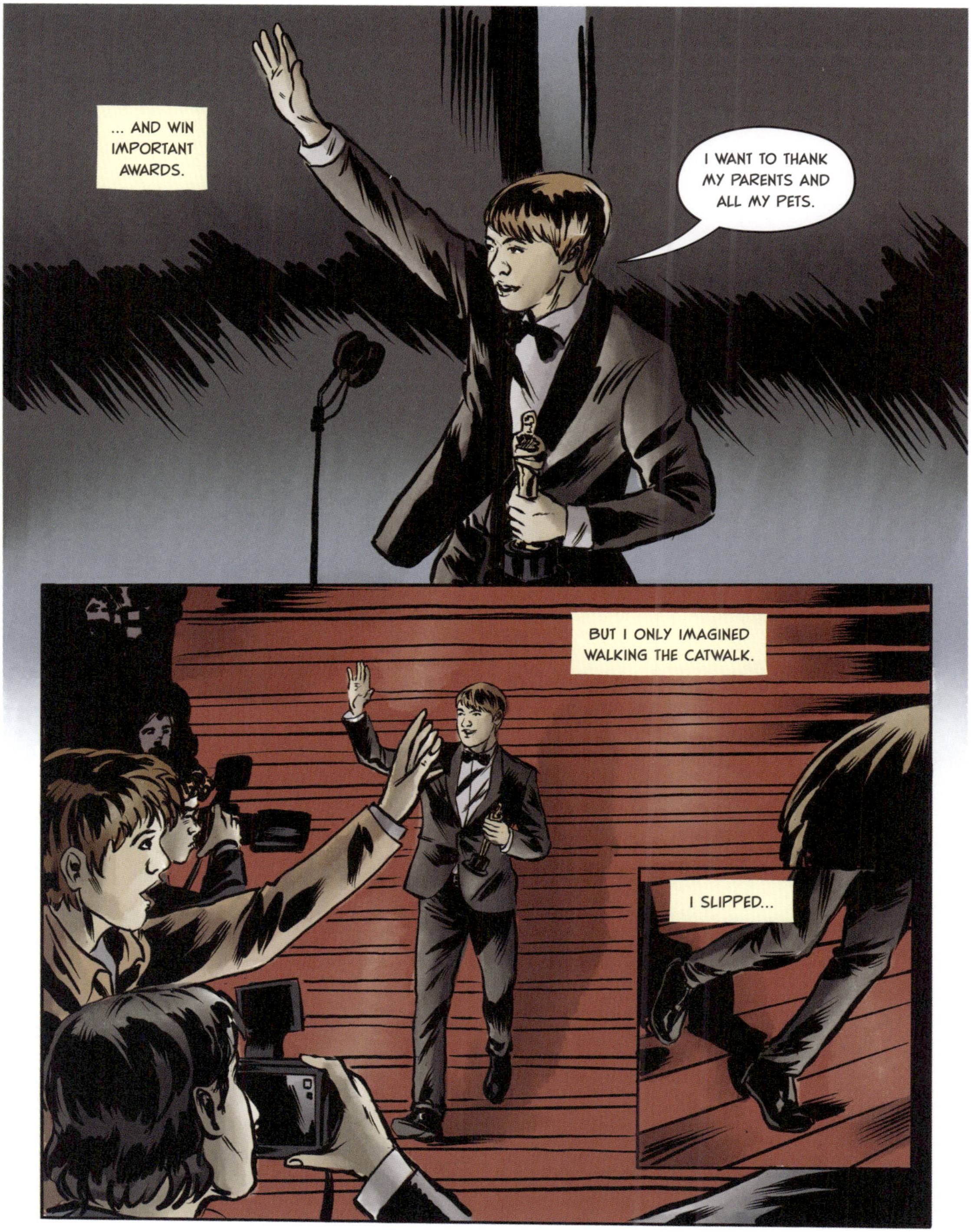
... AND WIN IMPORTANT AWARDS.
I WANT TO THANK MY PARENTS AND ALL MY PETS.
BUT I ONLY IMAGINED WALKING THE CATWALK.
I SLIPPED...

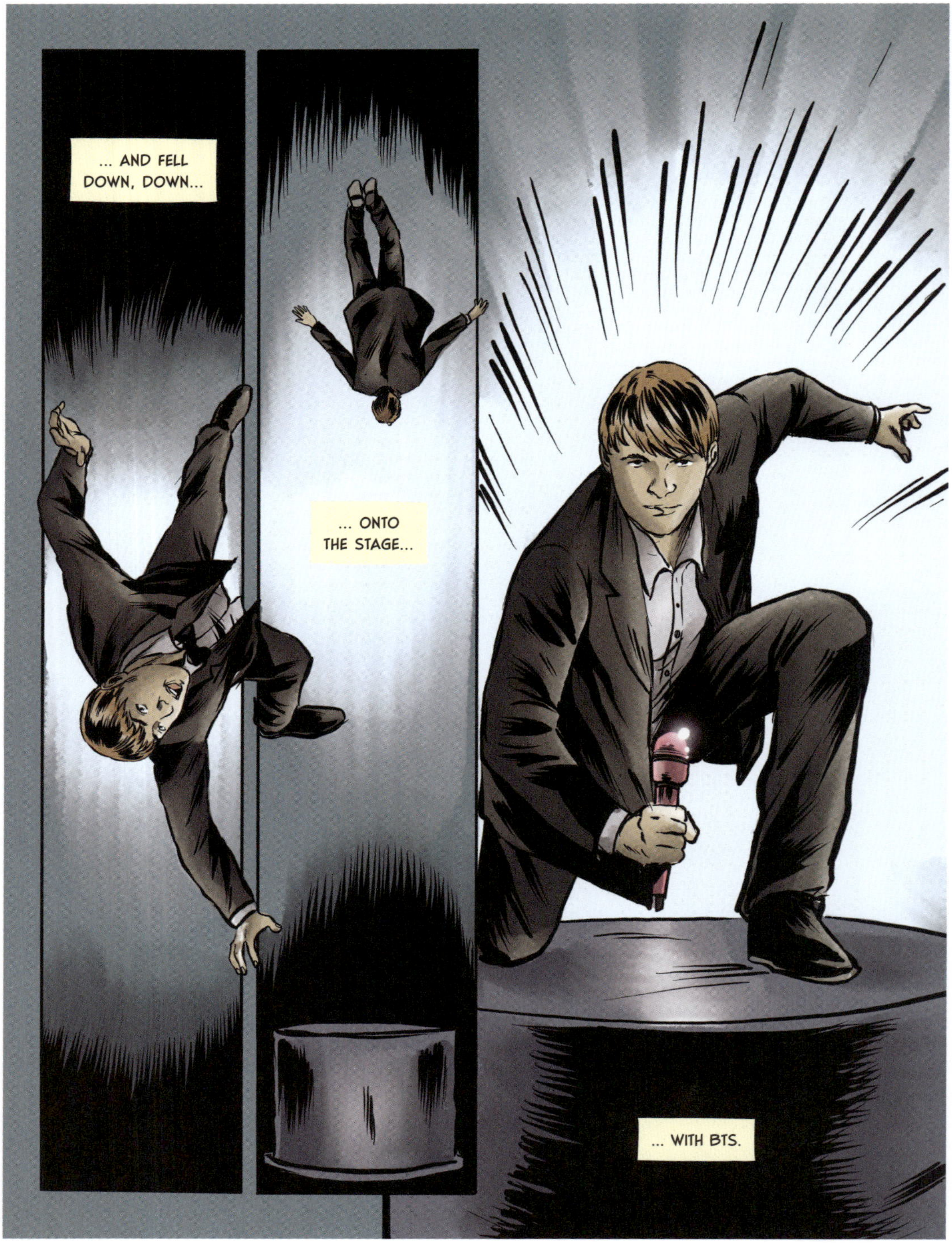
... AND FELL DOWN, DOWN...
... ONTO THE STAGE...
... WITH BTS.

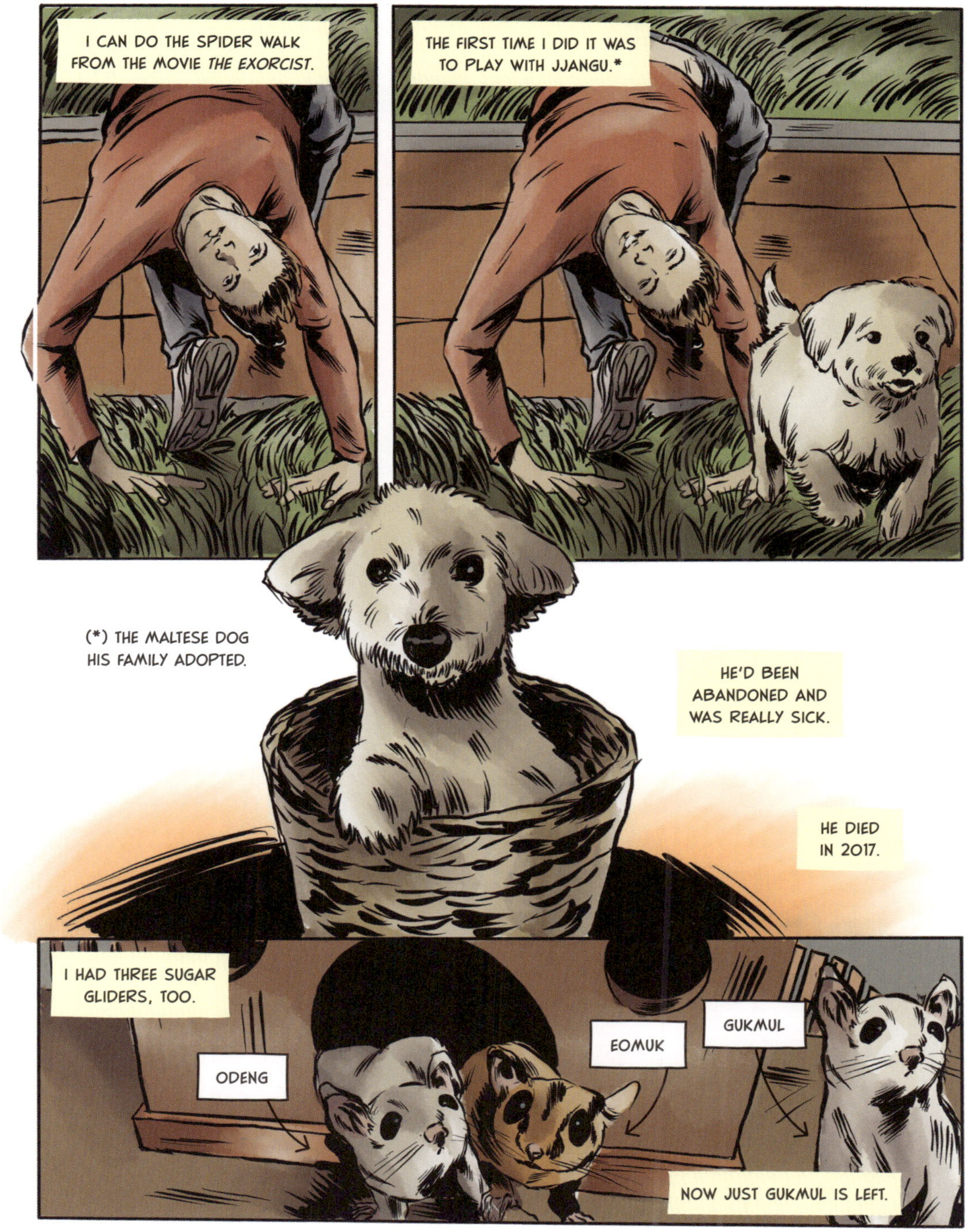
I CAN DO THE SPIDER WALK FROM THE MOVIE *THE EXORCIST*.
THE FIRST TIME I DID IT WAS TO PLAY WITH JJANGU.*
(*) THE MALTESE DOG HIS FAMILY ADOPTED.
HE'D BEEN ABANDONED AND WAS REALLY SICK.
HE DIED IN 2017.
I HAD THREE SUGAR GLIDERS, TOO.
ODENG
EOMUK
GUKMUL
NOW JUST GUKMUL IS LEFT.

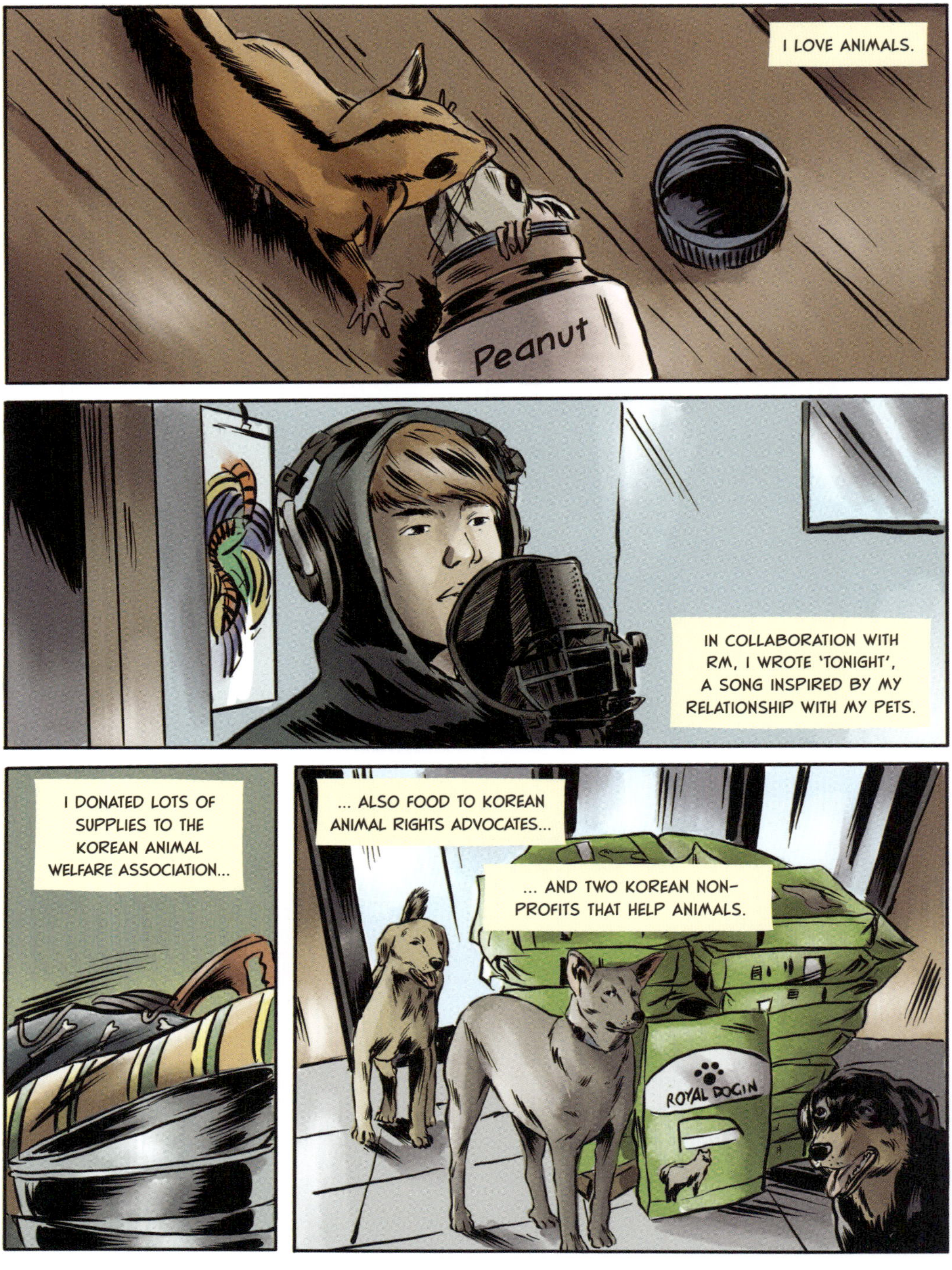
I LOVE ANIMALS.
Peanut
IN COLLABORATION WITH RM, I WROTE 'TONIGHT', A SONG INSPIRED BY MY RELATIONSHIP WITH MY PETS.
I DONATED LOTS OF SUPPLIES TO THE KOREAN ANIMAL WELFARE ASSOCIATION...
... ALSO FOOD TO KOREAN ANIMAL RIGHTS ADVOCATES...
... AND TWO KOREAN NON-PROFITS THAT HELP ANIMALS.
ROYAL DOGIN

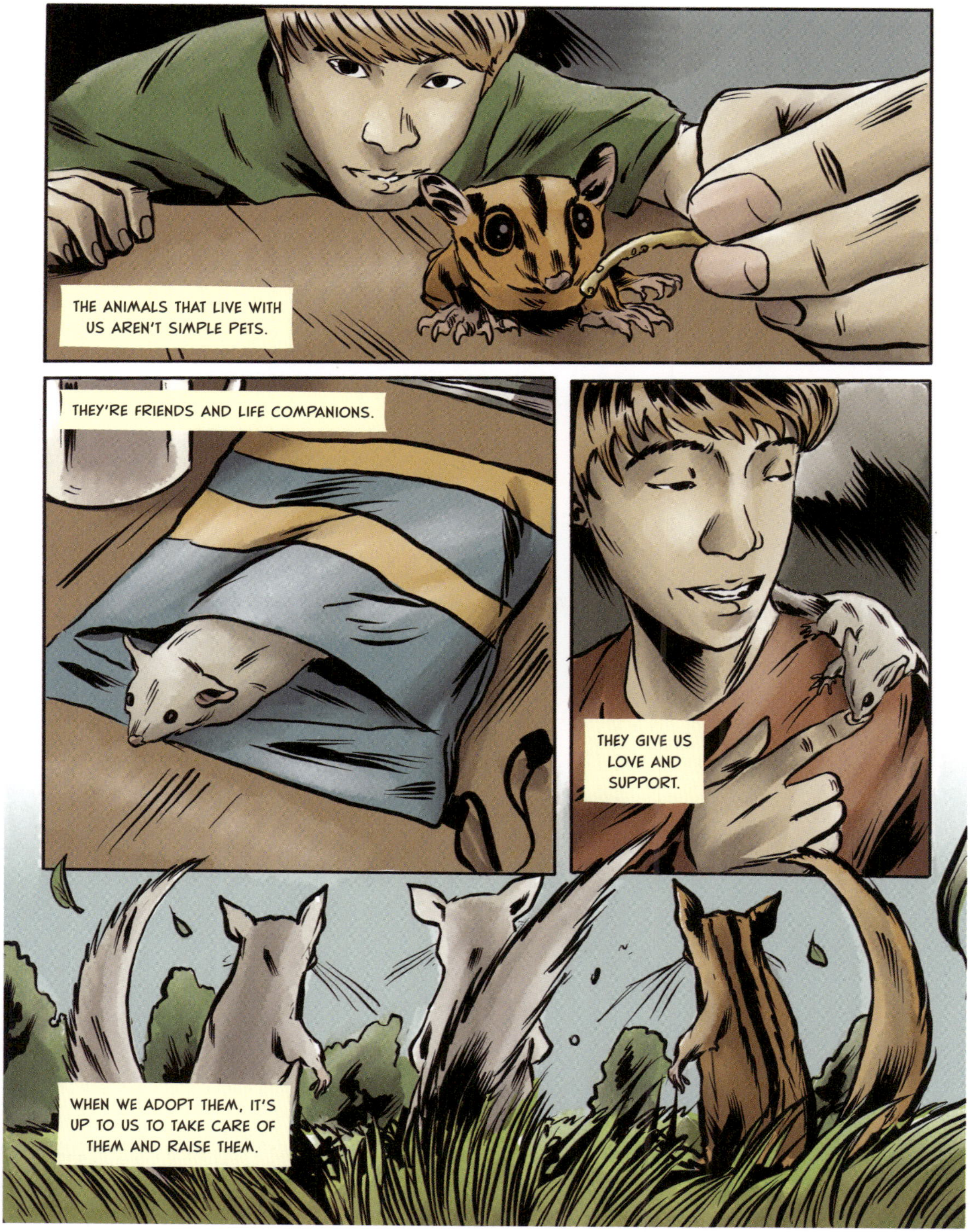
THE ANIMALS THAT LIVE WITH US AREN'T SIMPLE PETS.
THEY'RE FRIENDS AND LIFE COMPANIONS.
THEY GIVE US LOVE AND SUPPORT.
WHEN WE ADOPT THEM, IT'S UP TO US TO TAKE CARE OF THEM AND RAISE THEM.

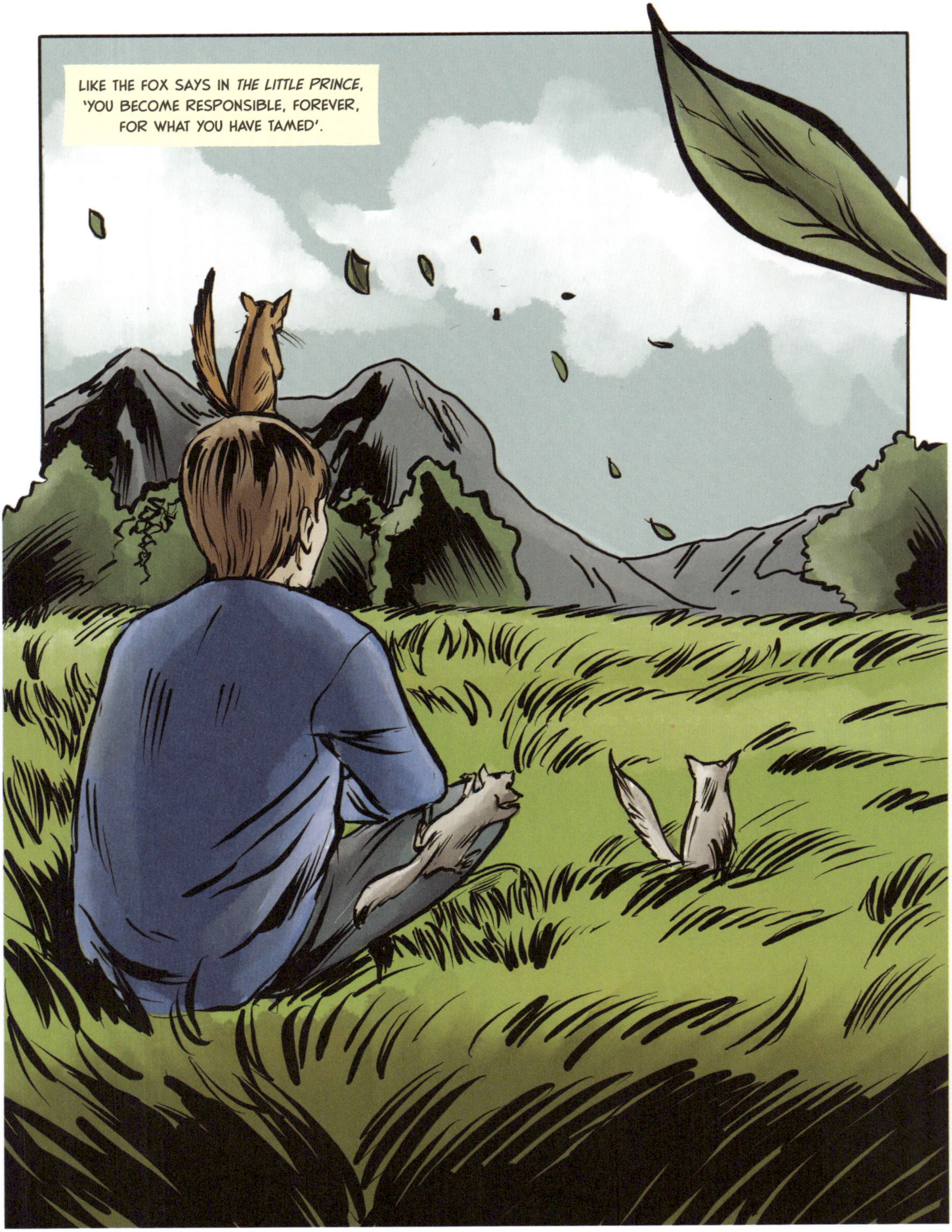
LIKE THE FOX SAYS IN *THE LITTLE PRINCE*, 'YOU BECOME RESPONSIBLE, FOREVER, FOR WHAT YOU HAVE TAMED'.

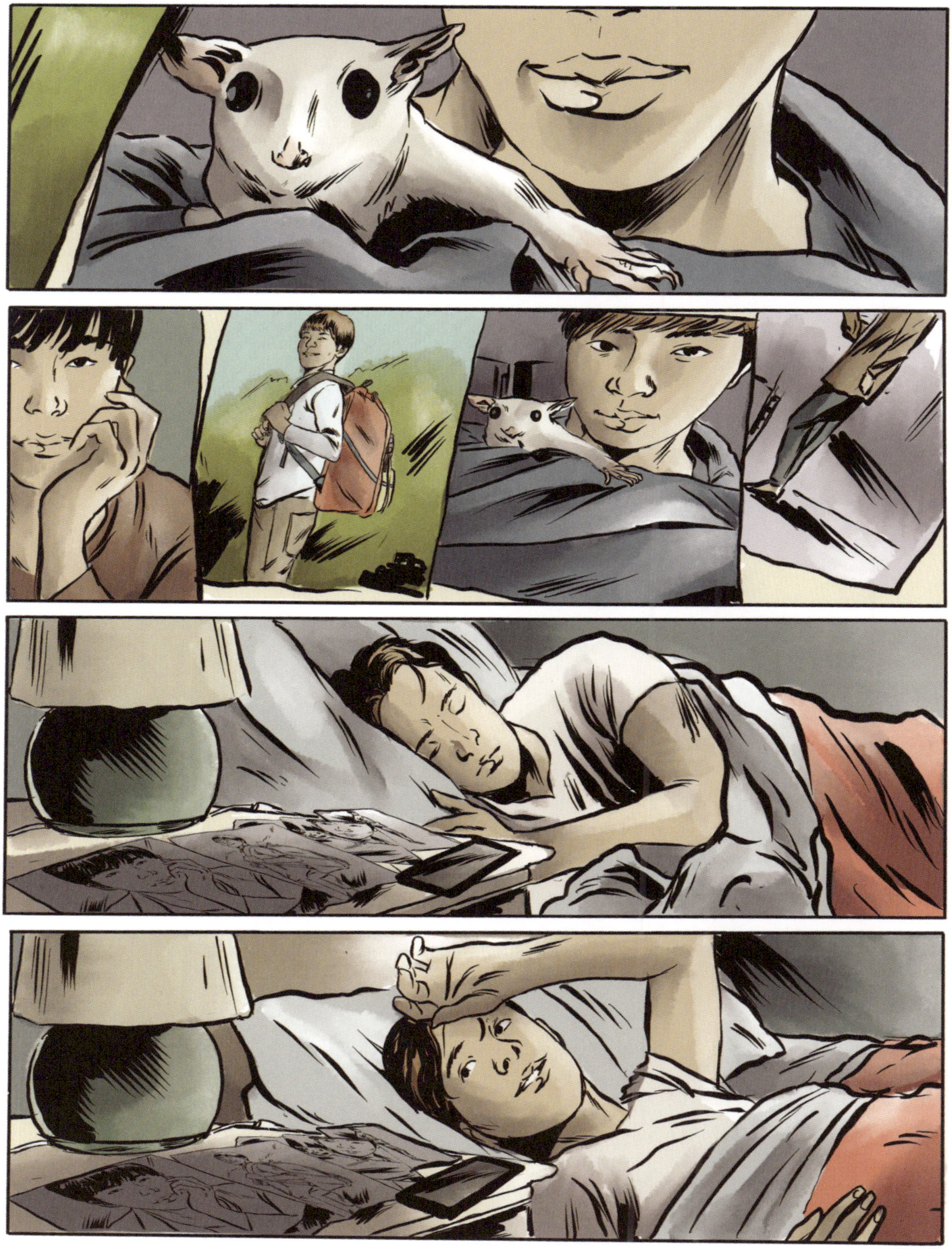

JIMIN

PARK JI-MIN

FROM ASPIRING DANCER AND PERFORMER TO IDOL, VIA THE JUST DANCE ACADEMY AND THE BUSAN HIGH SCHOOL OF ARTS.

JIMIN, AS A GUEST ON *THE TONIGHT SHOW STARRING JIMMY FALLON* IN NEW YORK, RECALLS THE GENESIS OF HIS PASSION FOR DANCE AND WHEN AND HOW HE TOOK HIS FIRST STEPS.

WITH A SOFT, GENTLE VOICE AND SMOOTH, PRECISE MOVES, HE HAS SPREAD TRADITIONAL KOREAN FAN DANCE (BUCHAECHUM) AROUND THE WORLD.

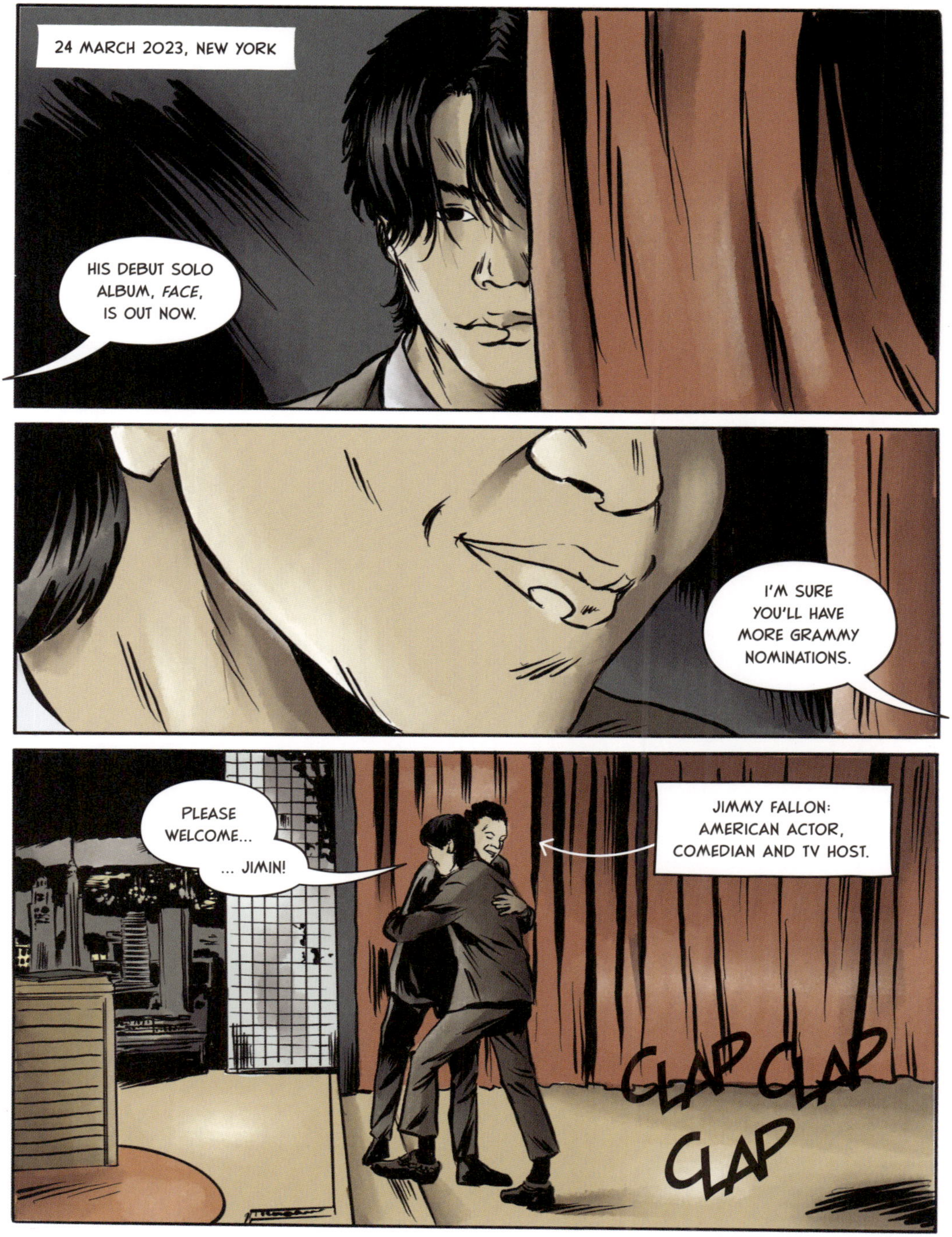
24 MARCH 2023, NEW YORK
HIS DEBUT SOLO ALBUM, *FACE*, IS OUT NOW.
I'M SURE YOU'LL HAVE MORE GRAMMY NOMINATIONS.
PLEASE WELCOME...
... JIMIN!
JIMMY FALLON: AMERICAN ACTOR, COMEDIAN AND TV HOST.
CLAP CLAP CLAP

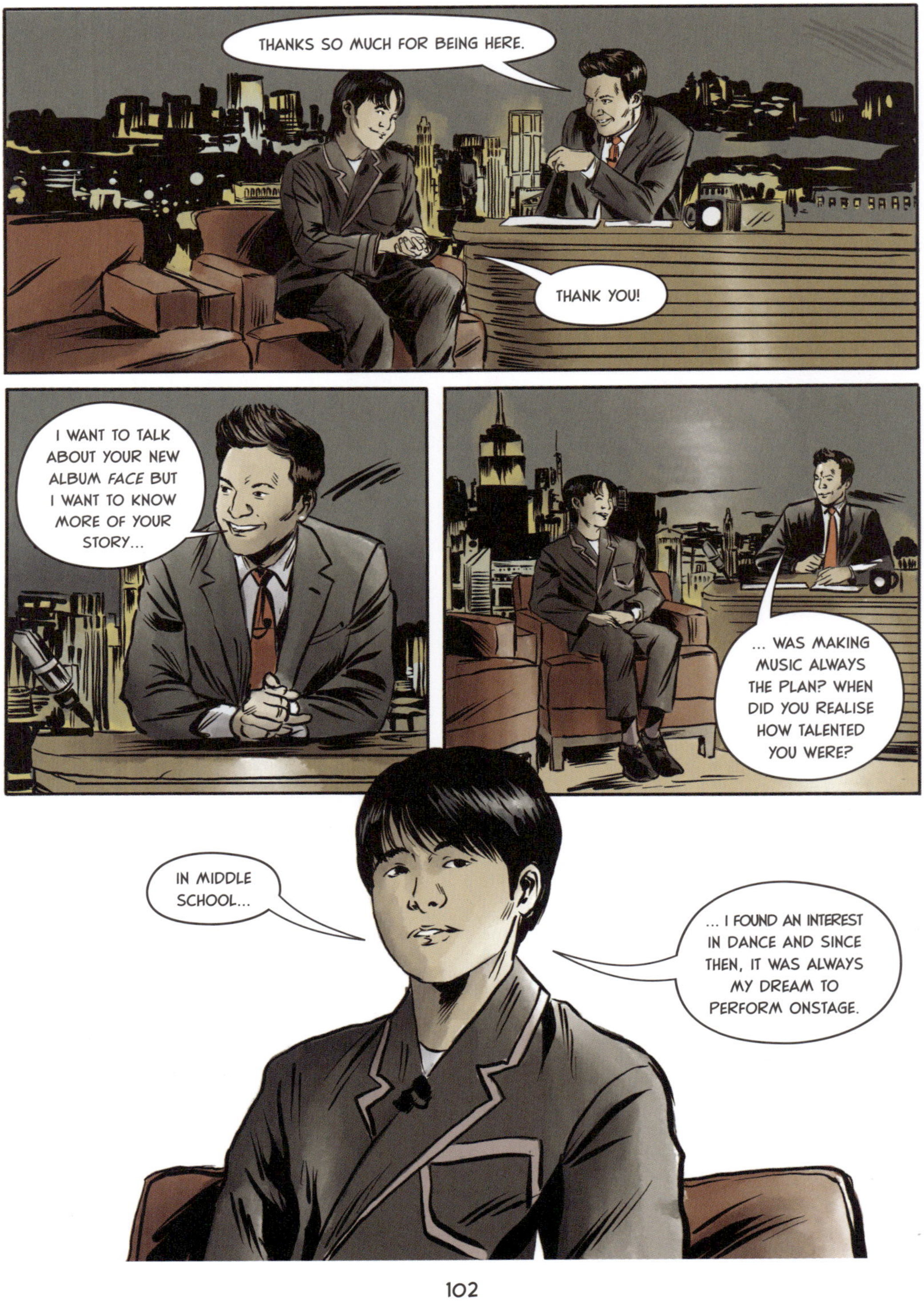
THANKS SO MUCH FOR BEING HERE.
THANK YOU!
I WANT TO TALK ABOUT YOUR NEW ALBUM *FACE* BUT I WANT TO KNOW MORE OF YOUR STORY...
... WAS MAKING MUSIC ALWAYS THE PLAN? WHEN DID YOU REALISE HOW TALENTED YOU WERE?
IN MIDDLE SCHOOL...
... I FOUND AN INTEREST IN DANCE AND SINCE THEN, IT WAS ALWAYS MY DREAM TO PERFORM ONSTAGE.

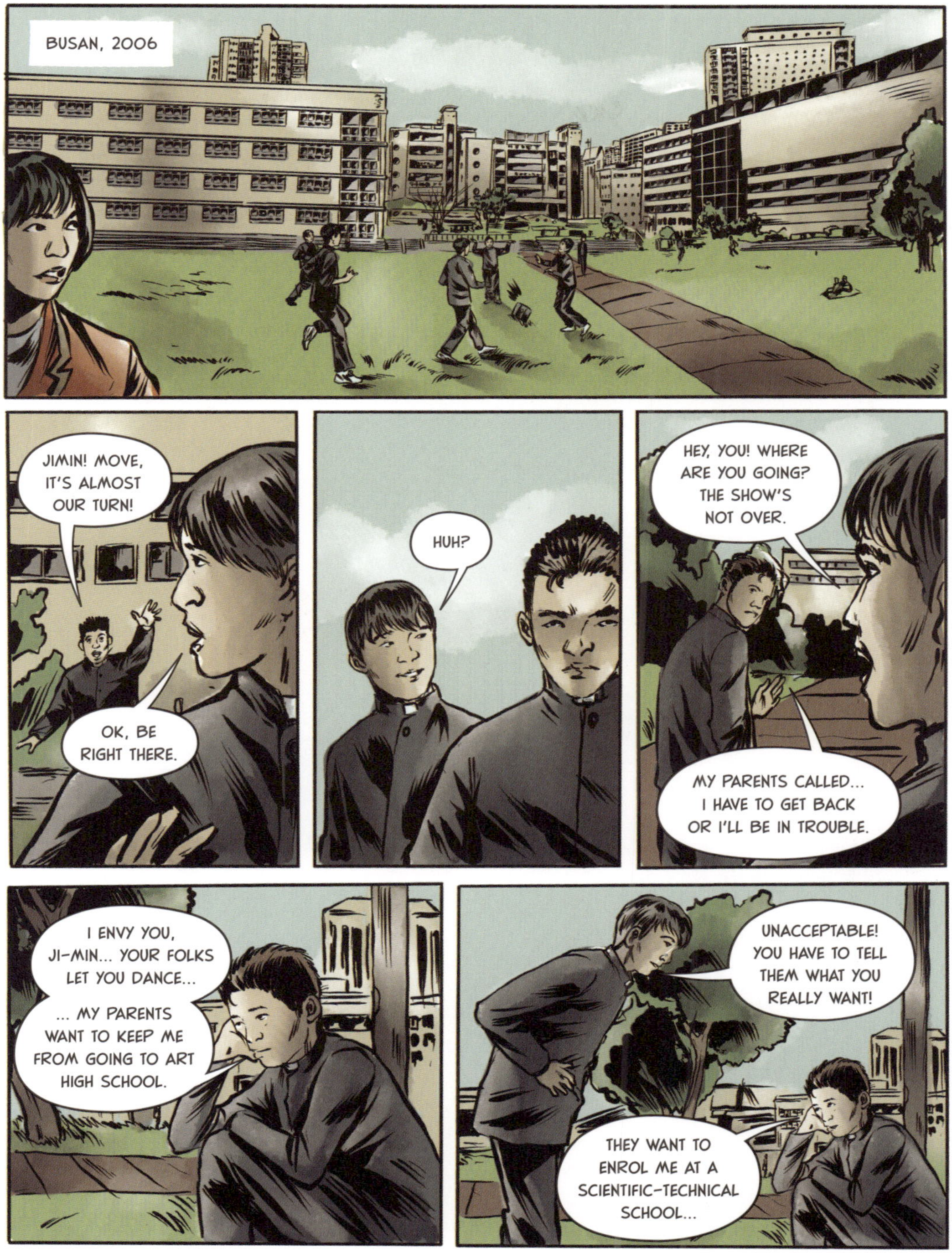
BUSAN, 2006
JIMIN! MOVE, IT'S ALMOST OUR TURN!
OK, BE RIGHT THERE.
HUH?
HEY, YOU! WHERE ARE YOU GOING? THE SHOW'S NOT OVER.
MY PARENTS CALLED... I HAVE TO GET BACK OR I'LL BE IN TROUBLE.
I ENVY YOU, JI-MIN... YOUR FOLKS LET YOU DANCE...
... MY PARENTS WANT TO KEEP ME FROM GOING TO ART HIGH SCHOOL.
UNACCEPTABLE! YOU HAVE TO TELL THEM WHAT YOU REALLY WANT!
THEY WANT TO ENROL ME AT A SCIENTIFIC-TECHNICAL SCHOOL...

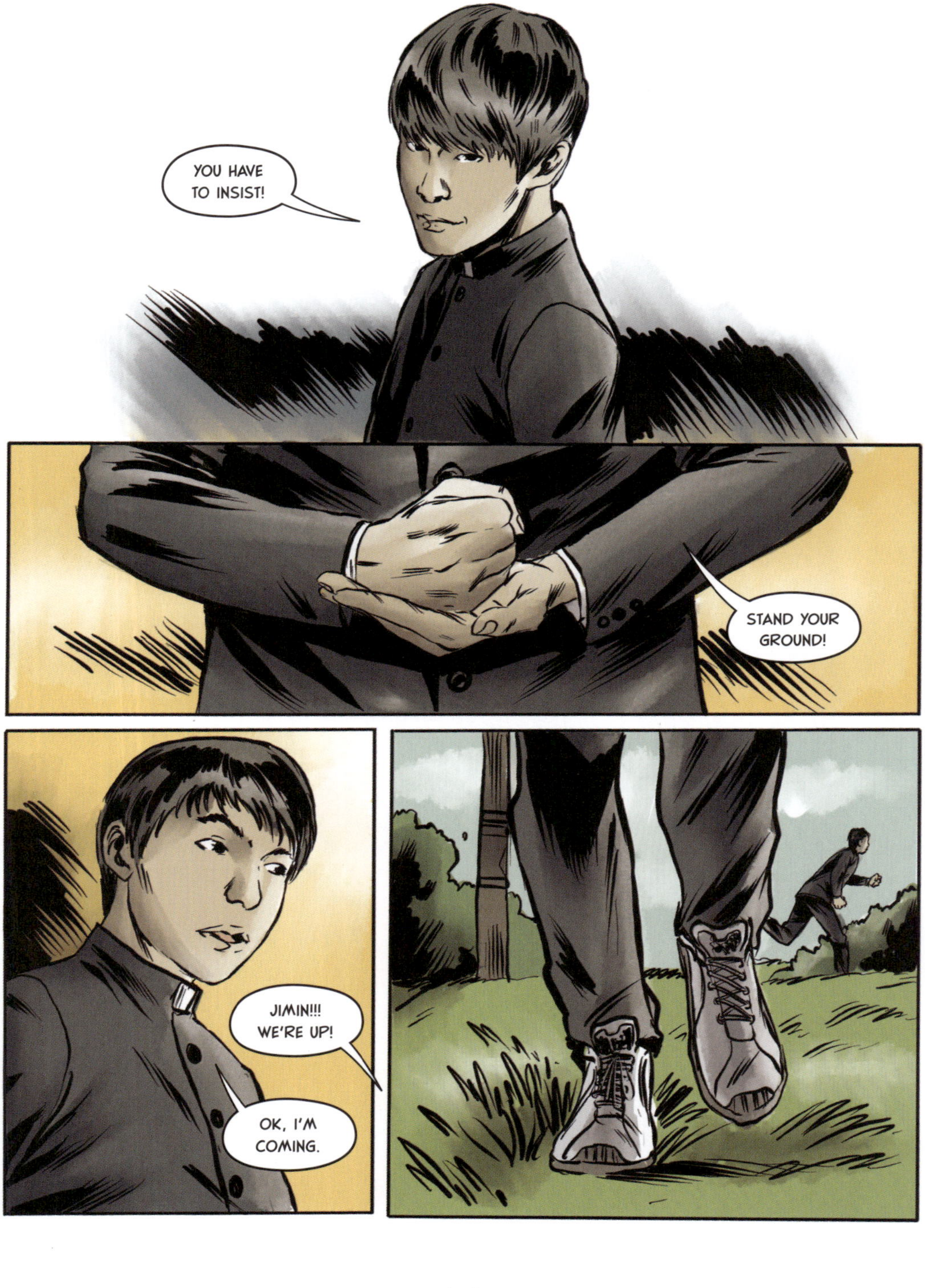
YOU HAVE TO INSIST!
STAND YOUR GROUND!
JIMIN!!! WE'RE UP!
OK, I'M COMING.

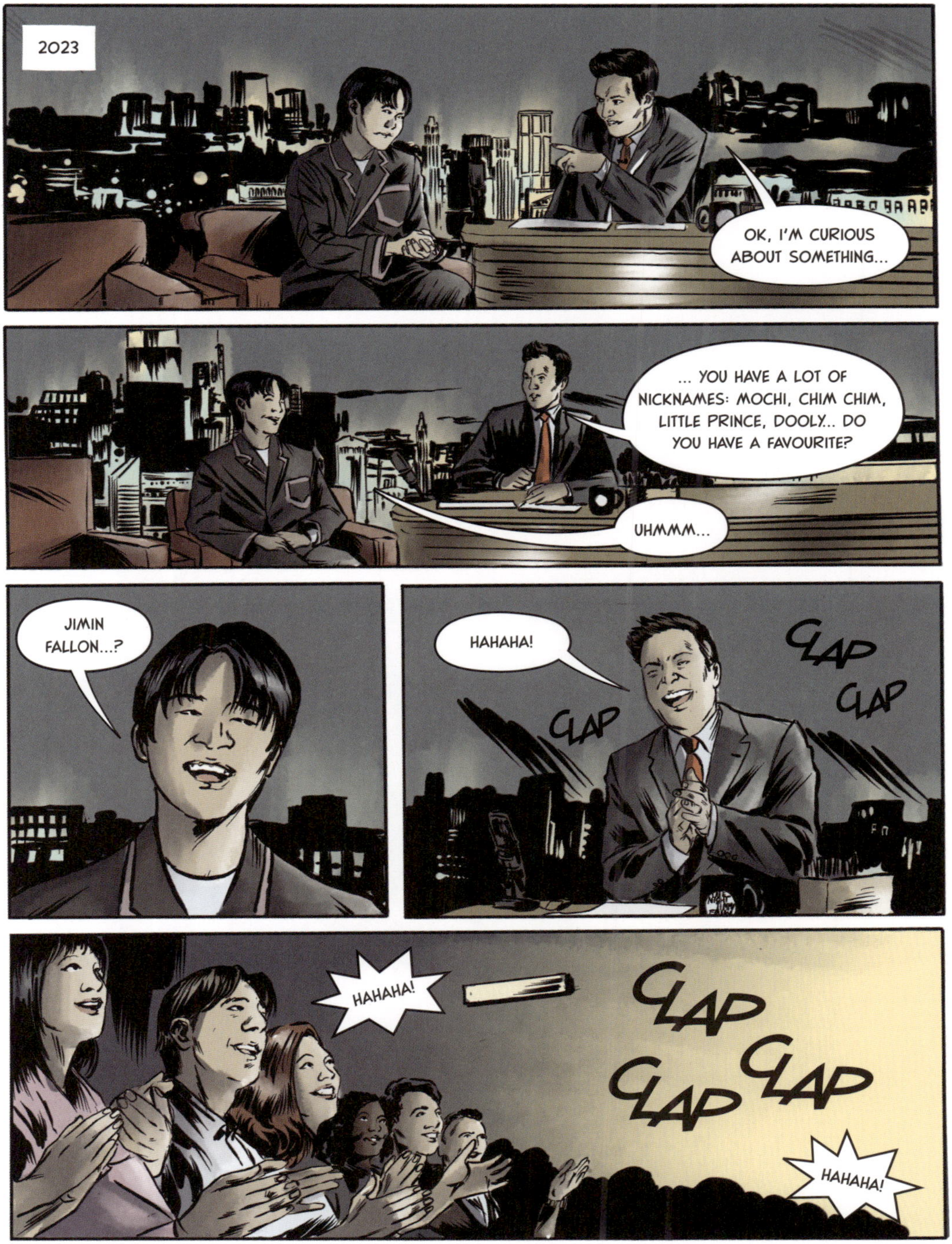
2023
OK, I'M CURIOUS ABOUT SOMETHING...
... YOU HAVE A LOT OF NICKNAMES: MOCHI, CHIM CHIM, LITTLE PRINCE, DOOLY... DO YOU HAVE A FAVOURITE?
UHMMM...
JIMIN FALLON...?
HAHAHA!
CLAP
CLAP
CLAP
HAHAHA!
CLAP
CLAP
CLAP
HAHAHA!

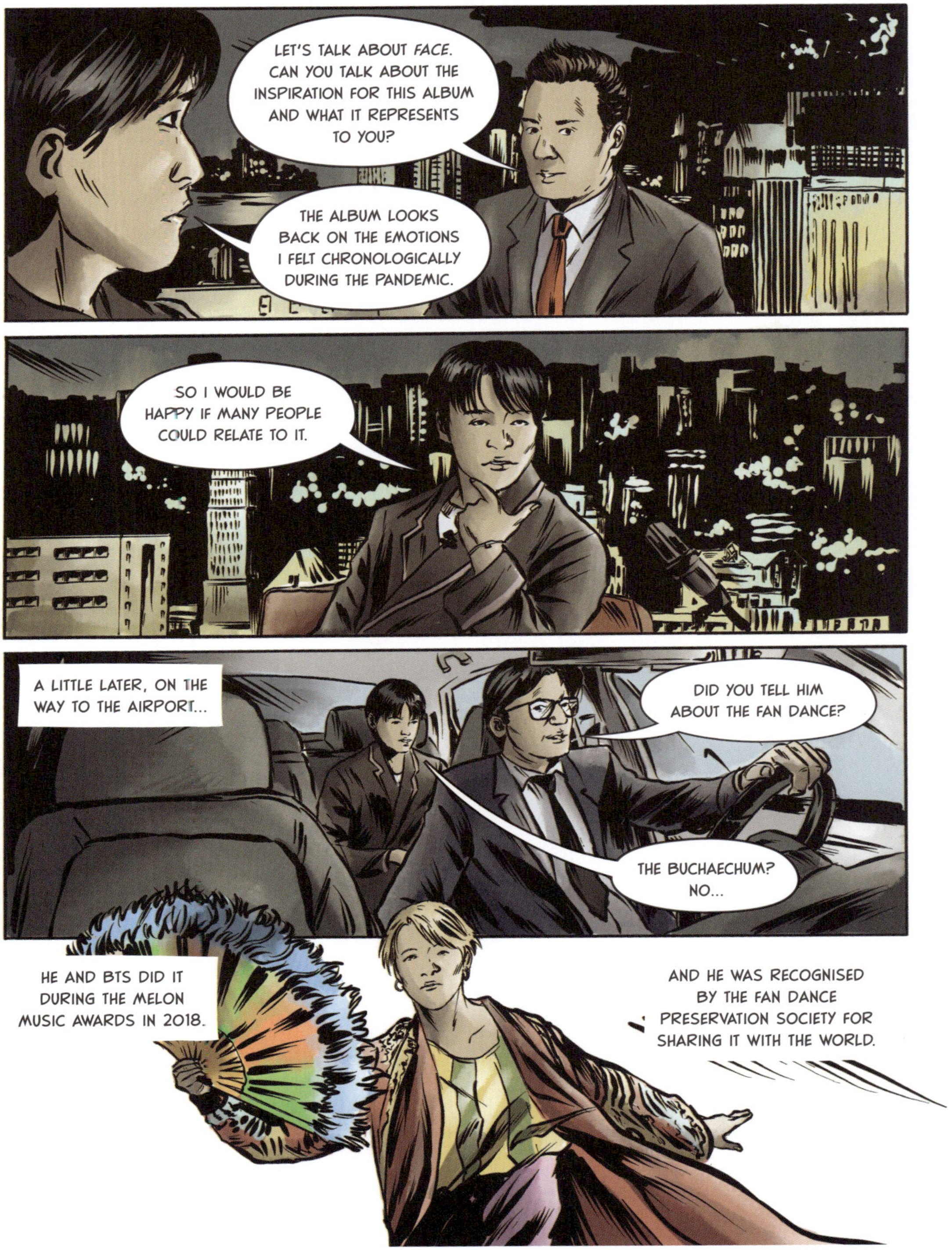
LET'S TALK ABOUT *FACE*. CAN YOU TALK ABOUT THE INSPIRATION FOR THIS ALBUM AND WHAT IT REPRESENTS TO YOU?
THE ALBUM LOOKS BACK ON THE EMOTIONS I FELT CHRONOLOGICALLY DURING THE PANDEMIC.
SO I WOULD BE HAPPY IF MANY PEOPLE COULD RELATE TO IT.
A LITTLE LATER, ON THE WAY TO THE AIRPORT...
DID YOU TELL HIM ABOUT THE FAN DANCE?
THE BUCHAECHUM? NO...
HE AND BTS DID IT DURING THE MELON MUSIC AWARDS IN 2018.
AND HE WAS RECOGNISED BY THE FAN DANCE PRESERVATION SOCIETY FOR SHARING IT WITH THE WORLD.

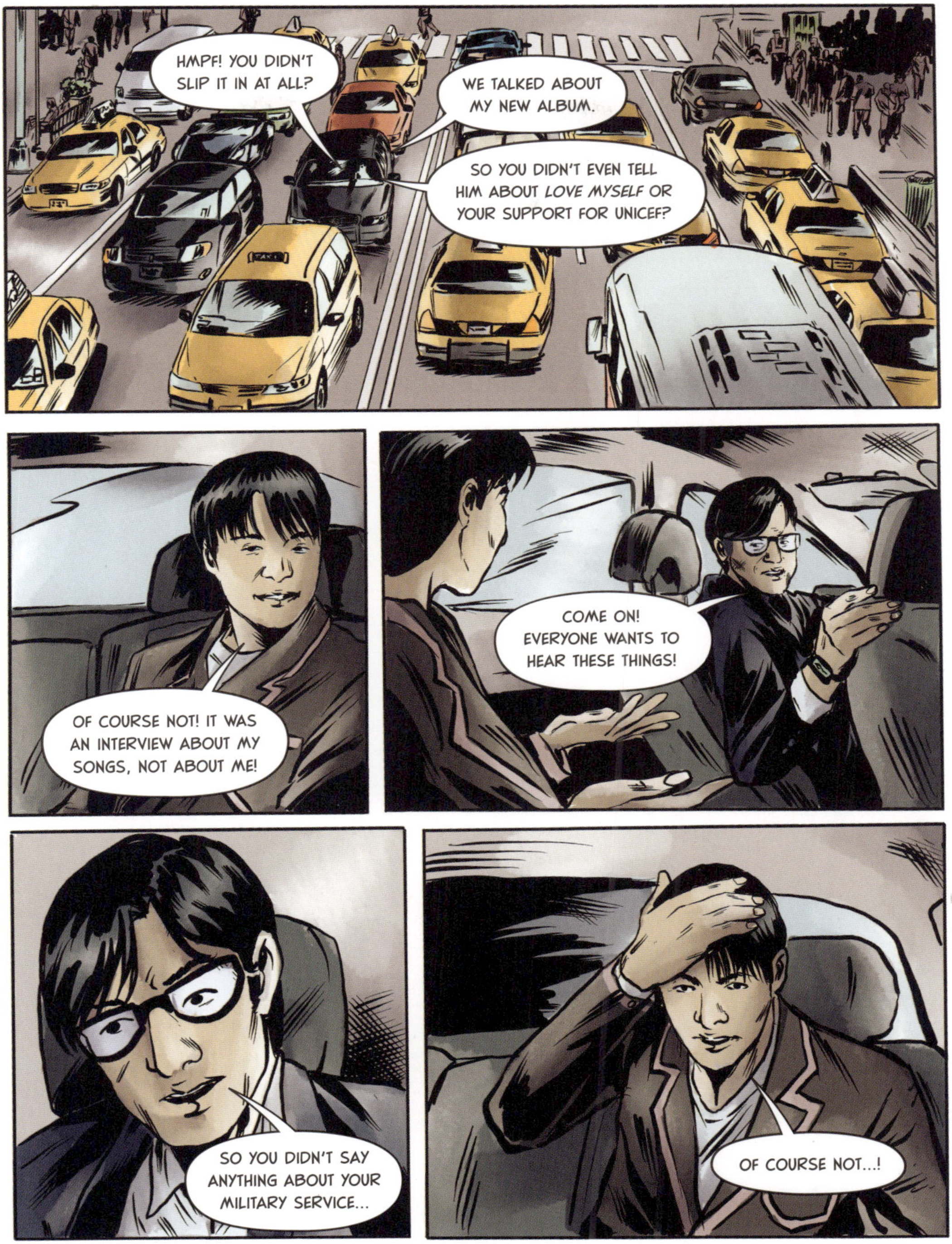
HMPF! YOU DIDN'T SLIP IT IN AT ALL?
WE TALKED ABOUT MY NEW ALBUM.
SO YOU DIDN'T EVEN TELL HIM ABOUT *LOVE MYSELF* OR YOUR SUPPORT FOR UNICEF?
OF COURSE NOT! IT WAS AN INTERVIEW ABOUT MY SONGS, NOT ABOUT ME!
COME ON! EVERYONE WANTS TO HEAR THESE THINGS!
SO YOU DIDN'T SAY ANYTHING ABOUT YOUR MILITARY SERVICE...
OF COURSE NOT...!

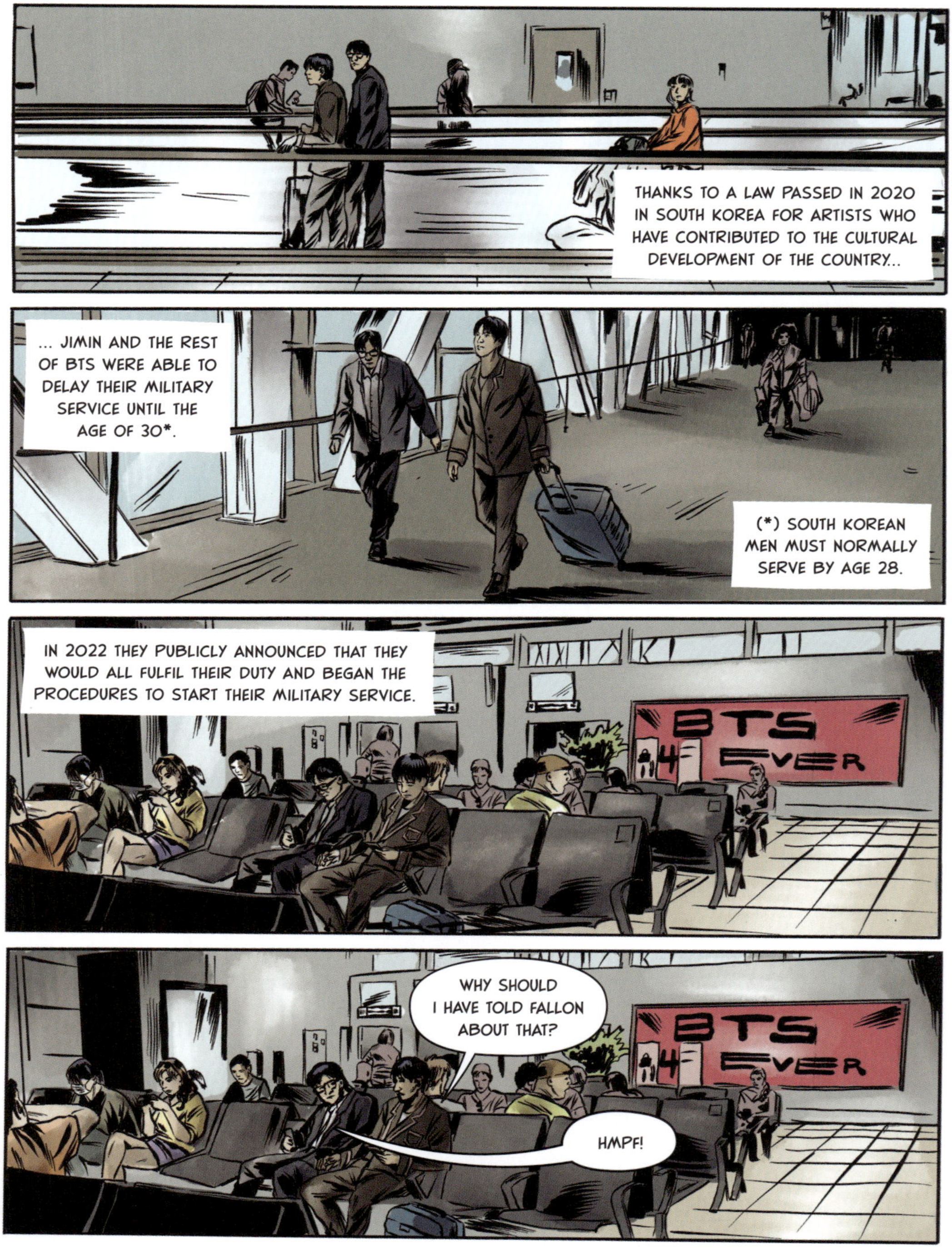
THANKS TO A LAW PASSED IN 2020 IN SOUTH KOREA FOR ARTISTS WHO HAVE CONTRIBUTED TO THE CULTURAL DEVELOPMENT OF THE COUNTRY...
... JIMIN AND THE REST OF BTS WERE ABLE TO DELAY THEIR MILITARY SERVICE UNTIL THE AGE OF 30*.
(*) SOUTH KOREAN MEN MUST NORMALLY SERVE BY AGE 28.
IN 2022 THEY PUBLICLY ANNOUNCED THAT THEY WOULD ALL FULFIL THEIR DUTY AND BEGAN THE PROCEDURES TO START THEIR MILITARY SERVICE.
BTS 4-EVER
WHY SHOULD I HAVE TOLD FALLON ABOUT THAT?
HMPF!
BTS 4-EVER

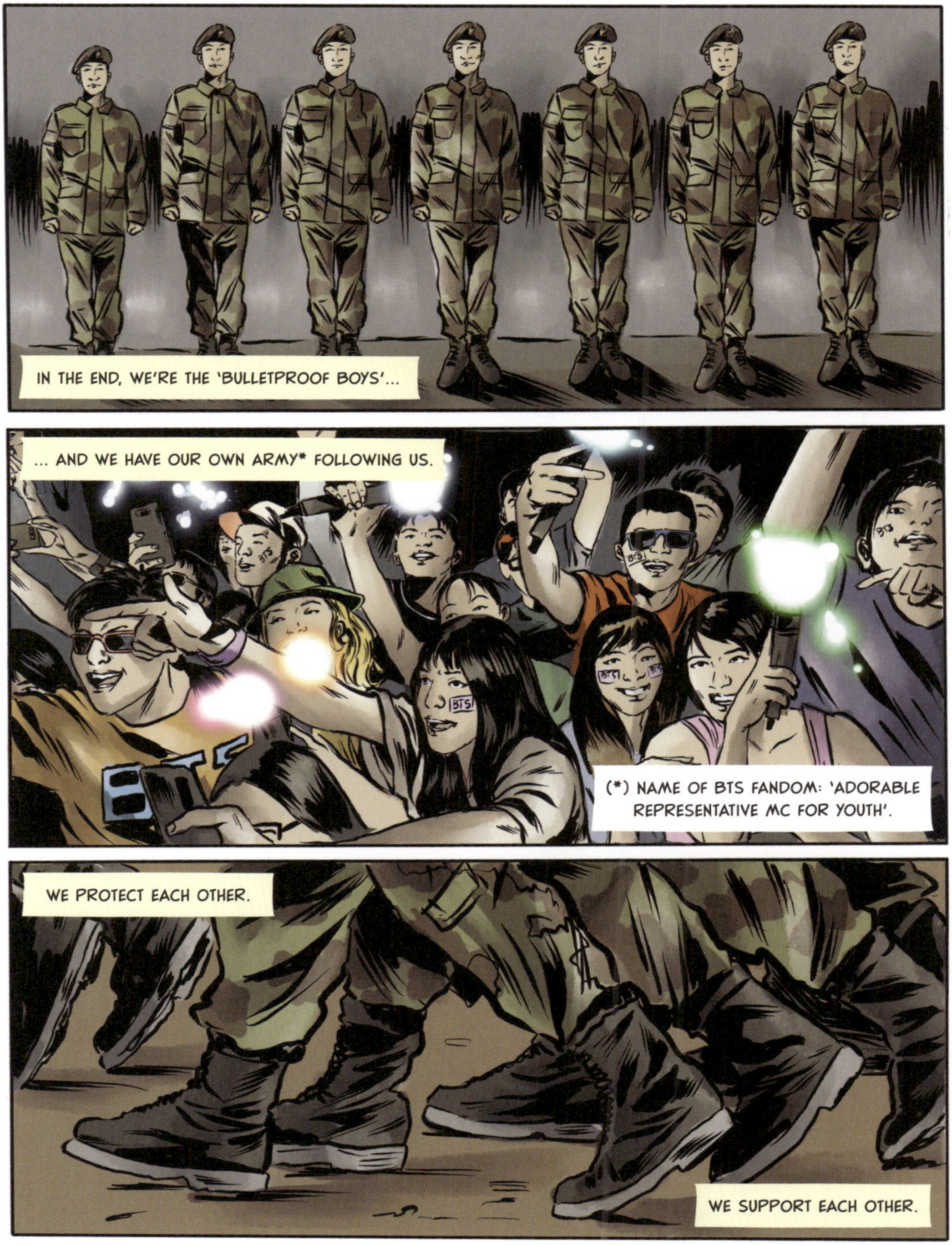
IN THE END, WE'RE THE 'BULLETPROOF BOYS'...
... AND WE HAVE OUR OWN ARMY* FOLLOWING US.
BTS
(*) NAME OF BTS FANDOM: 'ADORABLE REPRESENTATIVE MC FOR YOUTH'.
WE PROTECT EACH OTHER.
WE SUPPORT EACH OTHER.

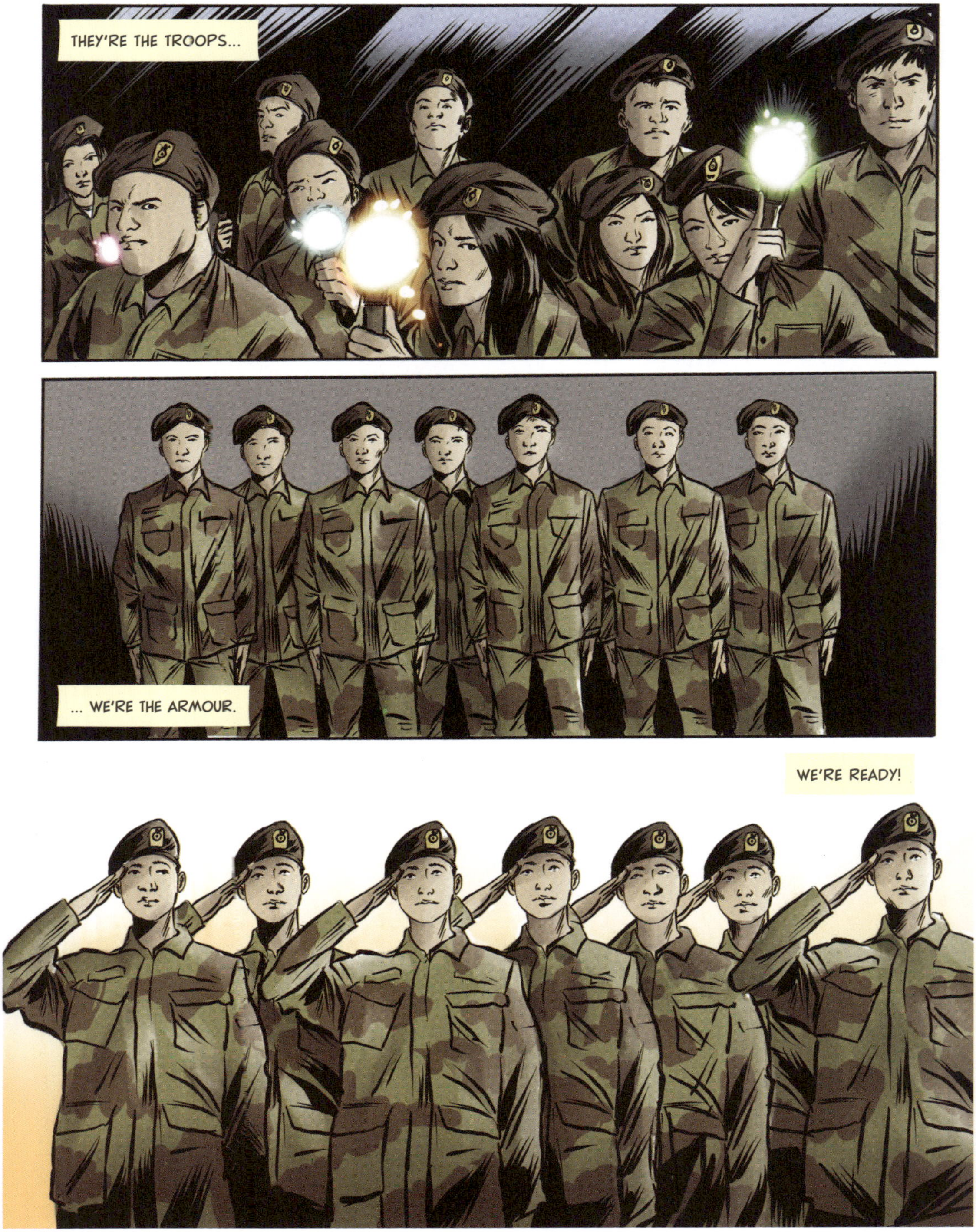
THEY'RE THE TROOPS...
... WE'RE THE ARMOUR.
WE'RE READY!

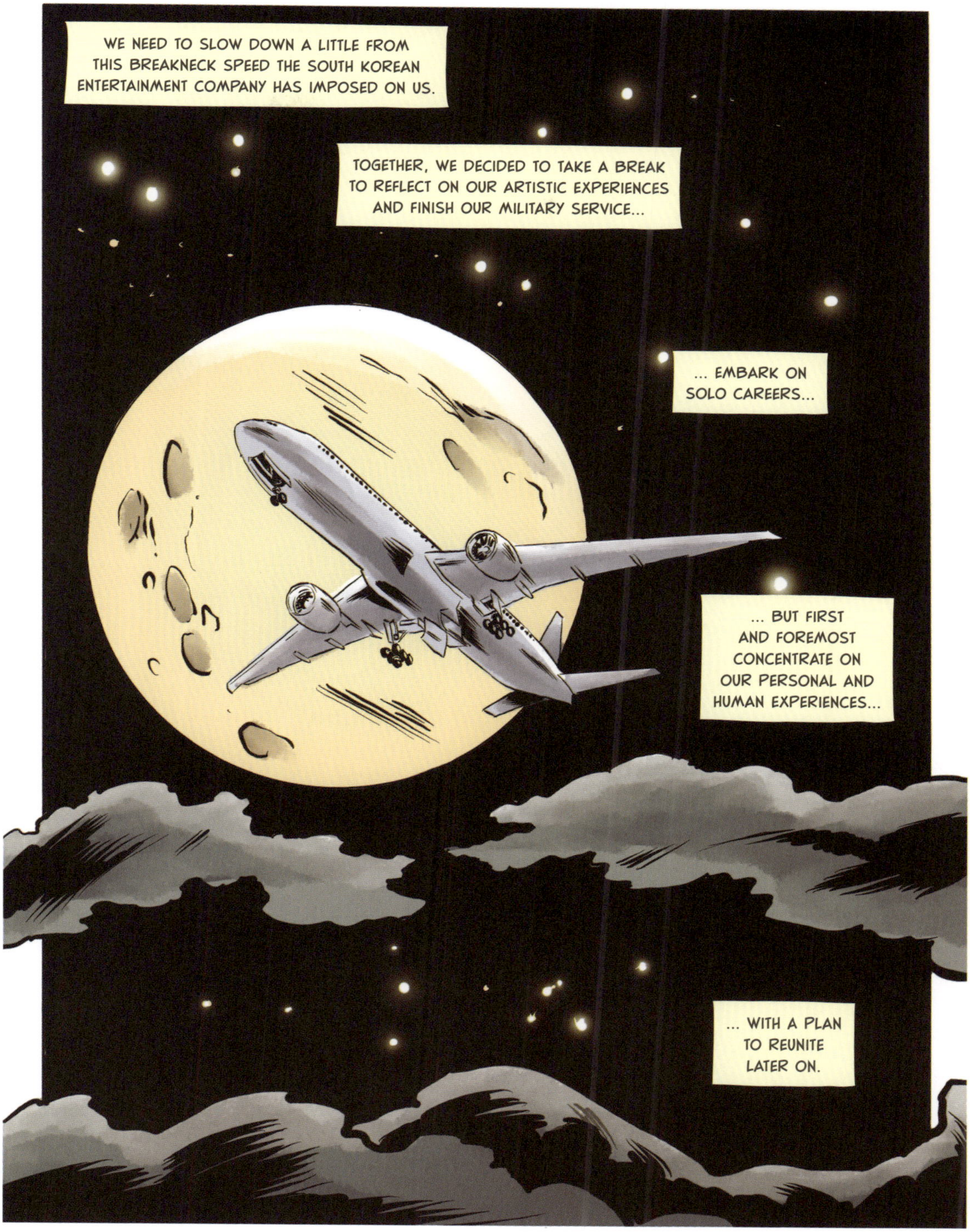
WE NEED TO SLOW DOWN A LITTLE FROM THIS BREAKNECK SPEED THE SOUTH KOREAN ENTERTAINMENT COMPANY HAS IMPOSED ON US.
TOGETHER, WE DECIDED TO TAKE A BREAK TO REFLECT ON OUR ARTISTIC EXPERIENCES AND FINISH OUR MILITARY SERVICE...
... EMBARK ON SOLO CAREERS...
... BUT FIRST AND FOREMOST CONCENTRATE ON OUR PERSONAL AND HUMAN EXPERIENCES...
... WITH A PLAN TO REUNITE LATER ON.

EPILOGUE

BEYOND THE SCENE

13 JUNE 2013: BTS MAKES THEIR OFFICIAL DEBUT ON A MUSIC BROADCAST.

AFTER THE RELEASE OF THE *SCHOOL TRILOGY* AND THE BAND'S GROWING POPULARITY, THE 'MAGNIFICENT SEVEN' BEGAN TO COMPOSE, PRODUCE AND CHOREOGRAPH ALBUMS UNTIL THEY MADE THE AMERICAN *BILLBOARD* CHARTS.

IN 2017, THEY BEGAN TO WIN AWARDS AND ACCOLADES, KICKING OFF THEIR PERSONAL WORLDWIDE TAKEOVER: OFFICIAL AND UNOFFICIAL FAN CLUBS, OFFICIAL AND UNOFFICIAL SOCIAL CHANNELS ARE BORN, HELPING TO MAKE BTS A GLOBAL PHENOMENON.

THE DEFINING DEMONSTRATION AND PINNACLE OF THE BAND'S POSITIVE INFLUENCE IS THE SPEECH THEY DELIVERED AT THE UN HEADQUARTERS IN NEW YORK ON 24 SEPTEMBER 2018.

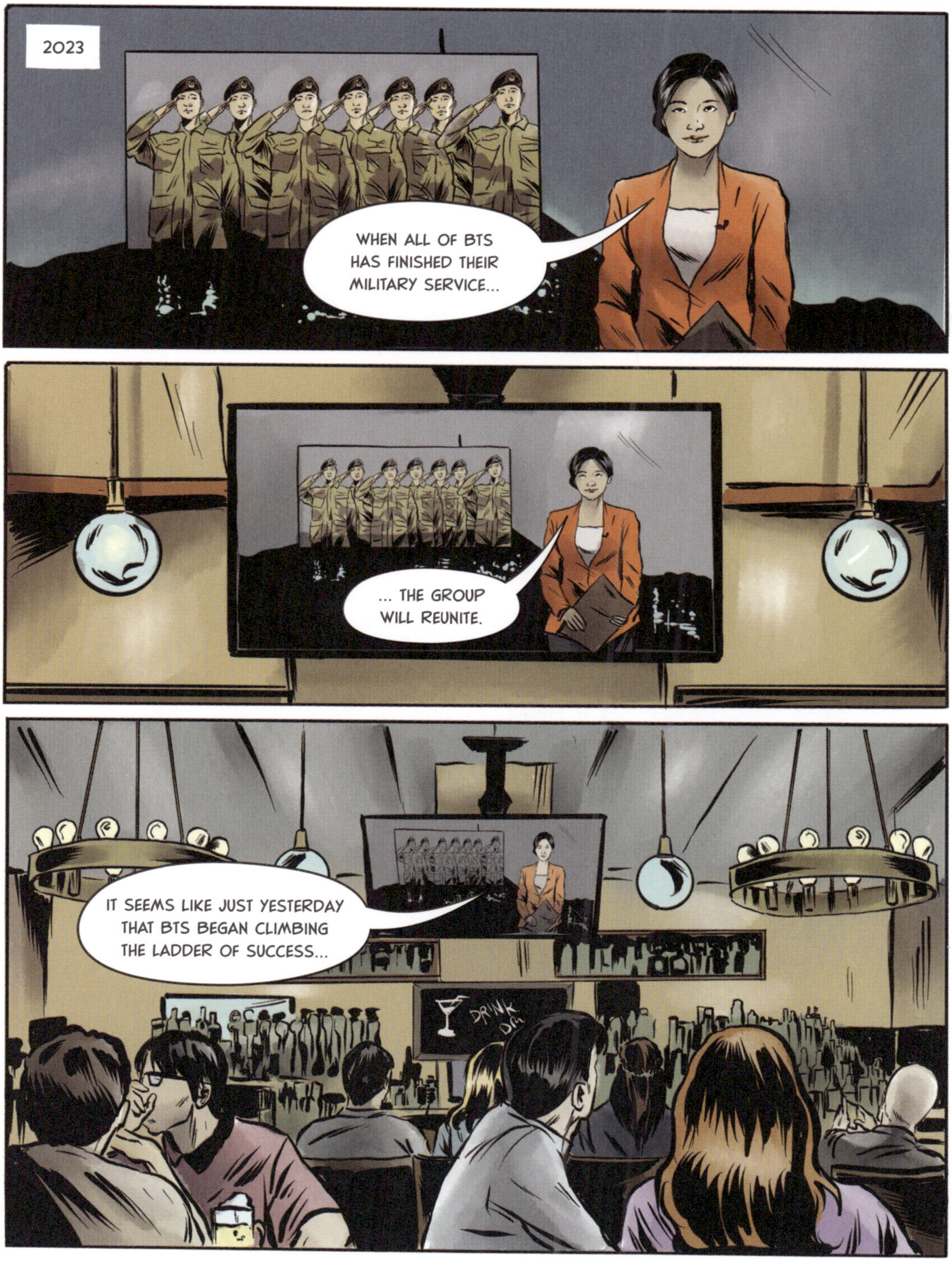
2023
WHEN ALL OF BTS HAS FINISHED THEIR MILITARY SERVICE...
... THE GROUP WILL REUNITE.
IT SEEMS LIKE JUST YESTERDAY THAT BTS BEGAN CLIMBING THE LADDER OF SUCCESS...
DRINK

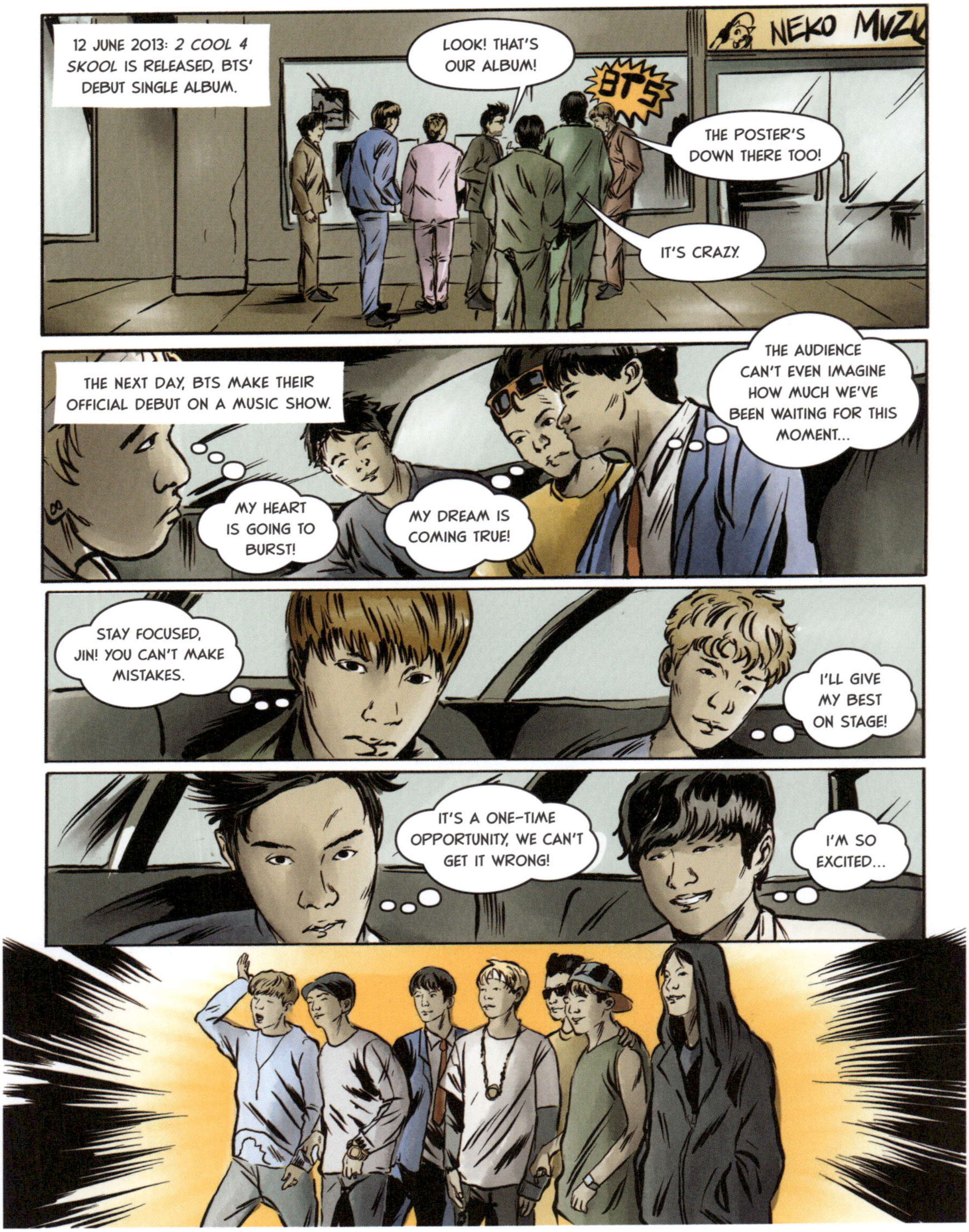
12 JUNE 2013: *2 COOL 4 SKOOL* IS RELEASED, BTS' DEBUT SINGLE ALBUM.
LOOK! THAT'S OUR ALBUM!
NEKO MUZ
BTS
THE POSTER'S DOWN THERE TOO!
IT'S CRAZY.
THE NEXT DAY, BTS MAKE THEIR OFFICIAL DEBUT ON A MUSIC SHOW.
MY HEART IS GOING TO BURST!
MY DREAM IS COMING TRUE!
THE AUDIENCE CAN'T EVEN IMAGINE HOW MUCH WE'VE BEEN WAITING FOR THIS MOMENT...
STAY FOCUSED, JIN! YOU CAN'T MAKE MISTAKES.
I'LL GIVE MY BEST ON STAGE!
IT'S A ONE-TIME OPPORTUNITY, WE CAN'T GET IT WRONG!
I'M SO EXCITED...

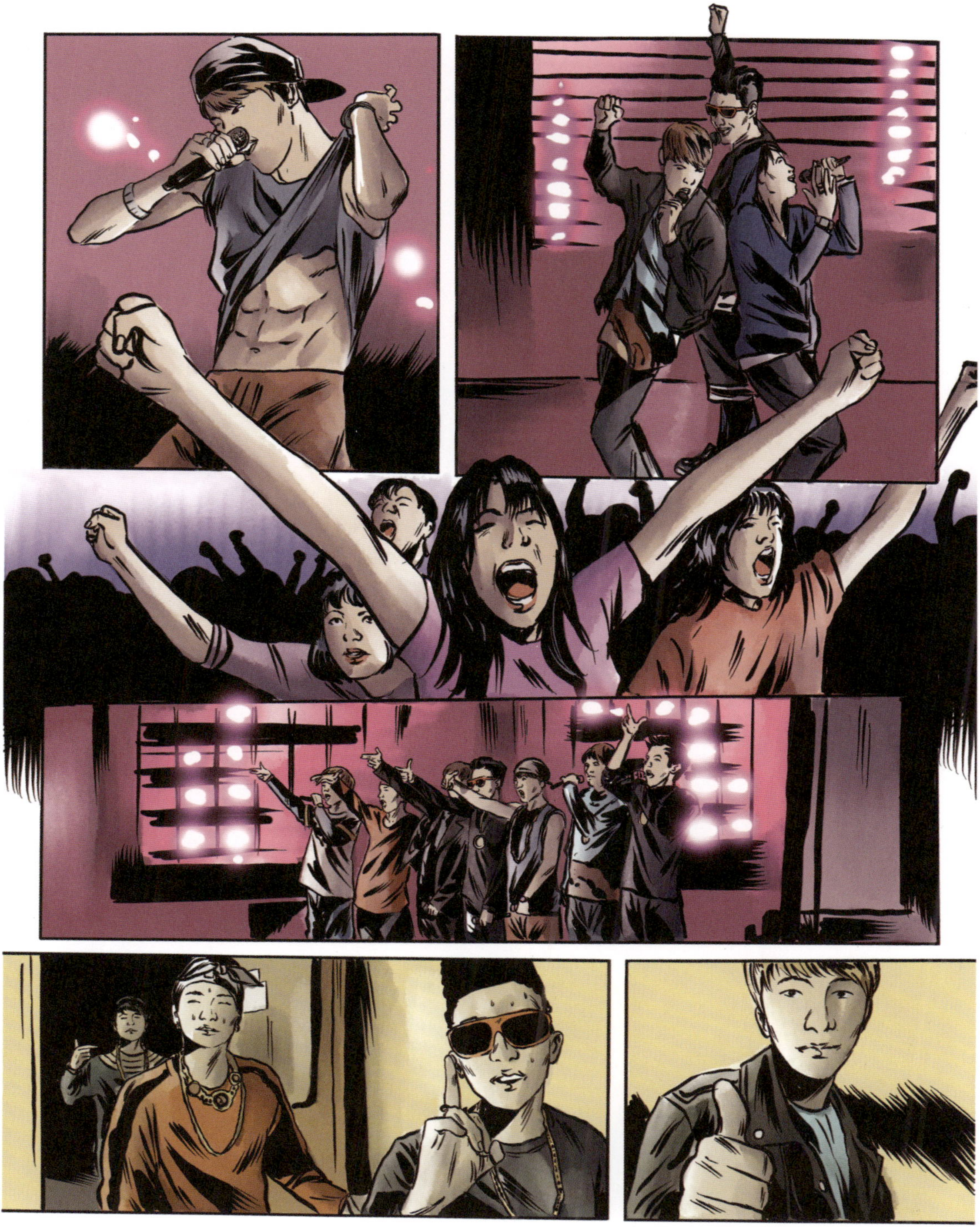

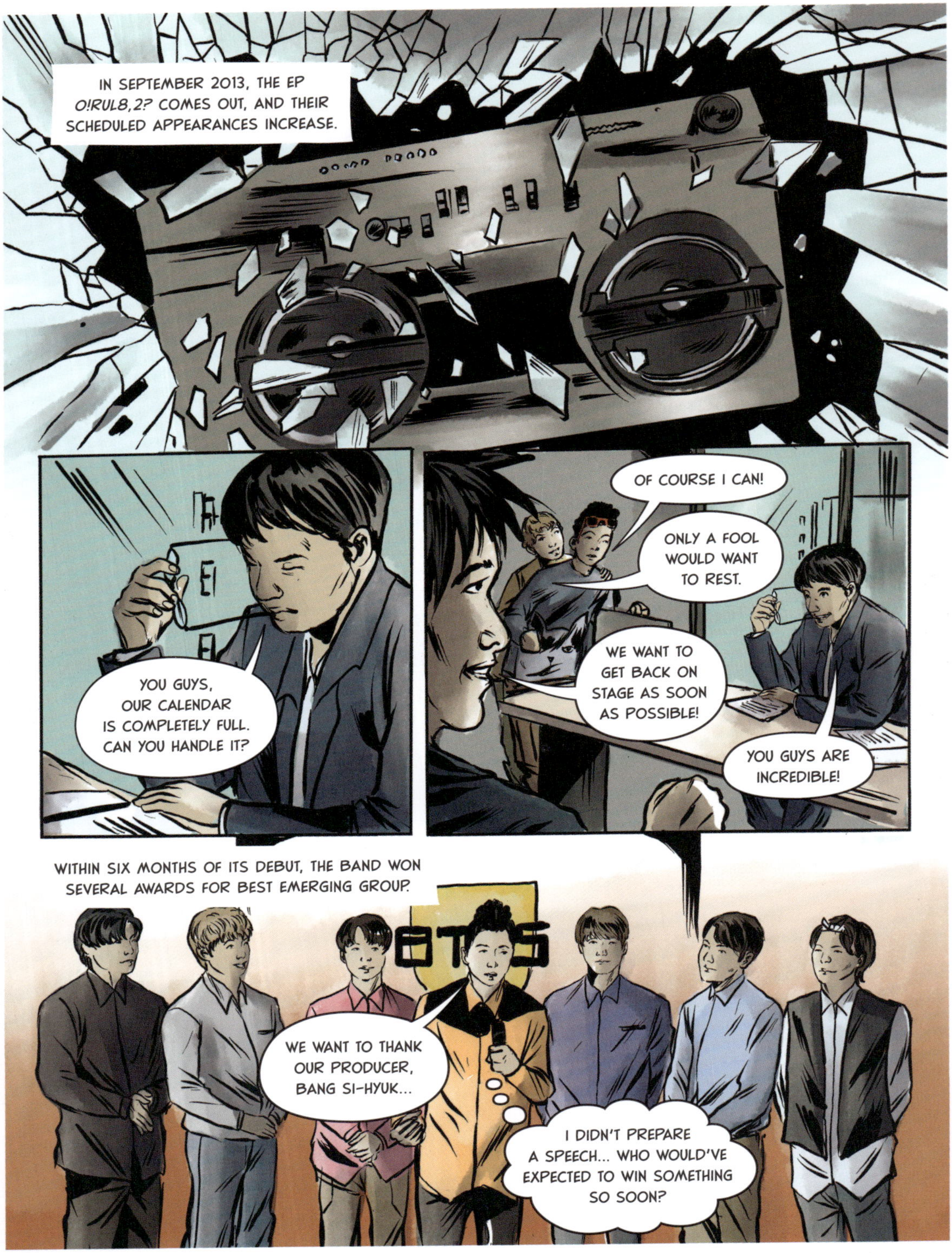
IN SEPTEMBER 2013, THE EP *O!RUL8,2?* COMES OUT, AND THEIR SCHEDULED APPEARANCES INCREASE.
YOU GUYS, OUR CALENDAR IS COMPLETELY FULL. CAN YOU HANDLE IT?
OF COURSE I CAN!
ONLY A FOOL WOULD WANT TO REST.
WE WANT TO GET BACK ON STAGE AS SOON AS POSSIBLE!
YOU GUYS ARE INCREDIBLE!
WITHIN SIX MONTHS OF ITS DEBUT, THE BAND WON SEVERAL AWARDS FOR BEST EMERGING GROUP.
WE WANT TO THANK OUR PRODUCER, BANG SI-HYUK...
I DIDN'T PREPARE A SPEECH... WHO WOULD'VE EXPECTED TO WIN SOMETHING SO SOON?

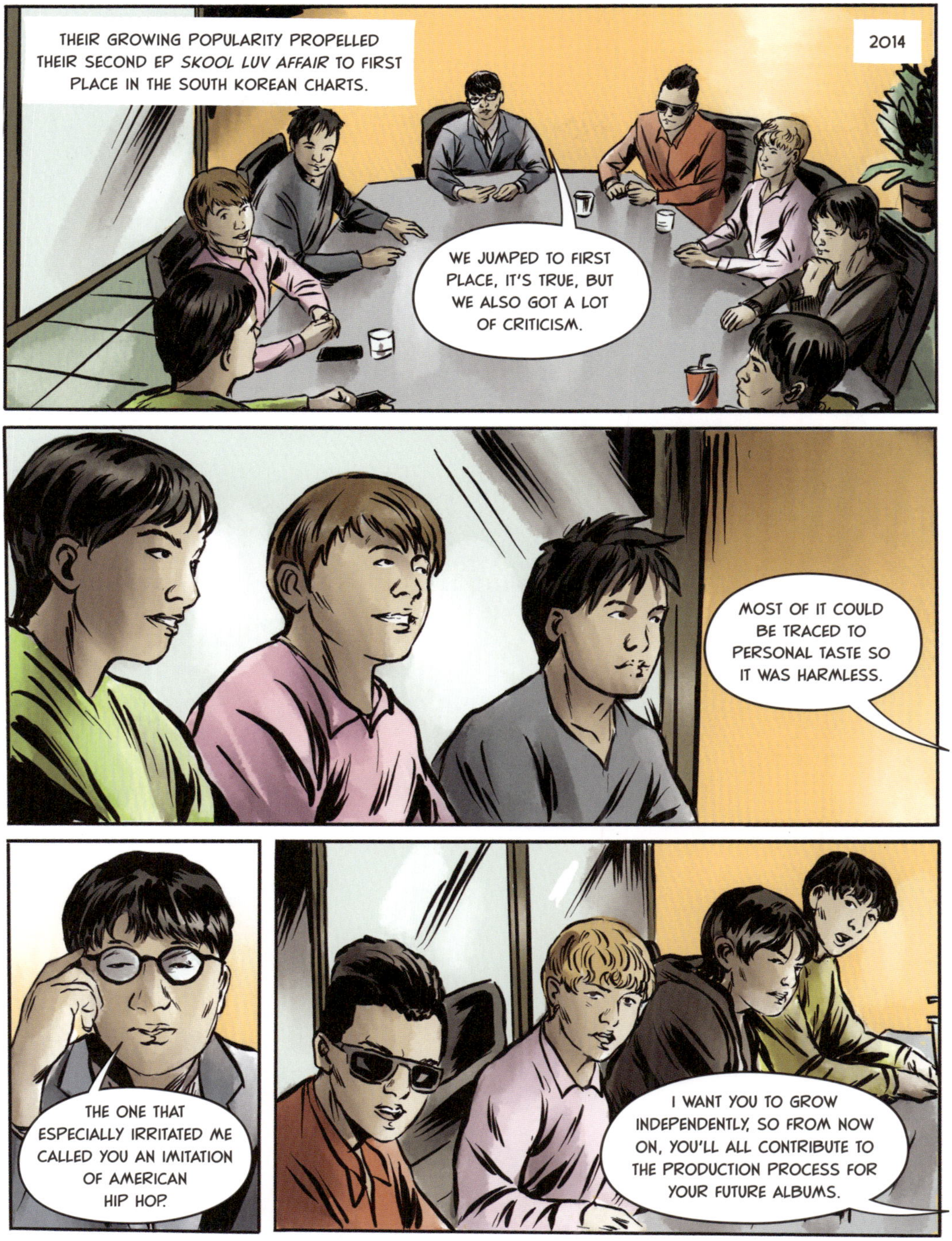
THEIR GROWING POPULARITY PROPELLED THEIR SECOND EP *SKOOL LUV AFFAIR* TO FIRST PLACE IN THE SOUTH KOREAN CHARTS.
2014
WE JUMPED TO FIRST PLACE, IT'S TRUE, BUT WE ALSO GOT A LOT OF CRITICISM.
MOST OF IT COULD BE TRACED TO PERSONAL TASTE SO IT WAS HARMLESS.
THE ONE THAT ESPECIALLY IRRITATED ME CALLED YOU AN IMITATION OF AMERICAN HIP HOP.
I WANT YOU TO GROW INDEPENDENTLY, SO FROM NOW ON, YOU'LL ALL CONTRIBUTE TO THE PRODUCTION PROCESS FOR YOUR FUTURE ALBUMS.

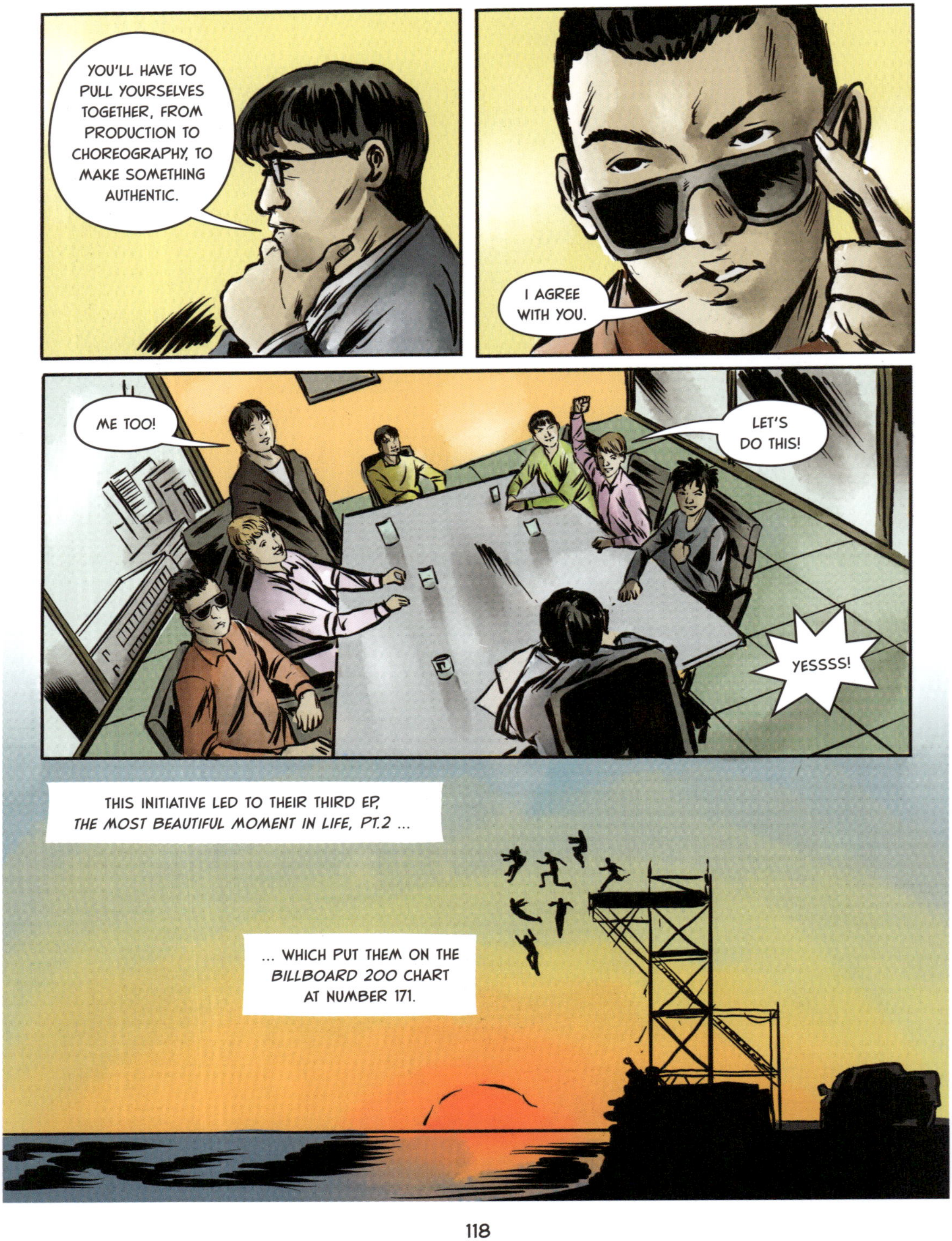
YOU'LL HAVE TO PULL YOURSELVES TOGETHER, FROM PRODUCTION TO CHOREOGRAPHY, TO MAKE SOMETHING AUTHENTIC.
I AGREE WITH YOU.
ME TOO!
LET'S DO THIS!
YESSSS!
THIS INITIATIVE LED TO THEIR THIRD EP, *THE MOST BEAUTIFUL MOMENT IN LIFE, PT.2* ...
... WHICH PUT THEM ON THE *BILLBOARD 200* CHART AT NUMBER 171.

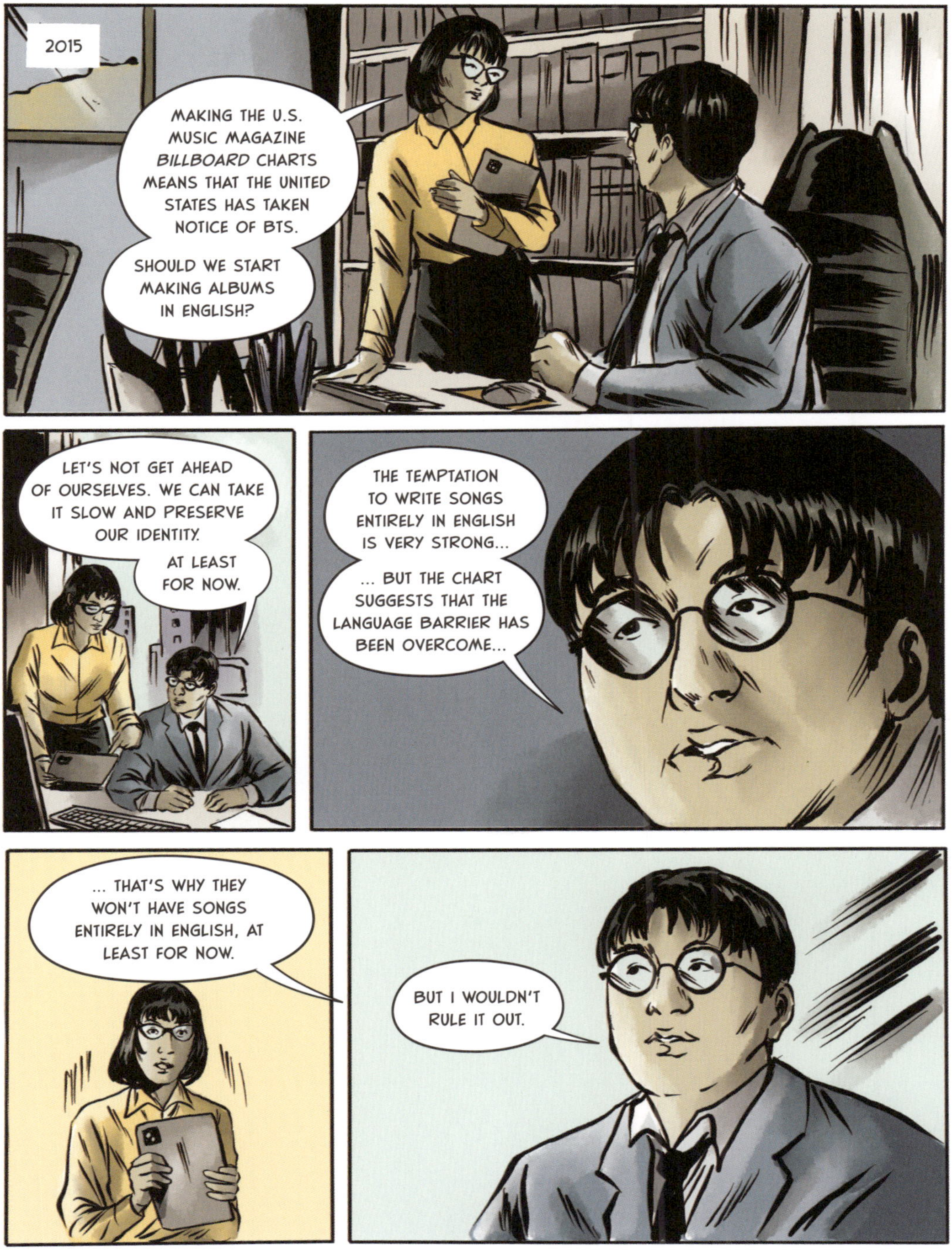
2015
MAKING THE U.S. MUSIC MAGAZINE *BILLBOARD* CHARTS MEANS THAT THE UNITED STATES HAS TAKEN NOTICE OF BTS.
SHOULD WE START MAKING ALBUMS IN ENGLISH?
LET'S NOT GET AHEAD OF OURSELVES. WE CAN TAKE IT SLOW AND PRESERVE OUR IDENTITY.
AT LEAST FOR NOW.
THE TEMPTATION TO WRITE SONGS ENTIRELY IN ENGLISH IS VERY STRONG...
... BUT THE CHART SUGGESTS THAT THE LANGUAGE BARRIER HAS BEEN OVERCOME...
... THAT'S WHY THEY WON'T HAVE SONGS ENTIRELY IN ENGLISH, AT LEAST FOR NOW.
BUT I WOULDN'T RULE IT OUT.

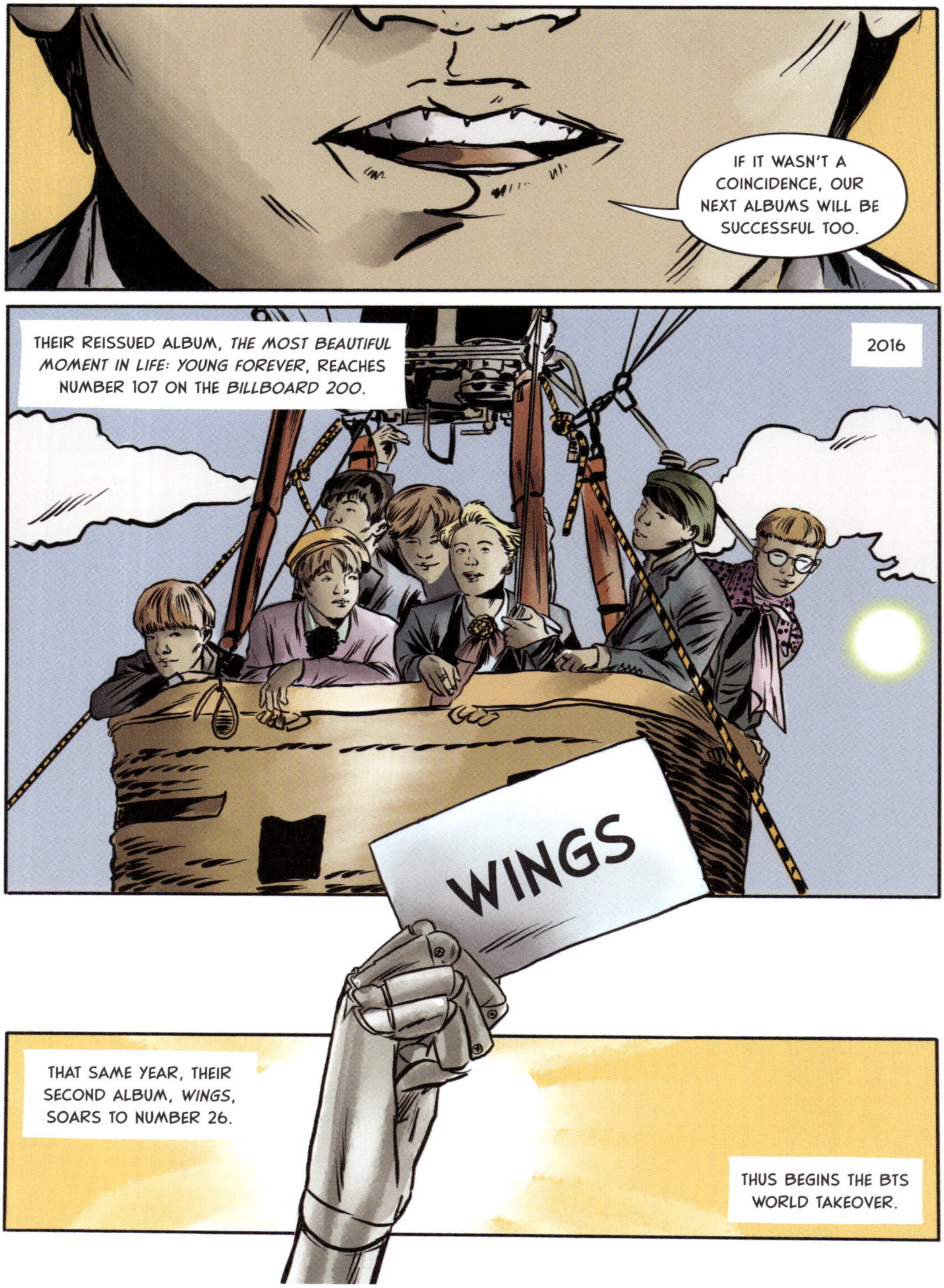

IF IT WASN'T A COINCIDENCE, OUR NEXT ALBUMS WILL BE SUCCESSFUL TOO.
THEIR REISSUED ALBUM, *THE MOST BEAUTIFUL MOMENT IN LIFE: YOUNG FOREVER*, REACHES NUMBER 107 ON THE *BILLBOARD 200*.
2016
WINGS
THAT SAME YEAR, THEIR SECOND ALBUM, *WINGS*, SOARS TO NUMBER 26.
THUS BEGINS THE BTS WORLD TAKEOVER.

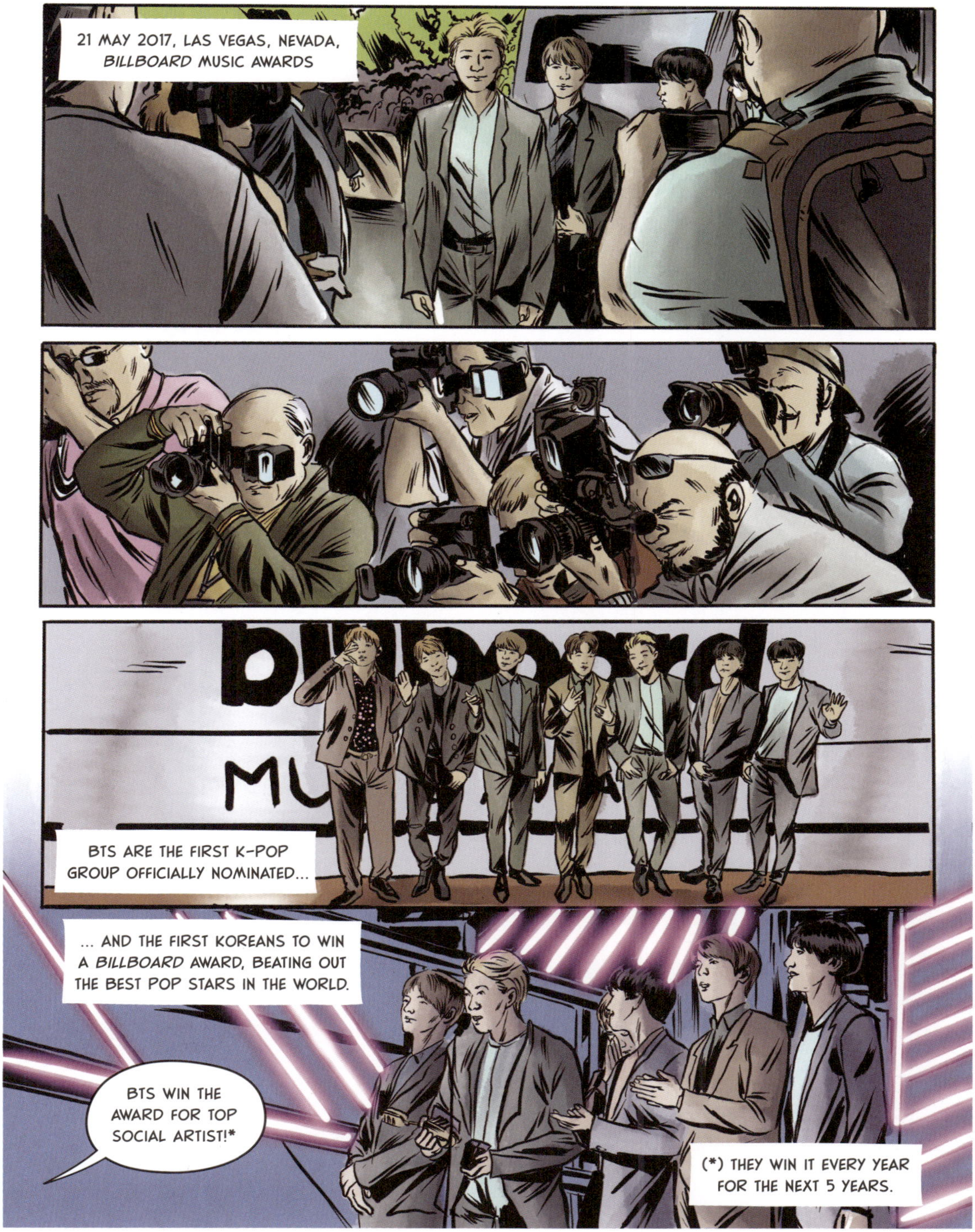
21 MAY 2017, LAS VEGAS, NEVADA, *BILLBOARD* MUSIC AWARDS
BTS ARE THE FIRST K-POP GROUP OFFICIALLY NOMINATED...
... AND THE FIRST KOREANS TO WIN A *BILLBOARD* AWARD, BEATING OUT THE BEST POP STARS IN THE WORLD.
BTS WIN THE AWARD FOR TOP SOCIAL ARTIST!*
(*) THEY WIN IT EVERY YEAR FOR THE NEXT 5 YEARS.

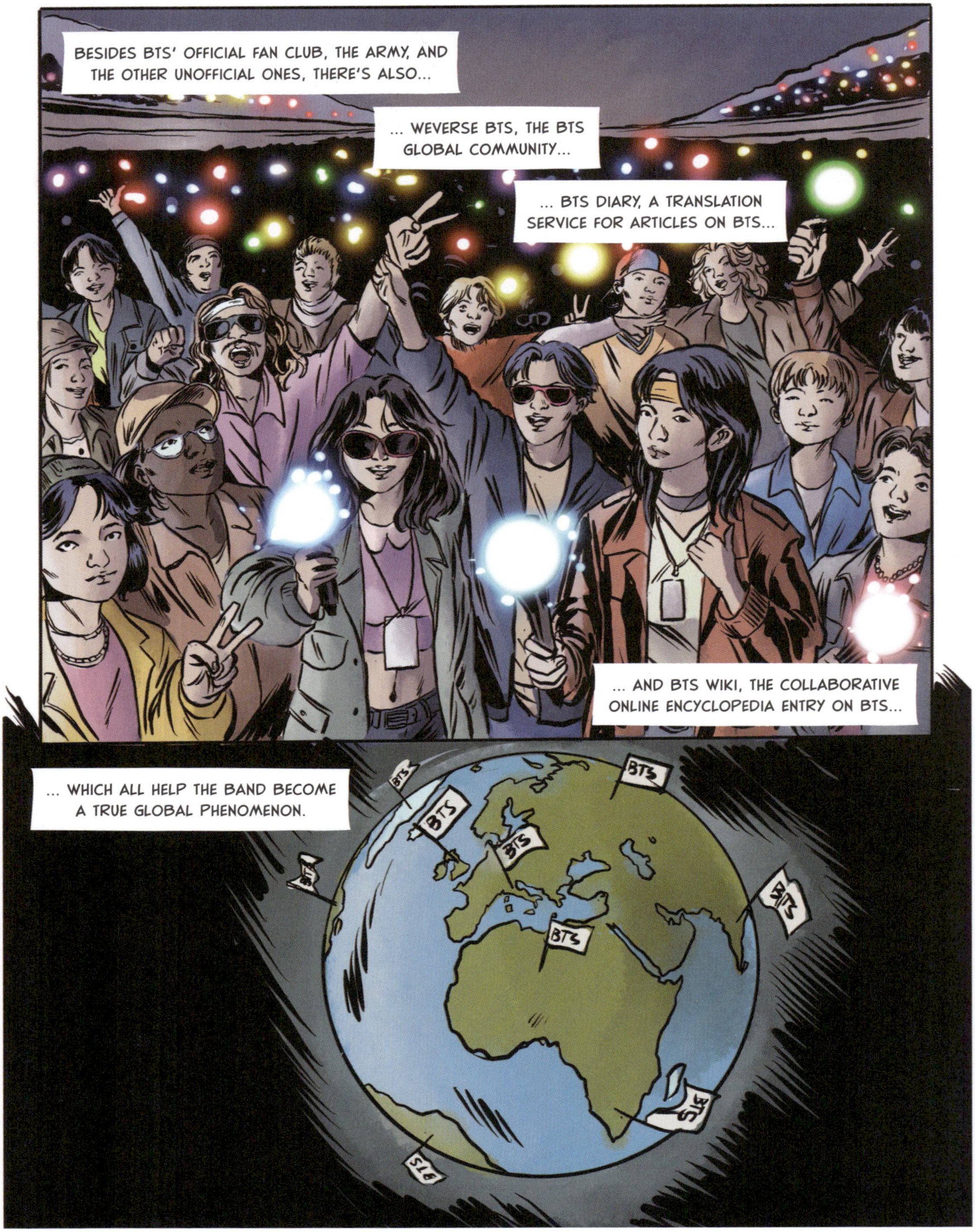
BESIDES BTS' OFFICIAL FAN CLUB, THE ARMY, AND THE OTHER UNOFFICIAL ONES, THERE'S ALSO...
... WEVERSE BTS, THE BTS GLOBAL COMMUNITY...
... BTS DIARY, A TRANSLATION SERVICE FOR ARTICLES ON BTS...
... AND BTS WIKI, THE COLLABORATIVE ONLINE ENCYCLOPEDIA ENTRY ON BTS...
... WHICH ALL HELP THE BAND BECOME A TRUE GLOBAL PHENOMENON.
BTS
BTS
BTS
BTS
BTS
BTS
BTS
BTS

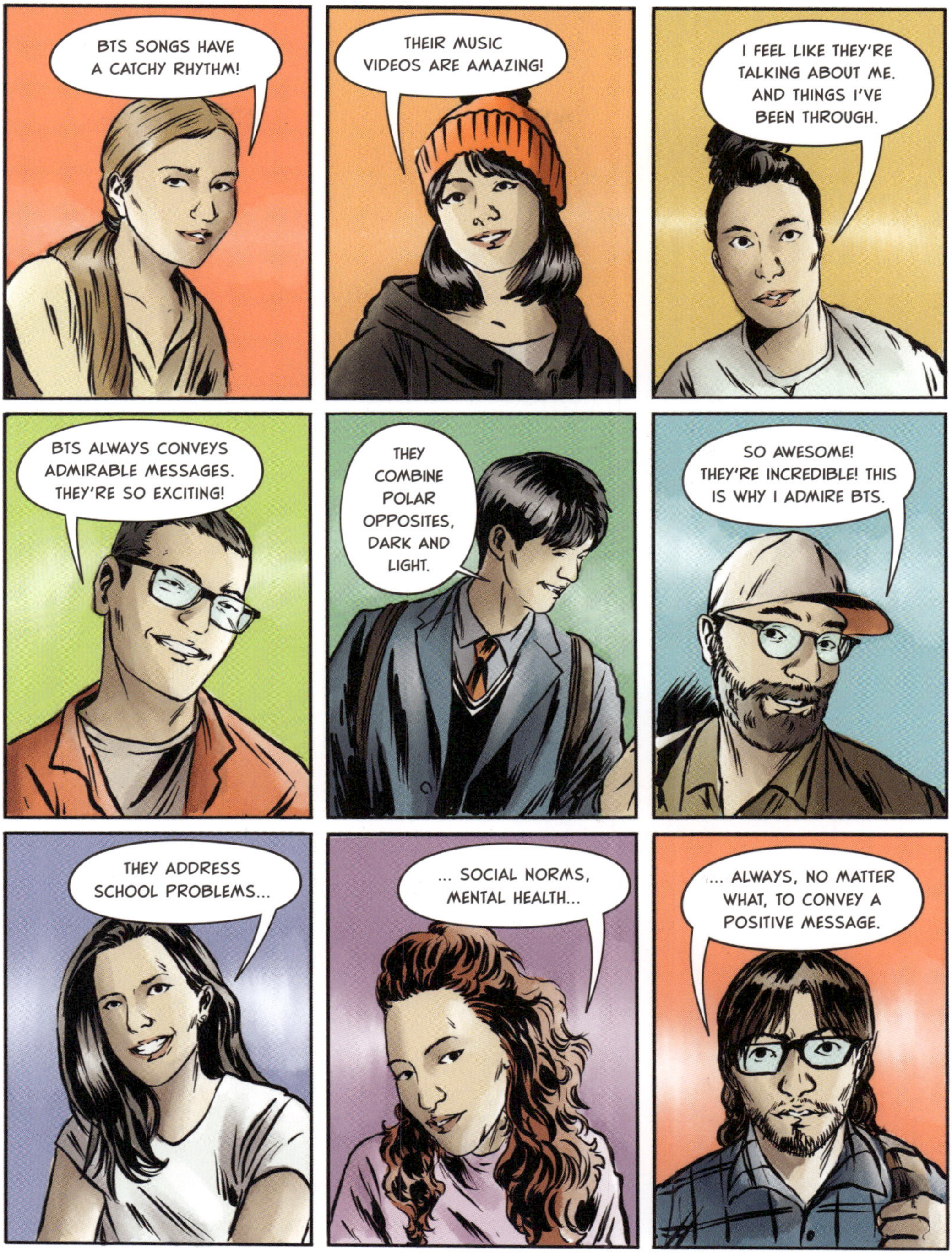
BTS SONGS HAVE A CATCHY RHYTHM!
THEIR MUSIC VIDEOS ARE AMAZING!
I FEEL LIKE THEY'RE TALKING ABOUT ME. AND THINGS I'VE BEEN THROUGH.
BTS ALWAYS CONVEYS ADMIRABLE MESSAGES. THEY'RE SO EXCITING!
THEY COMBINE POLAR OPPOSITES, DARK AND LIGHT.
SO AWESOME! THEY'RE INCREDIBLE! THIS IS WHY I ADMIRE BTS.
THEY ADDRESS SCHOOL PROBLEMS...
... SOCIAL NORMS, MENTAL HEALTH...
... ALWAYS, NO MATTER WHAT, TO CONVEY A POSITIVE MESSAGE.

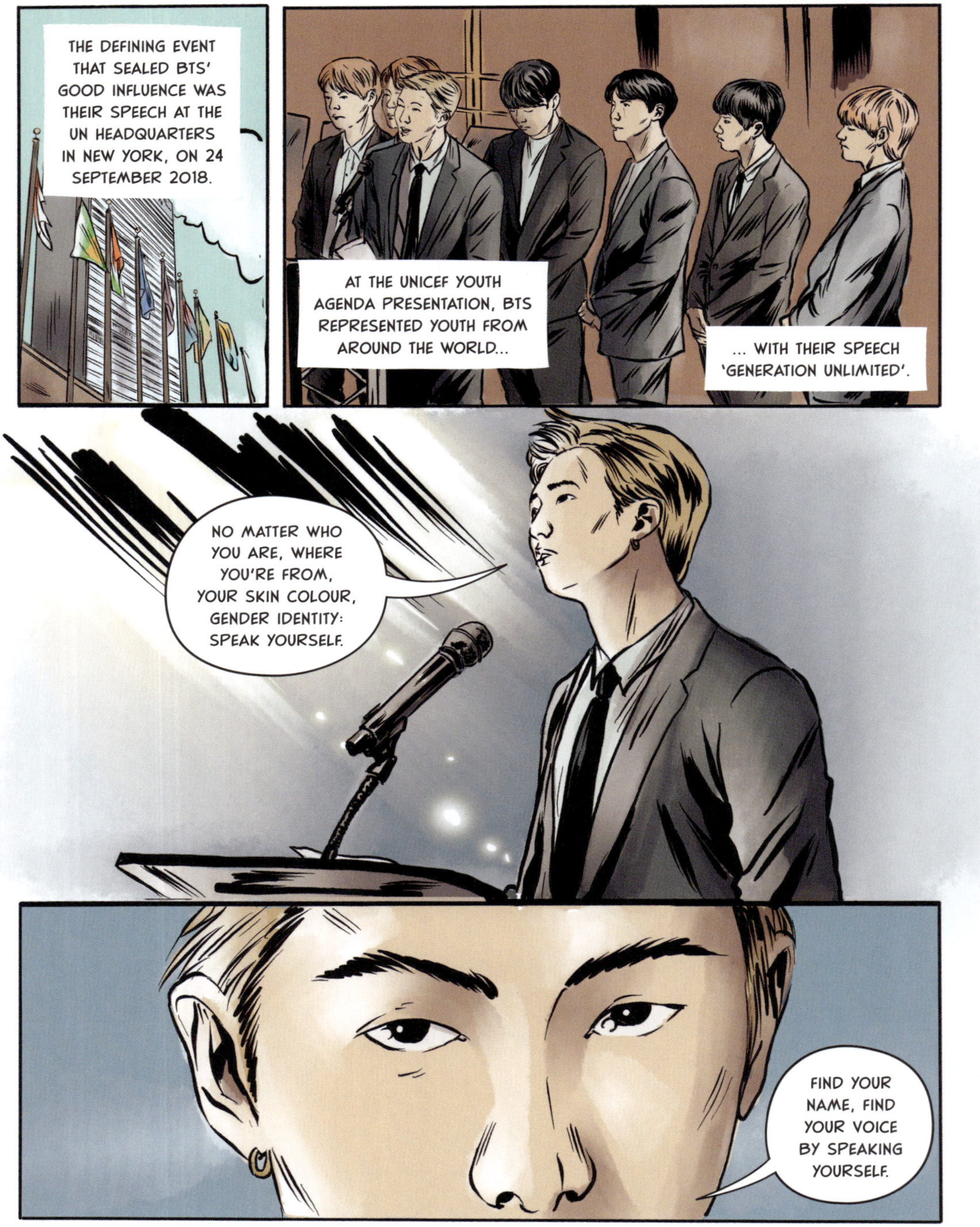
THE DEFINING EVENT THAT SEALED BTS' GOOD INFLUENCE WAS THEIR SPEECH AT THE UN HEADQUARTERS IN NEW YORK, ON 24 SEPTEMBER 2018.
AT THE UNICEF YOUTH AGENDA PRESENTATION, BTS REPRESENTED YOUTH FROM AROUND THE WORLD...
... WITH THEIR SPEECH 'GENERATION UNLIMITED'.
NO MATTER WHO YOU ARE, WHERE YOU'RE FROM, YOUR SKIN COLOUR, GENDER IDENTITY: SPEAK YOURSELF.
FIND YOUR NAME, FIND YOUR VOICE BY SPEAKING YOURSELF.

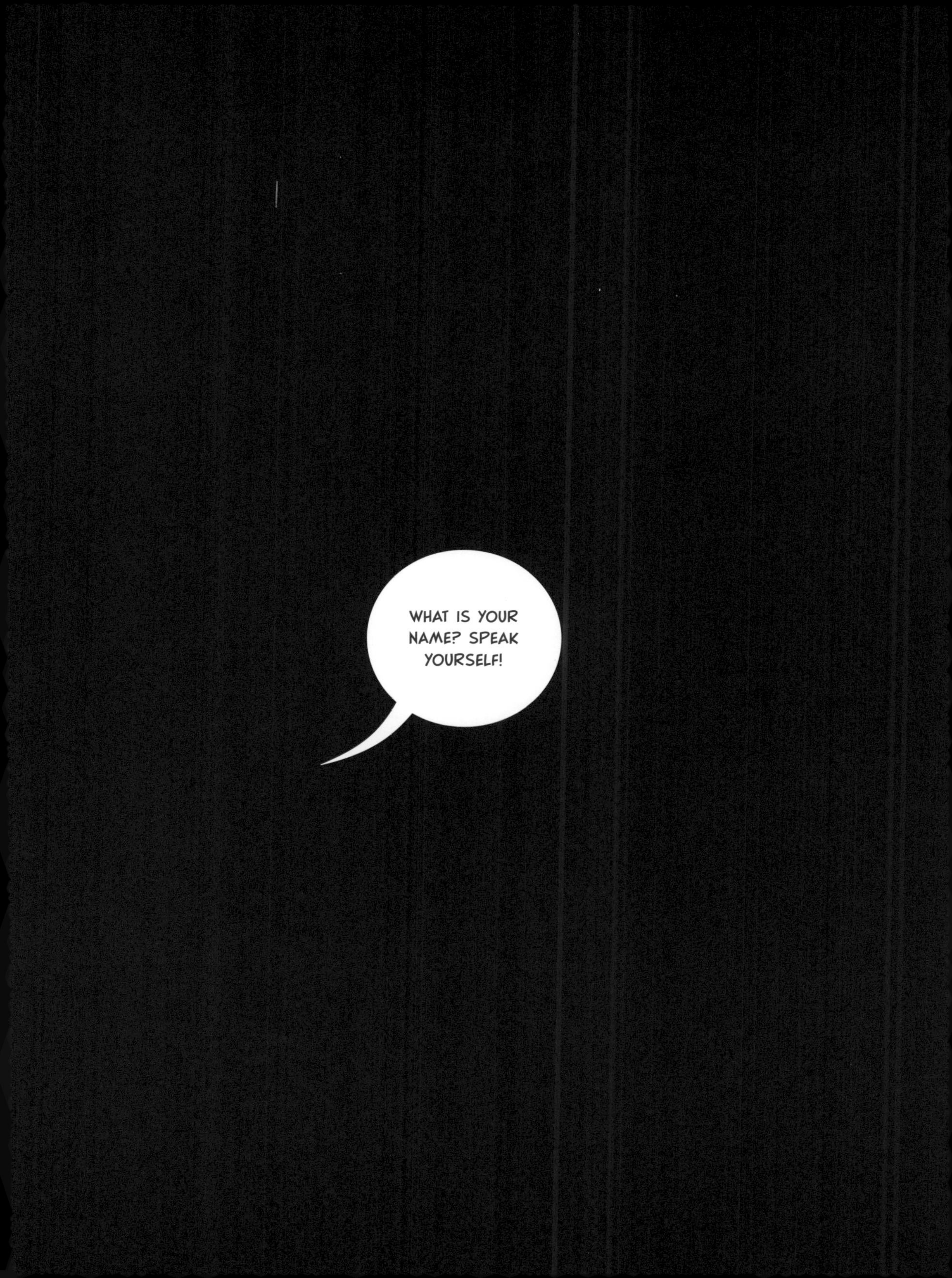
WHAT IS YOUR NAME? SPEAK YOURSELF!

DISCOGRAPHY

STUDIO ALBUMS

2014 – Dark & Wild
2014 – Wake Up
2016 – Youth
2016 – Wings
2018 – Face Yourself
2018 – Love Yourself: Tear
2020 – Map of the Soul: 7
2020 – Be

EXTENDED PLAYS

2013 – O!RUL8,2?
2014 – Skool Luv Affair
2015 – The Most Beautiful Moment in Life, Pt. 1
2015 – The Most Beautiful Moment in Life, Pt. 2
2017 – Love Yourself: Her
2019 – Map of the Soul: Persona
2020 – Dynamite
2021 – Butter (Hotter, Sweeter, Cooler)

SINGLE ALBUMS

2013 – 2 Cool 4 Skool
2021 – Butter

COMPILATION ALBUMS

2014 – 2 Cool 4 Skool/O!RUL8,2?
2016 – The Most Beautiful Moment in Life: Young Forever
2017 – The Best of BTS
2018 – Love Yourself: Answer
2021 – BTS, the Best
2022 – Proof

TOURS

2014/15 – The Red Bullet Tour
2015 – Wake Up: Open Your Eyes Japan Tour
2015/16 – The Most Beautiful Moment in Life On Stage Tour
2017 – The Wings Tour
2018/19 – Love Yourself World Tour

FILMOGRAPHY

FILM

2018 – Burn the Stage: The Movie, directed by Park Jun-soo
2019 – Love Yourself in Seoul, produced by Big Hit Entertainment/CJ CGV Screen X
2019 – Bring the Soul: The Movie, directed by Park Jun-soo
2020 – Break the Silence: The Movie, directed by Park Jun-soo
2022 – BTS: Permission to Dance On Stage – LA, directed by Sam Wrench and Park Jun-soo
2023 – BTS: Yet To Come in Cinemas, directed by Oh Yoon Dong

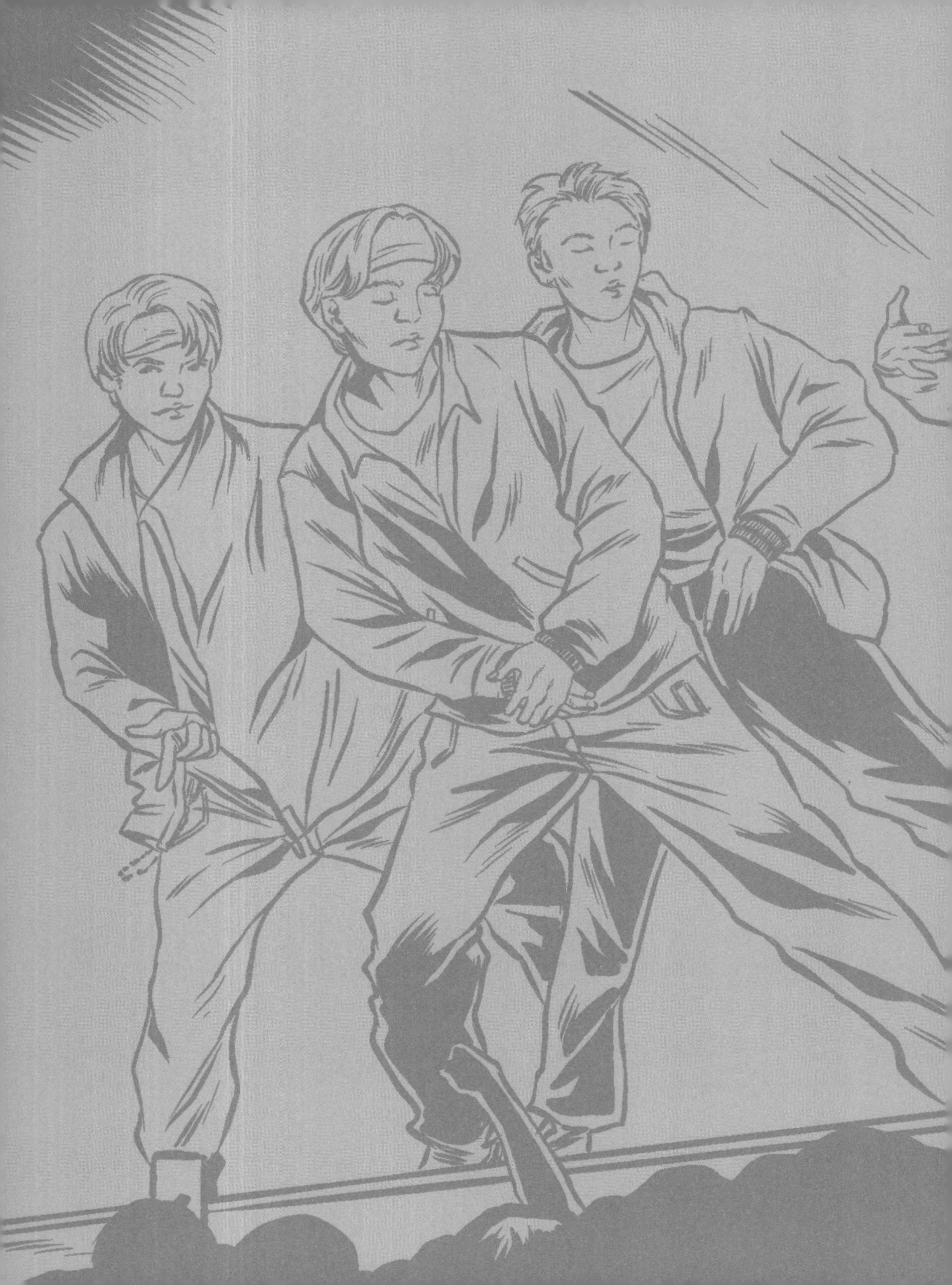